⸱⸱❧ THE MIDDLE AGES ❧⸱⸱

EDWARD PETERS, *General Editor*

Christian Society and the Crusades, 1198–1229. Sources in Translation, including The Capture of Damietta by Oliver of Paderborn. Edited by Edward Peters

The First Crusade: The Chronicle of Fulcher of Chartres and Other Source Materials. Edited by Edward Peters

The Burgundian Code: The Book of Constitutions or Law of Gundobad and Additional Enactments. Translated by Katherine Fischer Drew

The Lombard Laws. Translated, with an Introduction, by Katherine Fischer Drew

Ulrich Zwingli (1484–1531). Selected Works. Edited by Samuel Macauley Jackson. Introduction by Edward Peters

From St. Francis to Dante: Translations from the Chronicle of the Franciscan Salimbene (1221-1288). G. G. Coulton. Introduction by Edward Peters

The Duel and the Oath. Part I and II of Superstition and Force, Henry Charles Lea. Introduction by Edward Peters

The Ordeal. Part III of Superstition and Force, Henry Charles Lea. Introduction by Edward Peters

Torture. Part IV of Superstition and Force, Henry Charles Lea. Introduction by Edward Peters

Witchcraft in Europe, 1110–1700: A Documentary History. Edited by Alan C. Kors and Edward Peters

The Scientific Achievement of the Middle Ages. Richard C. Dales. Introduction by Edward Peters

History of the Lombards. Paul the Deacon. Translated by William Dudley Foulke. Introduction by Edward Peters

Monks, Bishops and Pagans: Christian Culture in Gaul and Italy, 500–700. Edited, with an Introduction, by Edward Peters

The World of Piers Plowman. Edited and translated by Jeanne Krochalis and Edward Peters

Felony and Misdemeanor: A Study in the History of Criminal Law. Julius Goebel, Jr. Introduction by Edward Peters

Women in Medieval Society

꒦꒷꒦꒷꒦꒷꒦꒷꒦꒷꒦꒷꒦꒷꒦꒷꒦꒷꒦꒷꒦꒷

Brenda M. Bolton

Stanley Chojnacki

Emily Coleman

Heath Dillard

Barbara A. Hanawalt

David Herlihy

Jo-Ann McNamara

Susan Mosher Stuard

Sue Sheridan Walker

Suzanne F. Wemple

WOMEN
IN
MEDIEVAL SOCIETY

Edited, with an Introduction,
by **SUSAN MOSHER STUARD**

University of Pennsylvania Press/1976

Copyright © 1976 by The University of Pennsylvania Press, Inc.
All rights reserved

Second printing 1977

Library of Congress Catalog Card Number: 75-41617

ISBN (cloth): 0-8122-7708-2
ISBN (paper): 0-8122-1088-3

Printed in the United States of America

Contents

Acknowledgments

The idea for this volume was born at the Medieval Institute, Kalamazoo, Michigan, in May, 1974. This conference, sponsored by Western Michigan University, provides an opportunity for presenting new studies on medieval subjects and fosters profitable communication between scholars. A special word of thanks should be given to the Director, Professor John Sonnenfeldt. He had planned to publish the joint paper by Jo-Ann McNamara and Suzanne Wemple, "Marriage and Divorce in the Frankish Kingdom," in the Collected Papers of the Medieval Institute. He graciously released the paper to us to permit earlier publication. The first and second Berkshire Conferences on the History of Women have been another fine opportunity for women scholars to present their studies on the history of women, and they have provided the paper by Sue Sheridan Walker. Professor Edward Peters of the University of Pennsylvania has supplied excellent advice and editorial comment. Above all I wish to thank the author of the second article in the volume, Emily Coleman. She has been the editor's editor, doing an outstanding job, reading and commenting to good purpose on a number of the articles and suggesting others for inclusion. Her perception and fine judgment are evident throughout, but, of course, I remain responsible for any errors of fact or judgment.

Susan Mosher Stuard

⁕ Introduction

Social history aids in understanding women's condition in any age; it is particularly essential for comprehending women in the Middle Ages, an era remote enough from our own so that common social presumptions do not pertain. As a discipline it demands that information gleaned from research be understood in the social context of the day, integrating knowledge at the expense, perhaps, of glamorous misconceptions of an earlier and exotic age. Such an approach dwells upon the ordinary with barely a mention of some of the more spectacular figures of the day, St. Joan, Eleanor of Aquitaine, and that host of saints, abbesses, princesses, and queens who come to mind at the mention of the Middle Ages. Instead it deals with the position of women, the roles assumed by women, and their importance within their social context, which often meant their importance within the family. Frequently these articles bring forward new information about women's lives; just as often they establish a more adequate context for comprehending previously available data.

Inheritance provides a good example. For generations scholars have noted women's inheritance rights in the medieval period, but the problem lay in interpreting what such rights meant in a woman's life. Certainly there existed no such simple equation deriving high social status from inheritance rights. The complexities of the problem, however, can be investigated by social history. Inheritance of land or of non-servile status meant enhancing a woman's desirability as a marriage partner in ninth-century French peasant society but at a price—her relative scarcity, as Emily Coleman's study of infanticide indicates. Heath Dillon shows that, in Spain, women's traditional right to inherit lay at the heart of the social restrictions which came to surround women's lives. In late medieval Venice, women's right to inherit and bequeath property established patterns distinct from male gifts, be-

1

quests, and dowry grants. As Stanley Chojnacki relates, it played an important role in determining the patterns of social cohesiveness of the patriciate.

It is this sort of problem which the authors of the anthology address. They are such manifestly important issues that one justly questions why so little has been done in the guise of scholarly investigative social history of women to date. The answer lies in the historiographical dilemma of women's history. Eleanor Shipley Duckett, a Cambridge-trained medievalist with considerable skills, exemplifies the difficulty. As she noted about her first study of medieval history, completed in the early decades of the century, "There it was, dull as ditchwater but my own. A godparent, I decided, might help catch a publisher and since I was not wise enough to know better I carried it to an eminent scholar. Would he of his charity read it? With courteous voice and complete British sincerity he replied, 'Do you want me to judge it on its own merits or as the work of a woman?'"[1]

Her lack of wisdom, she had learned, lay in not realizing that an unbridgeable gulf lay between work by and about women and the serious concerns of the scholarly community. Few women bridged that gulf. They learned their lesson far too well and simply refused to reach for that deeper level of comprehension which integrates women's position into the texture of social history. If their audience wished biography, anything from factual to romanticized or, on occasion, downright fictionalized accounts of women's lives, they supplied them. In fact the most remarkable women from the medieval period are the victims of this tendency. A great number of the pages written about them obfuscate rather than clarify their roles. Usually the notable woman is viewed as an anomaly, extraordinary in vigor and ambition, an exception to her age. More pertinent issues such as why these remarkable figures were produced and tolerated in their age, and the nature of the social context which fostered their talents, were seldom raised.

A number of sound works which related their findings to the history of women failed to reach, or impress, the scholarly world sufficiently, a reflection of the low esteem in which their subject was held. Bertha Phillpotts' brilliant study of *Kindred and Clan* had to wait well over a generation to find an appreciative audience.[2] Other historians who could have offered sound studies on women shied away from the field because it involved too many serious interpretive difficulties and would not win approbation from their scholarly colleagues. Eileen Power, whose work in social and economic history qualified her for such a task, was genuinely reluctant to undertake it. She finally assented to write a brief essay on women, and its slim pages, completed in 1926, stood as the only general synthesis on medieval women for nearly a half century.[3]

A corollary difficulty lies in finding adequate resource material for the history of medieval women. Along with biography, the other major scholarly field to concern itself with women was literary history. These studies contributed thorough analyses of role expectations for women within the epics, chansons, fabliaux, and other vernacular works of early Europe. But an interpretive difficulty arose whenever literary historians attempted to reconstruct those significant changes in role expectation which occurred in the medieval period, given manuscript material dating, for the most part, from the twelfth century or later. Some of the most significant questions concerning women were relegated to that largely speculative area concerning what might have constituted women's role before literary redaction. Bits and shards of recorded behavior had been retained, quite at odds with a heroine's late medieval characterization, but how does the critic go about interpreting such inconsistencies of characterization? Literary historians raised the appropriate questions concerning changing social expectations, but, given their sources, the questions often remained unanswered.

Ecclesiastical women of the early medieval period probably received the most sympathetic historical treatment. Lina Eckenstein produced her fine study, *Women Under Monasticism*, in 1896.[4] Women under the Rule were a source of wonder and fascination to modern women scholars. Reviewing the history of abbesses who served as administrators of double (that is, male and female) monasteries, who wrote scholarly treatises, philosophy, and literature, and were respected for it, intrigued and baffled modern women whose own administrative and scholarly talents were underutilized by the society in which they lived. Emily Putnam in her foreword to *The Lady* stated a prevalent theory to explain the disparity. She isolated the twin causes of chastity and distance from male-dominated society as the reasons for the Lady Abbess's success, and, with many of her early twentieth-century colleagues, founded, administered, and taught in women's colleges with such a model in mind. But the cloister was not the sole influence operating to produce those outstanding early ecclesiastical women. A more realistic model might have been available had Emily Putnam and her contemporaries understood the social environment outside the monastery walls. Their unconfirmed belief that early medieval society was a cruel, even vicious, male-dominated environment from which a sensible woman escaped, underestimated the spiritual commitment of those who entered the Orders and maligned the social conditions under which they lived.[5]

The following essays in social history state their findings so adequately that there is no need to introduce them here. Therefore this introductory essay is addressed to the sorts of problems which specifically relate to women's lives—in particular to women's life cycle, a public vs. a "privatized" or domestic existence, conditions of the material life as they relate to women, women's control of their reproductivity, the social history of religious opinion as it pertains to women, and the accomodation of legal principles to social needs as it affects women. All these factors are fundamental to creating understandings which affect the broader social issues of family, class, occupation (and medieval women frequently had occupations), and a rural or urban environment.

Birth, death, and the rites of passage between are points in life when women are most likely to leave a written record. Furthermore the events which punctuate a life, birth, infancy, possibly education, very likely betrothal and marriage or entry into a religious order, begetting children, divorce, widowhood, last testaments and death, reveal much about social priorities. Dowries, the preliminary step to marriage, are a particularly sensitive instrument for detecting social values. From early medieval society and the traditional Germanic male-awarded dowry to the development of the female dowry and its inflation into an extraordinary economic device in the late medieval city-state, dowries mark changes in women's social status. There are a host of related issues: who provides the dowry, who receives it? Even if a woman's marriage is the occasion of giving a dowry, will she control it in any fashion or upon any occasion in her life? There is an astonishing variety of answers to these questions, even in the limited examples of time and place covered in this volume. The variety signifies a fluidity in social usage that still existed in the Middle Ages. Tradition had yet to solidify into the unyielding patterns which characterize later centuries.

But women do not appear in the surviving manuscripts only at significant moments in their lives. Historians often remark about how frequently women appear in the medieval record, and in such a wide variety of functions. Early medieval women, to borrow a term from contemporary radical feminism, do not appear to have been "privatized," that is, relegated to a domestic existence where their functions are determined by, or subordinated to, their sexual capacities. My attention was drawn to women in the charters of Ragusa (Dubrovnik) for this reason. It was evident that women participated in public life in disregard of Statute Law, which, in being enforced, would have strictly limited their lives to the private or domestic sphere. David Herlihy makes an even stronger case for the early Middle Ages, 700–1200, noting in particular women's role in the economy. Although it is a sparsely documented era, a significant number of the surviving sources refer to women, and to their public acts. Now this had implications for society at large: with greater opportunity to use their capacities women became a more positive force in society. These essays should be read with the issue of women's public or private role in mind. An English woman of the feudal classes maintained a significant number of public capacities into the late Middle Ages. In Spain the greater privatization of women stood in conflict with the need to colonize newly reconquered territories. The degree of privatization of women varies by locale in Europe, with implications for the later development of national character.

A Syrian gentleman, Usāmah ibn Murshid, observing the behavior of Christian women on Crusade, was aghast at the freedom with which they appeared in public places and participated in the life of the community at large. He had aptly observed a striking peculiarity of western European society.[6] But in the late Middle Ages conditions conducive to women's public participation began to disappear in the Italian city-states, those pace setters for change in the medieval world. Richard Goldthwaite notes the disappearance of the tower and loggia in Florentine domestic architecture in the late fourteenth and fifteenth centuries, and the growing emphasis upon the bourgeois palace with its elegance of interior space. Complementary to this is a trend in painting toward depiction of the domestic scene, the madonna and child shown with infinite tenderness.[7] Despite the fascination with family, and women, and children within the isolated domestic setting, a woman's opportunities were significantly confined by shutting her away from the loggia, that window upon urban life. This is a significant loss of rights from the earlier medieval period, no matter how tenderly compensated by celebration of the domestic joys.

Participation in public life relates directly to women's occupations. Women's membership in artisan guilds, which were on occasion exclusively filled with women, depended upon the social right to participate in public life. The loss of this right came to be closely tied to class standing, as this anthology illustrates. But more research needs to be done on its relationship to economic cycles: periods of economic expansion when women were encouraged to participate in public occupations and periods of falling prices when unemployment relegated women to the domestic sphere. Sociologists note that a woman's standing in her family is heavily dependent upon her capacity to derive income from work outside the family unit. Therefore lack of employment would tend to reduce a woman's social standing, conditions which came to operate more and more in the depressed conditions of the Renaissance economy.

If social status is dependent upon freedom to participate in public life, what of women's capability to do the hard physical work required by medieval agriculture and artisan production? Most ages make clear sex distinctions, viewing women as different in kind, largely due to their lesser size and physical strength. Despite Tacitus' famous description of the terrible and powerful early German women and occasional place names like Ladysmith, are there any reasons to believe that in the early history of the West women were capable of performing tasks which most other ages in history thought appropriate to men only? In this respect, conditions of women's material life may influence their social and economic position. While comparative statistics on physical size and strength are not available for the medieval period, a shred of significant data on women's general well-being does exist; these are observations on the age of menarche. A recent review of the medieval literature on the topic indicates that while St. Thomas Aquinas had Aristotle's authoritative age of fifteen for menarche before him, he opted for the much earlier age of twelve.[8] Since age of menarche is an indication of general health determined largely by the protein content of the diet, it appears that Fernand Braudel's "wholly carnivorous" European man is matched by a protein-eating woman.[9] Of course, there are social priorities involved; apparently women were not discriminated against in the allocation of available protein, although distinctly different proportions of protein in the diets of men and women characterize other places and other times. Apportioning women a substantial amount of protein could increase women's capacity to reproduce, while, and this is the startling fact, leaving them further energies to perform other tasks not specifically related to child-bearing and child-rearing. This stands among the most salient facts about the growth of Europe in its early centuries.

Generally favorable conditions of the material life can operate on the female half of the population in many ways. It may be conducive to the control of fertility, for example. Studies of post-industrial societies indicate that the chief incentive for decreased birth rates are the relatively favorable or improved conditions of infant survival.[10] If medieval women could with some confidence expect their offspring to survive, largely because of their own good health maintained by an adequate diet, they might be expected to make some effort to control their fertility. This tendency would be strengthened if they knew they might participate in gainful employment in the public sphere. Himes, in his study of contraception, noted references to medieval contraceptive practice a generation ago.[11] John Noonan's excellent study of the church's position on contraception gives indication of the frequency with which the church legislated against contraception and abortion throughout the medieval period. He listed the numerous formulae for contraceptives and abortifacients.[12] It would be foolhardy to attempt an evaluation of their success, but as B. D. H. Miller has stated, "The evidence on contraception is often indirect: we have to infer that what was frequently prohibited was also frequently practised."[13] Contraception, then, reveals attitudes, and medieval women often showed positive attitudes toward the possibility of control over their fertility.

Our discussion of factors affecting women's lives in the medieval period can go no further without some discussion of the role played by religious, or ecclesiastical, opinion upon women's position in society. How was an ecclesiastical organization whose principles of morality were based upon the highly privatized conditions of women in the ancient Mediterranean world to adapt to the significantly different social and economic conditions under which medieval women lived? There is no better issue in which to weigh this problem than contraception: specifically, its meaning in the medieval world in contrast to its meaning within the context of late classical Mediterranean society. As classical women were almost entirely confined to a private domestic sphere, their use of contraceptives would indicate either a refusal to undertake the responsibilities of their reproductive, that is, their only socially productive, life or, possibly, their extra-marital activity. Both were anathema in the eyes of church authorities, and the declining birth rates of the late ancient world were seen as a particularly heinous social evil.

Applying ecclesiastical prohibitions on contraception, which were the product of such a social climate, to the lives of women of the Middle Ages was singularly inappropriate. Medieval women were not as completely privatized or as exclusively defined by their sexual nature. Contraception would be employed by them to limit the demands of family in relation to their other responsibilities. Population, despite the unsettled conditions of the early medieval period, reflected a tendency toward increase; despite contraception, famine, war, and disease, medieval women supported an overall increase. The church did accomodate somewhat in recognition of women's economic role. Burchard's *Decretum*, which is dependent upon opinions offered in the Venerable Bede and earlier sources, exacted a lighter penance for a woman "prohibiting conception" if her economic condition was poor.[14] This implies some recognition of the economic and social conditions affecting medieval women's lives, but it was not strong enough a tendency to block the ancient church's equation of contraception with homicide, and the harsher doctrine ultimately prevailed.

There are very few historical interpretations of the church's position on women's role in medieval society, and a thorough examination of the writings of the Church Fathers is needed. Such an investigation should keep in mind that women lived their lives in tension between the conditions of their social and material existence and the often conflicting dictates of the church. The church could sustain women in their roles or reduce their capacity to function in the public sphere and maintain control over their own lives. It reached women at the most significant moments in their lives; through its control of the sacrament of marriage the church had, perhaps, the most profound effect upon them. The article in this volume on early medieval marriage and divorce by Jo-Ann McNamara and Suzanne Wemple investigates the complex steps which led to the formulation of an orthodox position on canon marriage in the writings of the Carolingian authority, Hincmar of Rheims. In the process many traditional practices of proven social value were lost, not the least of which was the right to repudiate a marriage. Social institutions suited to the needs of the day were not likely to survive when pitted against the canons of sacred law or the validity of the sacraments.

Social history offers one cautionary lesson when dealing with church law or ecclesiastical opinion as it pertains to medieval women. Because the church prohibited, or chastised, or declared a penance does not mean that society conformed. Again, the church's directives were most likely to be influential among the upper classes and among the urban who were served by an effective ecclesiastical structure. The principle holds for civil law also.

Legal statutes can be obeyed to the letter, stretched beyond recognition, abused, misused, or ignored by society. Any study of the social history of religious opinion would then have to evaluate whether ecclesiastical judgments were actively and successfully enforced.

At least in regard to the church's opinion of women, the Middle Ages can be appropriately bisected by the Gregorian reform movement of the late eleventh century. This reform demolished the double monasteries of the earlier era and quite effectively walled women's houses off from the institutional hierarchy of the church. The great medieval churchwomen, Hild at Whitby, Leoba, Hildegard of Bingen, Roswitha of Gandersheim, all belong to the earlier period. As the influence of churchwomen waned, church writings on women showed a greater tendency to regard women as the "other," the basis for a growing misogyny and a violation of the orthodox Christian belief that all souls, without distinction of age, class, or sex, are equal in the eyes of God. Religious opinion in the medieval period travels a long distance from the generally sympathetic statements in the writings of Pope Gregory I, 590–604, to the late medieval bifurcation of women into spiritual or profane beings, the divine Mary or the seductive Eve. Even some of the least misogynous late medieval church philosophers, such as Vincent of Beauvais, whose supposedly enlightened theories on the education of women are thought to prefigure the Renaissance, did not escape the generally pessimistic attitudes toward women of his day. As Rosemary Tobin notes in her appraisal of his ideas on the education of women, "With all due deference to Vincent for qualifying some of the more extremely restrictive positions of his authorities, it is still quite evident that he is more concerned about the effects of a girl's behavior on others, whether family or society, than he is on her own soul."[15] His attempt to control women's impact upon society reveals the church's growing fear of women's drives and purposes. It serves to illustrate that as the ecclesiastical hierarchy grew more remote from women it encountered greater difficulty in comprehending women who participated in society. It was only truly at ease with that totally spiritualized image of the private and domestic woman, Mary, the Mother of God.

Brenda Bolton in her study, "Mulieres Sanctae," indicates the severity of the social problem which existed. Thirteenth-century women found the church ill-disposed to create insitutions for the expression of their deeply-felt devotion. The *Frauenfrage*, or Women Question, came to be an important religious issue, and one which was not answered very satisfactorily. The recognized danger for the church, of course, lay in devout women seeking the representatives of heretical movements for spiritual guidance. Heresy plays a significant role in women's history, and the heretical movements of the thirteenth century are no exception.

Canon law and civil statute became increasingly important in women's lives in the later Middle Ages. As social tradition was replaced by highly

specific statute law in the feudal kingdoms of the north and in the Mediterranean city-states, women confronted in civic guise those Roman legal
principles which had influenced the church's opinion on their position. If the
statute law of the Adriatic city-states can be taken as illustrative, and it suits
the purpose because it contains some of the most ancient codified urban law,
women lived strictly curtailed existences. They might be citizens, but they
were private citizens, unable to exercise the public rights enjoyed by their
fathers, husbands, and sons. Do such laws indicate that freedoms of earlier
centuries have disappeared? Social history, through examining the application of law, can investigate this problem. In Ragusa (Dubrovnik), for
example, I noted the law was disregarded so women might participate in the
public sector, and I concluded that women were too essential in a period of
economic growth to be excluded from a role in the family's economic
pursuits. This illustrates one of the most baffling difficulties for women's
studies: the attempt to determine whether legal principle and social custom
coincide. Historians dealing with women have grown increasingly wary of
accepting restrictive laws and misogynous interpretations of women's
position at face value. Women do not necessarily behave as if they accepted
either. In the context of Venetian patrician society, women appear to have
had considerable impact on inheritance and, through it, the economy.
Barbara Hanawalt, by investigating the behavior of female felons, reveals a
whole range of female behavior outside the law, behavior only apparent to
the historian's eye because the felons were apprehended and left a record in
the Court Rolls. Whether openly criminal, as in this case, or merely passively
resistant, women can be notorious scofflaws; the more privatized, the more
likely they are to be so. This makes their history elusive, but it should
sharpen our awareness of social undercurrents. Even under conditions which
severely limit their activity, women may enjoy considerable informal
freedoms and have a decisive impact upon the society in which they live.

The tendency, as the Middle Ages progressed, was toward a lessening of
the public activity of women, a lower place in ecclesiastical opinion, fewer
roles in guild organizations, and less agricultural administration if not less
agricultural labor. But such generalizations must be carefully qualified by
specific reference to locale, as this volume amply illustrates. But why did
women's generally favorable position during Europe's early and anarchic
centuries tend to worsen as medieval society developed? Various answers
have been offered. Some credit the early Germans with customs particularly
favorable to women. They offer as evidence the male dowry of the Germans
and the higher *wergild,* or bloodprice, of women in the Barbaric Law codes
of many of the German tribes.[16] Some note also that Christianity had yet to
make significant inroads into the still largely pagan customs of Europe north
of the Alps. This latter interpretation may do the early missionary church a
great disservice. The church's most notable accomplishment with regard to
women lay in incorporating them into its early monastic houses. Another

interpretation has been offered stressing the fact that early medieval women had not yet undergone those evolutionary steps into a patriarchal, male-dominated, capitalist, accumulating society, and they were, for the time being, relatively free. Frederick Engels, in his study of the *Origin of the Family*, struck this markedly romantic theme in his interpretation of Europe's barbaric age.[17] None of these arguments takes sufficient note of the failure of early medieval society to define rigidly a public and a private sphere, and relegate women to the latter. Nor do they note the relatively beneficent conditions of the material life which prevailed. Early medieval women had opportunity to make recognized public contributions to society; they were valued for that reason. We know from historical sources that women did receive recognition. Betty Bandel, in a note on English chroniclers' attitudes toward women before the Norman Conquest, pointed out that vigor, ambition, daring, and intelligence were recognized and commended. After the Conquest such behavior was regarded as inappropriate and unwomanly.[18]

The late eleventh and twelfth centuries stand in many ways as a watershed between the greater opportunity for women in early medieval times and the more confining circumstances of life in the later Middle Ages. But before we identify civil law codes or ecclesiastical opinions as the arch-villains in this change, some effort should be made to count the cost of relative freedom for women in the early Middle Ages. When inventories and similar sources yield comparative statistical data, we learn that early medieval women had notably higher (that is, earlier) mortality rates than men. Women in the early Middle Ages paid the price of early death for the valuable contributions of maintaining population growth and contributing to society in the public sphere. Historians must therefore take into account an individual's reasonable desire for a longer and less demanding existence. A privatized life might mean some reduction in the harsh demands of life, even if purchased at the price of lower social status. Here lies a difficult issue involving, possibly, changing mentalities. Does a peasant woman or a town-bred spinster feel bitter resentment if relieved of field work or excluded from a guild by an adequate supply of male labor? Does the Florentine bourgeois wife find ample satisfaction in her high-ceilinged palace and lovingly executed portrait to compensate for loss of participation in the family's civic and business concerns? Does a Provencal duchess shut out from the administration of her own lands by her husband's growing corps of bureaucrats enjoy the courtly songs and poems composed in her honor by lesser noblemen who have been as effectively dislodged from their bases of power as she has been from hers? These are the issues of changing mentalities and only in the latter instance, the courtly romance, are there adequate resources to begin the investigation of new and changing sensibilities.

By the later Middle Ages, in the most favorable (that is, urban) settings, women had increased their life spans, sometimes even outdoing the male segment of the population in longevity. Less difficult work seems to have exerted an influence here, but another factor is involved: certain women did not marry in the cities of the later Middle Ages, their comparatively long lives adding up to a statistical increase for all womankind. After centuries of population growth in which all but those few women who chose the monastic life married and propagated, single women began to appear in considerable numbers. Lack of dowries was trumpeted as the cause of this worrisome social situation, but it is also a symptom that population level increases were no longer particularly desirable. This complicated the celebrated *Frauenfrage*.[19] Women who did not marry were considered appropriately situated only when they were cloistered, an enormous burden upon the spiritual nature of the conventual orders and houses which existed.[20]

Although this volume does not purport to examine women's condition throughout all of medieval Europe, there is ample variety in the essays included to make useful comparisons by time and place. The medieval period will always attract notice because of curiosity about the origins of ideas and social traditions. But there are many more significant reasons to investigate women's position in the early centuries of the West. Possibly the greatest claim for early-European women's significance was put forward by David Herlihy.[21] He states that women were sufficiently capable to undertake the administration of the economy so that they might free men to undertake the geographical expansion of European society. No age is sufficiently understood until the contributions of women are made evident; this is particularly true of the Middle Ages.

NOTES

1. Eleanor Shipley Duckett, "Women and their Letters in the Early Middle Ages" (pamphlet, Smith College, Northampton, 1964), p. 1.

2. Bertha Phillpotts, *Kindred and Clan in the Middle Ages and After* (Cambridge, 1913).

3. Eileen Power, "The Position of Women in the Middle Ages," *The Legacy of the Middle Ages*, ed. C. G. Crump and E. F. Jacob (Oxford, 1926).

4. Lina Eckenstein, *Women Under Monasticism* (Cambridge, 1896).

5. Emily Putnam, *The Lady*, rev. ed. (Chicago, 1971), see author's foreword.

6. Philip Hitti, *Usāmah ibn Murshid, An Arab-Syrian Gentleman, 1095–1188*, (New York, 1929), pp. 164–66.

7. Richard Goldthwaite, "The Florentine Palace as Domestic Architecture," *American Historical Review* 72 (1972): 1011.

8. Darrel W. Amundsen and Carol Jean Diers, "The Age of Menarche in Medieval Europe," *Human Biology* 45 (1973): 363–68.

9. Fernand Braudel, *Capitalism and the Material Life*, trans. by Miriam Kochas (New York, 1973), pp. 127–37.

10. E. A. Wrigley, *Population and History*, (New York, 1969), pp. 180-202.

11. N. E. Himes, *A Medical History of Contraception* (Baltimore, 1936), pp. 135-69.

12. John Noonan, *Contraception* (Cambridge, 1965), pp. 143-300.

13. B. D. H. Miller, "She who hath Drunk any Potion," *Medium Aevum* 31 (1962): 188.

14. Burchard, *Decretum, Patrologiae cursus completus* (Latin series), ed. by J. -P. Migne, vol. 140, col. 972 (Paris, 1880), p. 19; for discussion, see Noonan, *Contraception*, p. 161.

15. Rosemary Barton Tobin, "Vincent of Beauvais on the Education of Women," *Journal of the History of Ideas* 35 (1974): 486.

16. For example, see Henry Adams, "The Primitive Rights of Women," *Historical Essays* (New York, 1891), pp. 1-41.

17. Frederick Engels, *The Origin of the Family*, trans. Ernest Utermann, (New York, 1902).

18. Betty Bandel, "The English Chroniclers' Attitude toward Women," *Journal of the History of Ideas* 16 (1955): 113-18.

19. For a review of this literature see David Herlihy, "Women in Medieval Society," (pamphlet: The Smith History Lecture, 1971, University of St. Thomas, Houston, Texas), and Josiah Cox Russell, *Late Ancient and Medieval Population* (Philadelphia, 1958).

20. Ernest McDonnell, *The Beguines and Beghards in Medieval Culture* (Brunswick, New Jersey, 1954).

21. See the first selection in this volume.

David Herlihy

Land, Family, and Women in Continental Europe, 701–1200

In reconstructing the social and economic history of the early Middle Ages, perhaps the single, most salient obstacle to our research is the scant amount of information we possess concerning the household economy of the lay family: how the family managed its lands and divided its labors among its members. Our sources, overwhelmingly ecclesiastical in provenience, tell us fairly much of the organization of Church properties, and, through a few surviving royal records, we have some information too about royal estates.[1] But at all times in medieval Europe, non-royal lay families owned or controlled the larger portion of the soil. We must try to learn more about how these propertied families managed their estates, and how internal family structure may have been affected by, or in turn may have influenced broader economic and social changes.

In studying the management of lay patrimonies and its possible interaction with family structure, the subject of immediate interest is the woman, the position she held within the family, the role she played in the supervision of family property, and the relation between the two. For as we hope to illustrate in this article, the woman comes to play an extraordinary role in the management of family property in the early Middle Ages, and social customs as well as economic life were influenced by her prominence.

To be sure, much is already known of the legal rights of women in regards to land ownership and the administration of family property, as defined in late Roman law and the Germanic codes. The history of Roman law is the history of progressive improvement in the legal rights of the woman.[2] Within marriage, for example, the kind of near-parental power (the *manus mariti*) the husband exercised over his wife was not universally

Originally published in *Traditio* 18 (1962): 89–120, reprinted by permission of the author and Fordham University Press.

characteristic of Roman marriages even in the period of the Twelve Tables and by the time of the Principate had become practically non-existent. Formal tutelage (*tutela*) over adult women *sui iuris* continued longer, till about the time of Diocletian, and throughout the Imperial period a woman—as, for that matter, many men—might live under the continuing and restrictive legal authority of her father (the *patria potestas*). Still, by variety of legal resources, the enterprising woman could, if she wished, render the tutelage more fictional than real, and even the woman under paternal power could eventually hold and manage property of her own. Within marriage, too, the property she had owned before marriage was kept distinct from her husband's, and, should the marriage be dissolved, that property and also her dowry would be returned to her. Apparently, however, late Roman law did not yet admit of a true community of property between the marriage partners in a way that would have permitted the wife to claim, at the death of her husband and the division of family property, a share in the wealth that family enterprise might have gained. But certainly, in late Roman legal development, progress was being made towards it.

From what we know of Old Germanic law, the woman was (as in early Roman law) similarly considered to be lacking in juridical capacity to look after her own interests.[3] According to Lombard law (in this regard perhaps the most conservative of the Germanic codes), the woman, even as an adult, remained under the guardianship ("mundium") of a male relative (or failing such, the king), whose permission was required for any transaction involving her property. Within marriage Lombard law provided for a close union of the partners' properties under the control of the husband. The principle here seems to have been that a wife's property could neither increase, nor decrease in marriage, which means she did not share in family acquests but, should the marriage be dissolved, could claim back from it exactly what she had brought to it.

In regard to the guardianship of women and the status of their properties within marriage, the other Germanic codes are not always so clear. It is, however, certain that by the age of the barbarian kingdoms the traditional Germanic restrictions on a woman's capacity to inherit, own, and administer property were breaking down. The famous and still somewhat mysterious title of the Salic law (62.6), prohibiting women from inheriting "Salic" land, was modified by the Edict of Chilperic (561–84), which admitted daughters to the inheritance in the absence of direct male issue.[4] In Frankish law, too, (to judge by charters) the adult woman by Merovingian times was free of effective male tutelage. Visigothic law in particular is remarkable for the freedom it granted to the marriage partners, including the wife, to administer the respective "capital" they possessed before marriage, and Burgundian law was similarly liberal. Moreover, in Visigothic law, acquisitions gained after marriage were considered the community property of the family, and should that family be dissolved, the wife or her heirs could claim a share in family acquests. Should the husband die, the wife retained use of and administrative control over family property and indeed over the total patrimony of her minor children. Frankish, Alemannian, and Bavarian laws also provided for a close association of the partners' possessions, and the wife (though apparently not her heirs) could benefit personally from family acquests. It is, however, very difficult to judge if the often vague provisions of these codes as yet represented a true community property (as in the Visigothic law); but we may safely say again that progress was being made towards it.

Besides these contrasts among the various legal traditions, there are likewise evident certain uniformities worth pointing out. And uniformities are of course to be expected, given the all-pervasive influence of the Christian Church and given her strong notions on the proper position of the woman within the family.[5] In unequivocally asserting that men and women shared a common spiritual destiny and dignity, the Christian Church undoubtedly helped prevent the woman from anywhere becoming a chattel of her husband; in seeking to establish the sanctity and permanence of marriage, the Church helped confirm her importance as established mistress of her household. At the same time, Christian teaching was hardly such as to allow a real social matriarchy to develop anywhere in Europe. The Church Fathers characteristically thought of the woman as a weaker vessel, and considered a prominent role in affairs outside the family unsuited for her. In other words, under the levelling influence of Christianity, the position of women throughout Europe was kept within certain limits. She was everywhere more than chattel, and everywhere less than a matriarch. Specifically in regard to property, late Roman law and the Germanic codes were similar in recognizing that the woman could retain a personal title to property even within marriage, though the degree of freedom she possessed in administering it and the benefit she derived from further family gains differed considerably among the various legal traditions.

However, if the legal rights of women in regard to family property have already been pretty well explored, our picture still shows gaps. The laws deal largely with the great or extraordinary events in the history of medieval families: how they were created, what happened when they dissolved. They tell us rather little of the ordinary, day-by-day life of the family, how its property was administered, and the role women played in it. To investigate this, we may turn from legal codes to our so-called "documents of practice"—donations, sales, exchanges, leases, and so forth, which constitute a detailed and precise record of early medieval agrarian life. In Italy, Germany, and Northern France, such documents have survived in great numbers from the middle eighth century; in Southern France and Spain, from the early ninth. By 1200 they are counted by the tens of thousands.

In handling these documents, we shall try a statistical approach—not on the pretense of constructing a precise sociological survey but in an effort to more effectively survey our huge mass of material than could be done by random and impressionistic selection of a few documents out of thousands. Our statistics are directed, in other words, towards illustrating largely verbal contrasts and changes in our documents considered as a single corpus, in the hope that out of such an analysis a clearer view of woman's practical role in the family and in land administration might emerge.

Specifically, we shall construct three statistical indices, each based on a different kind of information but all reflective of the role women played in the family and in the administration of its property. Because that role varied in different parts of Europe, we shall construct these indices separately for each of the following five regions of continental Europe: Italy, Spain (including Portugal), Southern France (roughly south of the Loire River and including French Switzerland), Northern France (including the Low Countries), and Germany (including Austria, German Switzerland, Alsace, and Luxemburg).

One possible indication of the importance of the woman within the family is the use, by her children, of a matronymic rather than a patronymic. We have much material with which to evaluate the importance of the matronymic in continental Europe. For the scribe of course had to identify precisely the principals in and witnesses to his charters, and to this end he often gave a parent's name: "Petrus filius Silvestri," simply "Petrus Silvestri," occasionally "Petrus de Silvestro." Both men and women were commonly identified by a parent's name, even after the parent's death (indicated in the charters by such words as "quondam" or "bone memorie"). For Italy, between the early eighth century and 1200, we can extract from the chartularies and parchment collections listed in the Appendix over 80,000 patronymics. Our numbers from other regions are not so enormous, but they are still substantial. From Southern France we have close to 10,000; from Spain, nearly 19,000. In both areas, patronymics appear from the early ninth century, but remain sporadic until the eleventh. From Northern France we have over 6,000, and from Germany 700. In these regions our series becomes threadbare from the late ninth to the eleventh centuries—a period when our northern private charters are both relatively few in number and poorly informative.

Significantly for our purposes, many persons in the charters are identified not by the name of a father but of a mother: "Azo filius Formose," "Azo Formose," "Azo de Formosa." We shall try to illustrate this curious popularity of the matronymic by calculating what percentage of our total identifications by parent involves female names. In calculating that percentage, we take as a patro- or matronymic only the name of a male or female parent used to identify a particular individual. We do not consider as patronymics such phrases as "heredes Iohannis" and "filii Tancredi," in which the "heirs" or "sons" are unnamed. Nor do we take as a patronymic reference to a parent who also appears in the charter; thus, in such a phrase as "Petrus et Iohannes filius ipsius Petri," Petrus would not be counted. In instances where both parent and grandparent are named (e.g., "Iohannes de Petro Formose"), only the parent's name is counted. In instances where both father's and mother's names are given, only the father's is counted. In double names, the second is considered a patronymic when in the genitive case, unless it is evident from the context that it is not. Thus, "Guillelmus" is considered a patronymic in the name "Raimundus Guillelmi" but not in the name "Raimundus Guillelmus." Ambiguous cases (e.g., "in manu Raimundi Guillelmi") are excluded. Spanish second names in -z (e.g., "Petrus Lopez" and "Iohannes Gonzalez") are counted as patronymics. However, in such Spanish names as "Petrus Taresa," the "Taresa" is considered a matronymic. In such hybrid names as "Iohannes Guillelmi filius Matilde," we count only the parent's name following the "filius." Names of kings given to date the charter are not considered. Each particular patronymic is counted only once in each charter, no matter how many individuals may bear it.

Table 1 gives the results of our count on the basis of centuries for each of the five regions of continental Europe we are considering:

TABLE 1

Percentage per Century of Identifications by Matronymic

Region	8th	9th	10th	11th	12th
Italy	2	2	5	6	5
Spain	—	—	1	6	3
S. France	—	—	9	12	10
N. France	—	0	0	6	8
Germany	3	0	—	2	8

Source: Chartularies and parchment collections listed in the bibliographical Appendix. The figures on which these percentages are based can be found in Table 4, column 1.

Because of the wide regional differences in the use of patronymics and the notarial methods of expressing them, we ought not press these comparisons too closely. However, rough as our table undoubtedly is, there still emerges from it evidence of a remarkable use of matronymics in Southern France from the tenth through the twelfth century. In Spain the phenomenon is evident from the eleventh century, though Spanish matronymics are drawn, as we shall see, chiefly from particular kinds of charters. In Italy, matronymics become common from the second quarter of of the tenth century and reach their peak frequency (532 out of 6,062) in the early eleventh. Their relative numbers then decline, though they remain fairly plentiful through the twelfth century. In Northern Europe, the phenomenon becomes evident somewhat later than in the South, clearly so in Northern France, presumably so in Germany, though we have only few names with which to judge the incidence of matronymics before 1100 in Germany.

Graph 1, based upon our total of over 125,000 patronymics from all regions of the continent and plotted on the basis of twenty-five-year periods, affords a more accurate chronological perspective on this incidence of matronymics. It shows that the matronymic, rare from the eighth century to the middle tenth, becomes ever more common during the latter half of the tenth century and reaches its peak frequency in the early eleventh. Its incidence then falls off, though it remains relatively high through the twelfth century.

How are we to explain this marked preference of so many individuals in our charters to identify themselves with their mothers? We cannot of course discount the influence of notarial practices upon this incidence of matronymics. Occasionally the matronymic partook of the nature of a nickname. "Fasana the daughter of Sergius the priest," a Neapolitan charter of 1108 reads, "who is called de Maroccia."[6] In those areas where notarial tradition dictated particularly rigid formulas and strict procedures, the notary may well have suppressed such semi-popular sobriquets in favor of formal and consistent references to the father. The extreme rarity of matronymics in Milanese documents (for example, in comparison with those from other areas in Italy) may owe something to the peculiar strictness of the Lombard notarial procedures.

Still, while notarial usage may be a factor in explaining why matronymics are extremely rare in some areas, it cannot explain why they are plentiful in others. For we still need to know why, in the charters, so many men were identified with their mothers. Nor are there grounds for attributing the widespread increase in the incidence of matronymics after 950 to any evident and equally widespread change in notarial practices.

In some few instances, the matronymic seems to indicate that the father had remarried and had children by another wife. "Petrus Vilelmi," says a French document of 1138, "son of Dulciana and his brother Bertrand son of Lucia."[7] Then too, the matronymic could be conveniently used as a means of distinguishing a son from a like-named father or grandfather. A ninth-century charter identifies Charles the Bald (d. 877) as "son of Judith," whether to distinguish him from other Charles's in the Carolingian line or from his half-brothers Lother and Louis, whom his father Louis the Pious had had by earlier marriage.[8] However, even if we could presume that substantial numbers of those bearing matronymics in our charters had half-brothers or like-named fathers, we must still explain why, in most instances, the mother's name alone was sufficiently well known in the community to identify her children. That Charles the Bald could be identified by reference to his mother Judith, exclusively, shows that Judith, in her own right, was a

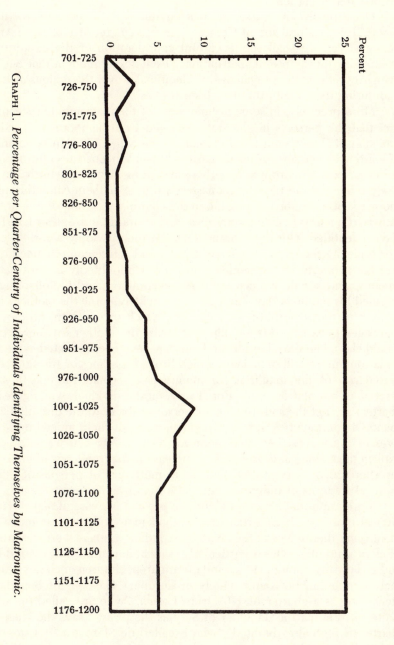

GRAPH 1. *Percentage per Quarter-Century of Individuals Identifying Themselves by Matronymic.*

famous lady. And from what we know of her prominent role in Carolingian history, that is certain.

Occasionally, of course, the matronymic is flatly indicative of illegitimacy. "John, natural son of Gemma," reads a charter of 1182 from Amalfi.[9] However, as we shall see, a careful consideration of the circumstances accompanying the use of matronymics excludes all thought that our index primarily reflects the prevalence of illegitimacy over the regions of Europe and during these centuries of its history.

More precisely, in some instances use of the matronymic reflected the fact that the person's juridic status derived from his mother. "Tersia, the daughter of Honoria our freedwoman," says a will of 739.[10] In a document of 874, listing eleven serfs of the monastery of San Vincenzo al Volturno, no less than four bear a matronymic, perhaps indicating illegitimate birth, but more likely reflecting the fact the monastery's title over them came through the mother.[11] So also, serfs appearing in the chartulary of Saint-Pierre at Ghent rather frequently bear matronymics, and sporadic examples of serfs and slaves identified with their mothers can be found widely across Europe.[12] For typically the child of a slave-woman and a freeman remained a slave and the property of his mother's master.[13] Undoubtedly liaisons between freemen and servile women were not uncommon, and the offspring who retained his mother's "law" may also have widely borne the mother's name, at least in the records of the seigneury which owned him. Moreover, in marriages between serfs of different lords, the mother's owner typically would claim half the offspring, and this may have been reflected in the use of a matronymic.[14] Still, marriages which broke class lines or transgressed the boundaries of the manorial community can account for only a minute fraction of our matronymics. For clearly, most individuals who figure in our charters are not the sons of serfs or persons subject to the discipline of the manorial community. They are freemen, many of them indeed representatives of the highest levels of medieval society. Nor can we satisfactorily explain the sudden and pronounced increase in the frequency of matronymics after 950 by a supposed increase in marriages of persons of different juridical status or of different manorial lords.

More important a factor behind this use and increase of matronymics is clerical marriage. It is certain that a good many of the men and women identifying themselves in the charters with their mothers were the products of clerical families. This is particularly evident in central Italy around Rome and in Tuscany, though clerics and the apparent children of clerics bearing a matronymic can be found widely in Europe. "The sons of Benedict the cleric," reads a charter of 1109 from Capua, "who are called the sons of Gaita."[15] "Fasana the daughter of Sergius the priest," says the Neapolitan charter of 1108 already cited, "who is called de Maroccia."[16] Ugo, son of Bishop Regembald of Florence, styled himself in a charter of ca. 1059 "son of Minuta."[17] In our central Italian and Tuscan charters, a disproportionate number of priests use a matronymic. Had they been raised in the vicinity of a church, to continue as adults their father's profession? In other words, the proliferation of matronymics after 950 would seem to some extent to measure the developing crisis in the Western Church over clerical marriage ("nicholaism"). So too, the decline in our index from the middle eleventh century to some extent shows the success of the Gregorian reform movement, which took as its supreme goal the restoration of celibacy as the fundamental rule of clerical living.

A discreet effort to conceal an uncanonical clerical marriage thus accounts for many of our matronymics. Still, such discretion cannot be the most general explanation for their use. Our charters do not give the impression of a careful reticence in regard to illegitimacy, and bastards, natural sons, or children of priests are often baldly labeled in them. In many charters, the father is recognized and his name stated (prayers may be asked for his soul), but the son or daughter still uses a matronymic.[18] Stranger still, in some instances the same individual will use a patronymic in one charter and a matronymic in another.[19] He changes his name as the circumstances of the contract, its locale, or the property involved in it, change. It is here evident that a matronymic is preferred because it better served to identify the principal, perhaps reflecting the fact that the mother was locally better known than the father or that her name was traditionally associated with property involved.

Moreover, clerical marriage by itself is an insufficient explanation for this profusion of matronymics. In Northern Italy, in Germany, in Northern France, and especially in Southern France and Spain, association with the mother is most strikingly characteristic not of the clergy but of the most prominent of laymen, the nobles and knights. In Spain, in the Aragonese charters by which vassals or châtelains are invested with their tenures or oaths of loyalty taken, both the vassal and his lord will usually identify themselves by matronymics.[20] Indeed, apart from these special (though numerous) charters, matronymics would have to be considered rare in Spanish documents. The similar acts of investiture and oath from Southern France are similarly characterized by a consistent use of matronymics to identify the principals. So strong is this tradition that in a charter from Maguelone, dated ca. 1155-1160, a vassal designated by a matronymic, swears a feudal oath, and it later emerges that the father too (along with the mother) is physically present and "ordering" his son so to act.[21] Is this consistent use of matronymics in association with feudal investitures and oaths only an example of a rigidified notarial practice in those areas? Perhaps; but again, these mothers must have been well known in their communities for their names to sufficiently identify their sons.

Moreover, in Southern France (unlike Spain), matronymics appear widely in other forms of charters too. So also in Italy, Northern France, and Germany, matronymics are found in all sorts of documents. The men who bear them are obviously socially prominent. They are often identified as knights: "Arduinus miles, filius Joscende nobilissime mulieris," "Artaldus miles de Calamont, filius Alatrudis."[22] Most of them are appearing as witnesses to the charters of great laymen or ecclesiastics. The women whose names they bear are socially prominent too, sometimes titled, often distinguished by the term "lady": "Don Pedro filio de dompna Cecilia," "Godesio Didaci de cometissa domna Geluira," "Guidoctus domine Navilie," "Iohannes de domna Maria."[23]

Here, there can be no question of disguising an illicit paternity. For several prominent families of Southern France—the Guillems of Montpellier, for example—we know quite well the genealogy of the male line.[24] But in each generation the members characteristically identify themselves not with their fathers (from whom they principally inherited their lands and status) but with their mothers: "Villelmus (V) filius Ermengarde," "Guillelmus (VI) filius Ermessendis," "Guillem (VII) filius Sibilie," and the like. Was the matronymic here used primarily in order to distinguish a succession of like-named Williams? Possibly; but such a device would still presume that these mothers were well known and long remembered in Montpellier.

A Poitevin charter is dated by reference to Guillaume V Aigret of Poitou (1039–1058), seventh duke of Aquitaine: "lord count William, son of countess Agnes, ruling."[25] Guillaume's father is well known and his legitimacy unquestioned. Can we be surprised when, in the dating of a thirteenth-century Poitevin charter, Louis IX, king of France, legitimate heir to the great Capetian line, is identified as "Louis, son of Blanche"?[26]

Why are these knights, nobles and kings associated with their mothers? Occasionally the reason would seem to be that their inheritance came from their mother. Alphonse VII, "the Emperor" (1126–1157), king of Castile, calls himself in several charters "son of Urraca," apparently for the reason that his Spanish inheritance devolved through her as daughter and heir of Alphonse VI rather than through his father Raymond of Burgundy. We can give an example, from Catalonia, of a son following his mother as tenant of a castle or fief, assuming, we may note, both her castle and her name.[27] In Southern France, Mary, viscountess of Béarn, succeeded her brother Gaston V. The Béarnais revolted and forced her and her husband to abdicate in favor of one of their sons. That son (Gaston VI) is called in a charter "son of Mary."[28]

Accordingly, the admissibility of women specifically to the inheritance of fiefs had some influence upon their status. In Catalonia and Southern France, it is evident from our charters that women were being widely admitted to feudal inheritances already from the tenth century.[29] In Italy, on the other hand, the "Edictum de beneficiis regni italici" (1037) of Emperor Conrad II expressly excluded women and cognate relatives from feudal inheritance; later emperors tried to impose a similar regimen in Germany, with indifferent success.[30] However, even in the twelfth century these customs governing feudal inheritance are still too amorphous and varying to have exercised a decisive influence on the prominence of women. It would be difficult to judge whether in Southern France or Catalonia, for example, such customs explain the high status of women, or the high status of women explains the development of the inheritance customs which were coming to favor them.

Moreover, the use of a matronymic in our charters does not consistently or even usually mean that the individual owed the major part of his inheritance to his mother. Guillaume V Aigret of Poitou did not inherit his lands from his mother Agnes (who was from Burgundy), nor did Louis IX receive France from his Spanish mother Blanche; yet in the charters we cited, both bear a matronymic. That Louis should be identified with Blanche of Castile would seem primarily recognition of the queen-mother's importance, of her role in the public eye, of the fact that she served as regent during her son's minority and continued to exert influence on royal policy. Agnes of Burgundy was similarly a *grande dame* of a previous century, whose role in Poitevin history was similarly prominent.[31]

For the patronymic or matronymic served no strictly juridical purpose in the charters and was not therefore strictly reflective of juridical factors. The scribe was primarily interested in identifying particular individuals, in the way consistent with established notarial practices which would make them easily recognizable to the readers of his charters. He did this usually by naming the family from which a person came, in the sense of mentioning the parent, the father or the mother, who at the time was better known or at least well known in the community.

The curious and considerable reputation of women within their communities, reflected in the matronymic—this to explain is the heart of our problem. And this much at least is obvious: a woman's reputation, fame, notability, and prominence, in the Middle Ages as today, could be built upon many factors. She could have sprung from a family long established in the community or of high social standing; she could have possessed in notable degree the feminine qualities of beauty, elegance, sensitivity, or simply the human qualities of intelligence, ambition, or energy. According to the etiquette of courtly love, the lover or troubadour was specifically enjoined to further the repute of his lady's physical and cultural distinctions and thereby add to her fame. And in Southern France, home of courtly love, there does seem to be a correlation between the work of troubadours in lauding ladies and the kind of community reputation reflected in our matronymics.

Many things could indeed make a lady famous. We are here interested in only one factor, her economic activities. We want to inquire if there is evident any correlation between the repute of women reflected in the matronymic and the economic functions they assumed in regard to family property. This is of course to lay emphasis on one factor out of many, but that factor would seem of indisputable importance. Medieval society was land-based; the status of a family was still pretty much determined by the lands it owned. The one most prominent in managing that land, who paid or collected the rent, who sold what surpluses the farm or estate produced or bought at the market place what is lacked, who participated in the various community functions that land management entailed—he would perforce become well known to his neighbors. When and if that manager was a woman, her reputation would be widespread. Then too, prominence in economic life may have enhanced a woman's influence on those activities supported by it: court life, court entertainments, and the qualities of the new vernacular literature therein developing. The possible correlation between social repute and economic functions of the lady is worth investigating.

We must first note, in general terms, that the woman during the Middle Ages everywhere and always had some importance in the management of the household economy. The wife characteristically supervised the household's "inner economy" (*Innenwirtschaft*), those activities carried on in or near the house, cooking, brewing, spinning, and weaving, usually too the garden and the raising and care of yard animals.[32] Conversely, the "outer economy" (*Aussenwirtschaft*), principally the work in outlying fields and the tending of herds, was the man's domain. However, the precise range of the woman's inner economy was flexible, expanding or contracting in relation to whether the man had assumed other functions which might keep him from home for lengthy periods or make him disdainful of agricultural labor. If we are to believe Tacitus' picture of the family life of the Germanic freemen on the eve of the invasions, the "best and bravest" of them left even agricultural labor to the women and made their contribution to the family fortunes by raids and wars. Tacitus elsewhere says that the Germanic warrior looked to collecting tribute from his housed slaves, but the other functions of home management, the *officia domus*, fell to the women and children.[33]

We need not attempt to assess the influence of the social arrangements Tacitus describes on later medieval development. For, fortunately, we have a picture of household management much closer to our period of interest, dealing not with common freemen but with the greatest of propertied laymen, the king himself. In 882 Hincmar of Rheims wrote for the instruction of the Frankish king Carloman an essay on the organization of the royal household, *De ordine palatii*, substantially incorporating into his text an earlier, similar treatise written by Adalhard of Corbie and dating from the reign of Charlemagne.[34] According to the *De ordine*, the royal treasurer, the *camerarius*, is directly under the queen. Moreover, the queen is responsible for giving to the knights their yearly gifts, the equivalent of their salaries. This heavy responsibility falls upon the queen in order to free her husband from "domestic or palace solicitude" and to enable him to give all his attention "to the state of the entire kingdom." So too, Agobard of Lyons mentions the Carolingian queen as being in a peculiar way responsible for the *honestas* of the palace.[35] Presumably this required too that the queen assume a similarly prominent role in supervising the economic activities which stocked the treasury, made possible the knightly gifts, and assured palatine *honestas*—specifically the workshops (*genitia*) on the royal manors and perhaps the manors themselves. Charlemagne's own *Capitulare de villis* mentions how instructions are given to manorial officials and accounts received from them by himself "or the queen."[36] Why else should that phrase "or the queen" be introduced into this administrative document if her role in regard to manorial administration was not a real one?

We have further hints that the importance of the woman was not limited to the royal administration but extended also to other great landed households, and that that importance did not change when grants of land rather than gifts became the principal payments for dependent knights. In the marriage donation (*sponsalitium*) made to Countess Adalmodis in Spain (1056), her husband specifically mentions the *mobile* or movables "which by agreement are to be given to the châtelains every year."[37] Like the Carolingian palatine knights, these Spanish châtelains would be beholden for their salaries to a woman. In Spanish charters of investiture, it is also occasionally evident that a male principal is absent, as his wife must promise that he will agree to the transaction "thirty days after Alamannus her husband comes."[38] The absent Alamannus, like the Carolingian king, had evidently found a way through which he could be largely relieved of "domestic or palace solicitude." About 1030 in Northern Italy, Waza, apparently the wife of the Margrave William III of Monferrat (d. before 1042), made a pious visit to the tomb of a saint.[39] She went "surrounded by knights," and a beggar beseeched her for alms. She refused, saying that she had not wealth abundant enough to suffice for herself "and all those seeking from me." The verb here used, *petere*, may perhaps be reminiscent of the juridic language of numerous Italian charters of benefice and lease, introduced by a formal "petition" for a grant of land.

Within the clerical or nicholaite family, women seem to have enjoyed a similar prominence. At Vercelli about 960, married priests ordered to put away their wives answered "that unless they were maintained by the hands of their women they would succumb to hunger and nakedness."[40] At Ravenna too, in 963, the priests could not live "regularly," i.e. celibately, "because of hunger and nakedness," implying that a wife assured them support not otherwise available.[41] In the 970's when Ratherius of Verona tried to introduce celibate living among his clergy, he found: "the excuse of almost everyone was 'this can in no wise be because of our poverty.'"[42] Apparently in these nicholaite families, women had assumed economic functions of critical importance. The presence of fair numbers of available, propertied, or at least economically resourceful women may have even aggravated the abuse of nicholaism within the tenth-century Church, as needy clerics sought a relief from their own poverty in advantageous liaisons. The sons of priests who use a matronymic were perhaps attempting to cover the ignominy of their fathers. But they also give illustration of the prominence and repute of their mothers within the life of the community. The important role which those women of Rome—the notorious Theodora and Marozia—played in the political history of that city in the early tenth century may perhaps be cited as further example of the prominence that women could achieve amid a largely nicholaite clergy.[43]

The economic functions of women are thus clearly important, most evidently among the warriors and the married clergy, the two chief propertied classes of early medieval Europe. Can we go on to discern particular areas or periods in which the economic status of the woman loomed especially large? To attempt this, we must return again to our documents of practice.

These documents do permit us to judge approximately the distribution of land ownership in the early medieval countryside and to assess the share that women may have claimed in it. The most satisfactory way by which we can make such an assessment is through field perambulations. To identify a piece of land, the scribe would often provide the names of the owners of contiguous property: "a field . . . which is terminated on the east by the land of Roclenus and Bernana and Bovo with his heirs . . . on the west [by the land of] Dodo and Tetuisa."[44] Wherever they appear, these perambulations follow pretty much a common model, and hence they permit sharper comparisons among areas and over time than that possible for our patronymics, affected as these latter are by variant notarial practices. From Italy we have over 63,000 names of contiguous lay owners, from Spain nearly 7,000, from Southern France over 13,000. For reasons we have elsewhere considered, our names from the North are much fewer, in both Northern France and Germany amounting only to a few hundred.[45] Comparisons between the North and South on the basis of contiguous owners are not possible beyond the Carolingian period, but at least for Southern Europe we have a good basis for judging the importance and extent of what we shall call women's lands.

For typically, in listing the contiguous owners, the scribe would distinguish among male owners, female owners and unnamed sons or heirs of an earlier owner, presumably now deceased. We can calculate what percentages of our total references to contiguous owners involve women or heirs. Such phrases as "terra Marie cum filiis suis" are counted as women's lands, but if a principal refers to the neighboring property of his own heirs, it is considered as his property.

Table 2 shows the importance of women and heirs as contiguous owners for the various regions of continental Europe we are considering.

TABLE 2

Percentage per Century of Women and 'Heirs'
Appearing as Contiguous Owners

W = Women	H = Heirs.									
Region	8th		9th		10th		11th		12th	
	W	H	W	H	W	H	W	H	W	H
Italy	6	9	3	10	3	12	3	20	4	15
Spain	—	—	7	9	17	2	13	4	8	8
S. France	—	—	8	1	9	1	9	2	6	2
N. France	—	—	7	0	4	1	2	4	—	—
Germany	18	1	2	3	—	—	—	—	—	—

Source: Chartularies and parchment collections listed in the bibliographical Appendix. The figures on which these percentages are based can be found in Table 4, column 2.

We may first of all note that German lands show a considerable proportion of women as contiguous owners in the eighth century (18 percent), though the only 300 references upon which this calculation is based may make the conclusion somewhat uncertain and the incidence seems to fall off in the ninth century. But consistently, the regions in which women appear with the greatest frequency as contiguous owners are Spain (17 percent of the total in the tenth century) and Southern France (almost 10 percent from the ninth through the eleventh centuries). In both areas the percentages fall off in the twelfth century. It is certain that much of this land was not exclusively female property but rather belonged to a woman and her minor sons, reflecting the generous provisions of the Visigothic and Burgundian laws which left to a widow use of and control over the family patrimony. It is also possible that some of these female owners were not so much the full legal owners as the administrators of an undivided family property acting for an absent husband, though of this we cannot be certain.

These high percentages from Spain and Southern France contrast sharply with low percentage of women's lands evident in Italy; there women constitute only 6 percent of the total owners in the eighth century, and thereafter only 3 or 4. However, in Italy we may note a proportionately greater importance of unnamed "sons" or "heirs" appearing as contiguous owners. This formula is unfortunately somewhat ambiguous. It could refer to an established and pretty well permanent consortery of adult owners. It could also characterize the property of minor children kept intact after the death of the father—the same kind of property which commonly figures as women's lands in French and Spanish sources. This formula seems, in other words, to mask somewhat the true extent of land in Italy under the control of women. This difference in terminology undoubtedly goes back to the contrasts between Lombard law on the one hand and Visigothic and Burgundian on the other. The widow, who in Lombard law did not enjoy a *potestas* over the patrimony of her minor children, also does not in the charters give her name to the land. Of course, within the fatherless family the woman undoubtedly could exercise an important voice, particularly if her children were of tender years. Still, the Italian widow hardly enjoyed the prominent recognition as head of her family and arbiter of its economic fortunes conceded her in Spain and Southern France.

Graph 2 illustrates for twenty-five-year periods the incidence of women's lands and heirs' lands for the whole of continental Europe.

A second way by which our charters permit us to estimate the importance of women as land owners and land managers is this: the frequency with which women appear as principal donors, sellers, or otherwise alienators of property within our charters. Of charters involving lay principals (excluding, however, kings and queens), we have over 20,000 from Italy, nearly 20,000 from Southern France, over 11,000 from Germany, and over 5,000 from Northern France and Spain respectively. We shall count as a woman's donation those charters in which a woman alone or a woman and her children figure as principals. Charters in which a husband and wife, or an adult son (mentioned first) and his mother are the principals are considered male donations. The numerous (particularly German) charters in which only serfs are conveyed are not considered, nor do we count commercial transactions not involving land. This method based on the importance of women as principal donors is obviously crude, since it may perhaps illustrate not so much the importance of women as property owners as their higher sense of piety and greater generosity towards churches, which in most instances are receiving the land. Still, the advantage of this approach is that it offers insight into periods and areas, particularly in Northern Europe, poorly illuminated by our other indices.

TABLE 3

Percentage per Century of Women
Appearing as Principal Alienators of Land

Region	8th	9th	10th	11th	12th
Italy	6	7	11	13	9
Spain	—	11	17	18	18
S. France	—	8	13	11	9
N. France	15	7	11	8	9
Germany	15	10	8	15	12

Source: Chartularies and parchment collections listed in the bibliographical Appendix. The figures on which these percentages are based can be found in Table 4, column 3.

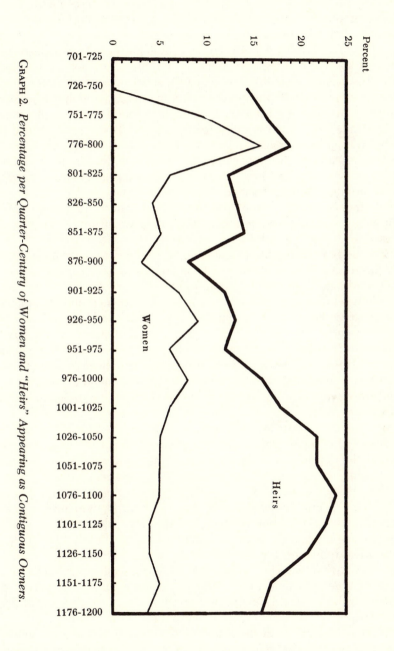

Graph 2. *Percentage per Quarter-Century of Women and "Heirs" Appearing as Contiguous Owners.*

Graph 3, as in our previous indices, illustrates the percentage of women appearing as principal donors for the whole European continent on the basis of twenty-five-year periods.

Is there a correlation between the prominence of women illustrated by our matronymics and their economic importance as owners or managers of land? We cannot of course pretend to a mechanical correspondence between our indices. Still, the increased frequency with which women appear as owners of land after 950 does seem to correspond with a similar increase in the incidence of matronymics for the same period. On a regional basis, Southern France is remarkable both for the extent of women's lands and the frequency with which the matronymic appears in our charters. In Spanish lands matronymics are found, as we have seen, chiefly in acts involving the feudal nobility, but at least among this important propertied class, the wealth and economic role of women would seem to have contributed to their own fame and promoted the utilization of a matronymic by their sons.

On the basis of our three indices and the literary texts we have cited, we may hazard a few general comments on the position of women in regard to family and land in the early Middle Ages.

Women appear with fair consistency as land owners and land managers and apparent heads of their families at all times and places in the early medieval period. Several factors explain this continuing prominence: the common principles of early medieval laws, which conceded even to the married woman a personal title to property; the influence of the Christian Church; and the practical role that the woman assumed as mistress of her own "inner economy"—a role which helped elevate and maintain her social and legal position.

At the same time, the position of the woman varied greatly according to her class, to her region, and even to the period in which she lived. According to class, the importance of the woman seems to advance as we ascend the social scale, becoming most pronounced among the warriors and the married clergy, the two chief propertied classes of early medieval Europe. This seems primarily attributable not to a distinctive juridical statute governing these classes but to the greater practical role the wife of a warrior or priest assumed in the economic support of her family. To fulfill their professional functions, both warrior and priest needed to some extent to be freed from what the *De ordine* calls "domestic solicitude." This in turn greatly enlarged the range of the woman's economic functions, increased her contacts with the world beyond her family, and gave her a social prominence frequently recognized in the matronymic borne by her sons.

Regional contrasts in the status of the woman are as pronounced as social differences. The economic role of women in Southern France and Spain, as measured by our last two indices, is particularly remarkable.

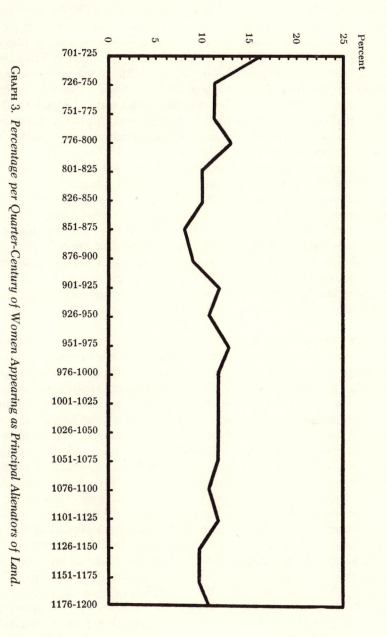

GRAPH 3. *Percentage per Quarter-Century of Women Appearing as Principal Alienators of Land.*

Undoubtedly, a significant reason for this are the peculiarly favorable provisions of the Visigothic and Burgundian laws, which placed no juridical restrictions on her freedom to administer her own property, to share in the administration of the family property or, as a widow, to assume administrative control over it. The principle of community property in Visigothic law likewise served to increase the personal wealth of the widowed woman. Conversely, in Italy Lombard law limited, though it could not entirely restrict, the freedom of the woman in the administration of land. So also, the exclusion of the woman from feudal inheritance in Lombardy, her admission to it in Southern France and Spain, are other juridical factors of importance in affecting her status.

Beyond law, we should mention the precocious development of the ideal of chivalry in Southern France, which in accentuating the professional specialization of the male as fighter simultaneously seems to have restricted his economic role within the family. Italy, on the other hand, reluctant and late in developing a true knighthood on the French pattern, does not see within the propertied family the same degree of specialization of the husband as fighter and his wife as largely responsible for the "solicitude" of household management. Northern France and Germany were initially more receptive than Italy to the notions of chivalry, and the role of the woman in those regions seems to have been proportionately more prominent.

Religion, law, social customs, the continuing concerns of household management are, however, relatively stable factors, and we have yet to explain how the importance of women in regard to land and family could apparently vary markedly over time, becoming particularly pronounced after 950 and reaching a sort of apex in the eleventh century. In this, another factor seems of some significance—the physical mobility of the population. Among those social classes (such as the medieval warrior nobility) whose mode of life involves considerable travel and movement, the man is the family member most frequently absent from home, while the wife, physically less mobile, is likewise more capable of assuming a continuous supervision over the family's fixed possessions. Moreover, in a social situation involving emigration or exodus, whether permanent or temporary, from the older centers of population, men tend to leave earlier and in proportionately greater numbers than women, as they are physically and socially better able to assume the risks and face the uncertainties of often hostile frontiers.

In leaving the community, they will need to make arrangements for the administration of their properties; frequently too, they will have to sell or mortgage their lands to finance their ventures. Emigration, in other words, provides an opportunity for the more stable elements within a community to assume a greater responsibility in the management of its lands. Thus, churches seem to have extended their lands considerably during periods of emigration. When the German warrior Riphwinus set forth in the 790s with

Charlemagne on his Italian campaign, he gave his property to his brother who was staying home, with the proviso that it be given to the monastery of Lorsch if he did not return.[46] The enormous increase in Church property in Carolingian times undoubtedly owed something to the extended campaigns of the great emperor, which took men like Riphwinus long and often permanently from home.[47] So likewise, that other great age of medieval military expansion—under way by the eleventh century and most dramatically expressed in the Crusades—seems similarly marked by an accumulation of lands in the hands of churches, able to extend mortgages on or to buy outright the properties of departing warriors.

The same largely monastic records which show against a background of military mobilization an extension of Church lands also seem to reveal an increase in the prominence of women as owners and managers of property. Sometime between 1060 and 1080, in the Vendômois in Northern France, the Lady Hersendis was forced to assume responsibility for her family's fortunes, "her husband having gone to Jerusalem." In company with some of her own dependent knights, she traveled to her and her husband's lord, the abbot of Marmoutier, there personally to implore the aid of St. Martin and secure the confirmation of her fief.[48]

The history of a family in Auch in Southern France offers a clear example of the economic enterprise of women in the absence of men.[49] Raymond Donat had three sons and two daughters. One of the sons and the heir of a second both went on crusade and mortgaged or sold their land to their sister Saura. The other son and the male heir of Saura's sister died (we are not told how) without issue, so Saura gathered together the total inheritance of her father for herself and her own son Bertrand.

Military mobilization, its expenses and its hazards, contributed importantly to the Lady Saura's successful reconstitution of her father's possessions. Did not the frequent departures, the extended absences of males, work generally to enhance the economic position of women as administrators, as heirs of those permanently gone? Liutprand of Cremona once commented how, in a single battle against Hungarian invaders (923), so many knights were killed that to his day (he was writing ca. 958–962) there existed a "permagna raritas" of knights in Lombardy.[50] Such default of males eventually would mean an accumulation of inheritances in the hands of women, even in areas such as Lombardy where prevalent custom was unfavorable to them.

And there does seem to be a correspondence between those periods of early medieval history marked by extensive mobilization of the population, vigorous military and geographic expansion, and those periods when women come most clearly to the fore as owners and managers of land. The Carolingian charters, particularly from Northern France and Germany, show a high percentage of women as donors and as contiguous owners. Our numbers of patronymics are too few for this period to draw firm conclusions from them; but at least we may note the significant fact that matronymics were known and used apropos of warriors even before 800 in those areas. The loss of male members of the population to wars, to new lands in process of settlement, simply to the floating population, the "army of wanderers" of which our Carolingian sources speak, seems directly related with the importance of women in the pattern of Carolingian land ownership.

From the late tenth century, a yet more vigorous wave of expansion takes shape in Europe, and this time it is Southern France and Spain which initially appear as the great centers of exodus.[51] French chivalry in particular seems touched with a passion for wandering; French knights pour across the Pyrenees on the great highway to Compostela, frequently to participate in the wars against the Moors. Spanish knights were hardly less mobile, given (as the epic of the Cid marvellously reveals) to bold raids along the Muslim frontier in search of material and spiritual profit. This ferment blends imperceptibly with the like ferment of the crusading movement (1095), which spreads it and extends it to all corners of Europe. St. Bernard, in preaching the Second Crusade (1147), supposedly emptied Europe's castles and cities of their men.[52] Did the largely man's world of distant pilgrimage and crusade help create a woman's world back home?—The troubadour poet Marcabru presents for us a touching lament of a "châtelaine" weeping for her lover, not dead, simply gone with King Louis on the Second Crusade, and all her other likely beaux with him.[53] Hers, to her sorrow, was a woman's world.

Religion, law, custom, the practical requirements of household management, and perhaps significantly too the social impact of Europe's great waves of military and geographic expansion, combined to raise the woman to a position of prominence, saluted to be sure in the charged sentiment of troubadour poetry, but as much saluted in the dry Latin of our thousand charters. The great, external, dramatic events of the day, the wars and crusades, are the work of active men. But their accomplishments were matched and perhaps made possible by the work of women no less active. And the achievements of both are joined together in a kind of alliance of accomplishment, fascinating in itself, and profoundly influencing the Western tradition.

APPENDIX

The statistical indices are based on the lists of chartularies and parchment collections published in *Speculum* 36 (1961): 100–102 and in other articles therein cited. The following lists are supplementary to them. The numbers in parentheses refer to the entries in H. Stein, *Bibliographie générale des cartulaires français* (Paris, 1907). Only those chartularies not listed in Stein are cited here in full.

I. *Italy.*

Italy—Placiti (*Fonti per la storia d'Italia* [= *FSI*] 92, 96 pts. 1 and 2). Ivrea—Libro rosso (*Bolettino della Società storica Subalpina* [= *BSSS*] 74). Jesi (*Carte diplomatiche iesine,* ed. A. Gianandrea [Ancona, 1884]). Osimo (*Carte diplomatiche osimane,* ed. G. Cecconi [Ancona, 1878]). Pistoia (L. Chiapelli, "L'Età longobarda e Pistoia," *Archivio storico Italiano* 79 [1921]: 227–338). Reggio—Liber grossus (*Liber grossus antiquus comunis Regii,* ed. F. Saverio Gatta [Reggio-Emilia, 1944]). Saluzzo (*BSSS* 15: pt. 2). Saluzzo—Marchesi (*BSSS* 16). *Santa Maria in Monasterio* (*Archivio della Società Romana di storia patria* 29). Tremiti (*FSI* 98). Trent—Codex Wangianus (*Codex Wangianus,* ed. R. Kink [Vienna, 1852]).

II. *Spain (including Portugal).*

Aragón—Chronica Adefonsi (F. Balaguer, "La chronica Adefonsi imperatoris," *Estudios de Edad Media de la corona de Aragón* [= *EEMCA*] 6 [1956]: 7–40). Aragón—Doña Talesa (F.Balaguer, "La vizcondesa del Bearn Doña Talesa," *EEMCA* 5 [1952]: 83–114). Aragón y Navarra—Pedro I (*Colección diplomática de Pedro I de Aragón y Navarra,* ed. A. Ubieto Arteta [Zaragoza, 1951]). Aragón y Navarra—Mandatos reales ("Mandatos reales navarro-aragoneses del siglo XII," *EEMCA* 2 [1946]: 425–31). Calatrava (F. R. de Uhagón, "Indice de los documentos de la orden militar de Calatrava," *Boletín de la Real Academia de la Historia* [*BAH*] 35 [1899]: 5–167). Egara (F. Torres Amat, "Egara [Tarrasa] y su monasterio de San Rufo," *BAH* 33 [1898]: 5–30; J. Solery Palet, "Cartulario del prioratu egarense," *BAH* 34 [1899]: 6–30). Madrid (*Documentos del archivo general de la villa de Madrid* [Madrid, 1888]). Portugal—Afonso Henriques (*Chancelarias medievais portuguesas,* vol. 1: *Documentos da chancelaria de Afonso Henriques,* ed. A. E. Reuter [Coimbra, 1938]). Santillana (*Colección diplomática: Documentos en pergamino que hubo en la real excolegiata de Santillana,* ed. M. Escagedo Salmón [Santoña, 1927]).

III. *Southern France (including French Switzerland).*

Aiguebelle (*Chartes et documents de l'abbaye de N.-D. d'Aiguebelle* [n. p., 1953]). Artige (270). Cellefrouin (*Cartulaire de l'abbaye Saint-Pierre de Cellefrouin,* ed. J. F. Chevalier [Ruffeo, 1936]). Chalon-sur-Saône—Abbaye de Saint-Marcel (839). Fontmorigny (*Le chartier ancien de Fontmorigny,* ed. A. Hubet [Bourges, 1936]). France—Trésor des chartes (*Layettes du trésor des chartes,* ed. A. Teulet, vol. 1 [Paris, 1863]). Hautcrêt (1677). La Sauve-Majeure ("Documents divers: Chartes de l'abbaye de La Sauve-Majeure antérieures au XIIIe siècle," *Archives historiques du département de la Gironde* 49 [1914]). Les Ecouges (2050). Marmoutier—Cartulaire blésois (2343). Marmoutier—Cartulaire tourangeau (2341). Marmoutier—

Livre des serfs (2352). Mauléon (2386). Nonenque (*Cartulaire et documents de l'abbaye de Nonenque*, ed. C. Couderc and J.-L. Rigal [Rodez, 1950]). Royan (3271). Saint-Cybard (*Cartulaire de l'abbaye de Saint Cybard*, ed. P. Lefrancq [Angoulême, 1930]). Saintes—Saint-Eutrope (3393). Sion (3711).

IV. *Northern France (including the Low Countries).*

Angers—Saint-Laud (130). Arras—Saint-Vaast (208bis). Beaumont-le-Roger (*Cartulaire de l'église de la Sainte-Trinité de Beaumont-le-Roger*, ed. E. Deville [Paris, 1912]). Beauvais—L'Hôtel-Dieu (*Cartulaire de l'Hôtel-Dieu de Beauvais*, ed. V. Leblond [Paris, 1919]). Beauvais—Saint-Lazare (*Cartulaire de la maladrerie de Saint-Lazare de Beauvais*, ed. V. Leblond [Paris, 1922]). Béthune (473). Cambron (776). Châlons-sur-Marne (838). Chartres—Grand-Beaulieu (*Cartulaire de la léproserie du Grand-Beaulieu*, ed. R. Merlet and M. Jusselin [Chartres, 1909]). Châteaudun (*Cartulaire de l'abbaye de la Madeleine de Chateaudun*, ed. L. Merlet and L. Jarry [Châteaudun, 1896]). Clairvaux (*Recueil des chartes de l'abbaye de Clairvaux*, ed. J. Waquet [Troyes, 1950]). Clermontois (984). Corbie (L. Levillain, *Examen critique des chartes mérovingiennes et carolingiennes de l'abbaye de Corbie* [Paris, 1902]). Eenaeme (1248). Flanders—Counts (*Actes des comtes de Flandre, 1071–1128*, ed. F. Vercauteren [Brussels, 1938]). Florennes (U. Berlière, "Chartes de l'abbaye de Florennes," *Documents inédits pour servir à l'histoire ecclésiastique de la Belgique*, vol. 1 [Maredsous, 1894]). France—Diplomata (*Diplomata chartae epistolae leges aliaque instrumenta*, ed. J. M. Pardessus [Paris, 1843–49]). Ghent—Saint-Bavon (1480). La Trappe (1917). Le Mans (*Actus pontificum Cenomannis in urbe degentium*, ed. G. Busson and A. Ledru [Le Mans, 1901]). Le Mans—La Couture (1979). Le Mans—Saint-Victeur (1998). Les Vaux-de-Gernay (2061). Liège—Saint-Lambert (2112). Liège—Saint-Jacques (P. Harsin, "Les chartes de Saint-Jacques du XIᵉ siècle," *Bulletin de la société d'art et d'histoire du diocèse de Liège* 22 [1930]: 53–72). Longpont (2217). Marmoutier—Cartulaire manceau (*Cartulaire manceau de Marmoutier*, ed. E. Laurain [Laval, 1911–45]). Mons—Sainte-Waudru (*Chartes du chapitre de Sainte-Waudru de Mons*, ed. L. Devillers [Brussels, 1899]. Montier-la-Celle (2552). Namur—Counts (*Actes des comtes de Namur de la première race, 946–1196*, ed. F. Rousseau [Brussels, 1937]). Ourscamp (2855). Paris—Saint-Martin-des-Champs (*Recueil des chartes et documents de Saint-Martin-des-Champs*, ed. J. Depoin [Paris, 1912]). Pontoise—L'Hôtel Dieu (3072). Poperinghe (3076). Rouen—La Sainte-Trinité (3236). Saint-Florent de Saumur—Livre noir ("Le Livre noir de Saint-Florent de Saumur," ed. P. Marchegay, *Archives d'Anjou* [Angers 1848], pp. 227–92). Saint-Leu d'Esserent (3468). Saint-Wandrille (F. Lot, *Etudes critiques sur l'abbaye de Saint-Wandrille* [Paris, 1913]).

V. *German lands (including Alsace, Austria, Luxemburg and German Switzerland).*

Bavaria—Monumenta boica (*Monumenta boica* [Munich, 1763ff.]). Carinthia (*Monumenta historica ducatus Carinthiae*, ed. A. von Jaksch [Klagenfurt, 1896]). Enns (*Urkundenbuch des Landes ob der Enns* [Vienna, 1852ff.]). Freiburg (*Freiburger Urkundenbuch*, ed. F. Hefele [Freiburg, 1940]). Freising (*Die Traditionen des Hochstifts Freising*, ed. T. Bitterauf [Quellen und Erörterungen zur bayerischen Geschichte (= QEBG) n.F. 4–5, Munich, 1905–9]). Göttweig (A. F. Fuchs, *Urkunden und Regesten zur Geschichte des Benediktinerstiftes Göttweig, 1. Theil 1058–1400* [Fontes Rerum Austriacarum (= FRA) 2. Abt. 51, Vienna, 1901]; *idem, Die Traditionsbücher des Benediktinerstiftes Göttweig* [FRA 2. Abt. 96, Vienna and Liepzig, 1931]). Halle (*Urkundenbuch der Stadt Halle*, ed. A. Bierbach [Magdeburg, 1930]). Klosterneuburg (*Codex traditionum ecclesiae collegiatae Claustroneoburgensis*, ed. M. Fischer [FRA 2. Abt. 4, Vienna, 1851]). Mainz (*Mainzer Urkundenbuch*, ed. M. Stimming [Darmstadt, 1932]). Neustift (*Das Traditionsbuch des Augustiner-Chorherrenstiftes Neustift bei Brixen*, ed. H. Wagner [FRA 2. Abt. 76, Vienna, 1954]). Passau (*Die Traditionen des Hochstifts Passau*, ed. M. Heuwieser [QEBG n.F. 6, Munich, 1930]). Salzburg (*Salzburger Urkundenbuch*, ed. W. Hauthaler [Salzburg, 1910]). Schäftlarn (*Die Traditionen des Klosters Schäftlarn, 760–1305*, ed. A. Weissthanner [QEBG n.F. 10, Munich, 1953]). Seitenstetten (*Urkundenbuch des Benedictinerstiftes Seitenstetten*, en. I. Raab [FRA 2. Abt. 23, Vienna, 1870]). Strassburg (*Urkundenbuch der Stadt Strassburg*, ed. W. Wiegand [Strassburg, 1879]). Tegernsee (*Die Traditionen des Klosters Tegernsee, 1003–1242*, ed. P. Acht [QEBG n.F. 9, Munich, 1952]). Tyrol (*Tiroler Urkundenbuch*, ed. F. Huter [Innsbruck, 1937]). Westpahlia (*Westfälisches Urkundenbuch*, ed. H. Erhard [Münster, 1847–51]). Worms (*Urkundenbuch der Stadt Worms*, ed. H. Boos [Berlin, 1886]. Xanten (*Urkundenbuch des Stiftes Xanten* [Bonn, 1935]). Zürich (*Urkundenbuch der Stadt und Landschaft Zürich*, ed. J. Escher and P. Schweizer (Zürich, 1888]).

TABLE 4

Master Table

M = Masculine   F = Feminine   H = Heirs   T = Totals

	Patronymics			Boundaries				Donors		
	M	F	T	M	H	F	T	M	F	T
701–725:										
Italy	8	0	(8)	1	1	0	(2)	15	1	(16)
N. Fr.	5	0	(5)	2	0	0	(2)	36	6	(42)
Germ.	16	0	(16)	1	1	0	(2)	36	9	(45)
	29	0	(29)	4	2	0	(6)	87	16	(103)
		F = 0%							F = 16%	

TABLE 4 (Cont.)

Master Table

M = Masculine   F = Feminine   H = Heirs   T = Totals

	Patronymics			Boundaries				Donors		
	M	F	T	M	H	F	T	M	F	T
726–750:										
Italy	124	2	(126)	55	9	0	(64)	65	8	(73)
S. Fr.	2	2	(4)					1	1	(2)
N. Fr.	5	0	(5)					15	2	(17)
Germ.	5	0	(5)					63	6	(69)
	136	4	(140)	55	9	0	(64)	144	17	(161)
		F = 3%			H = 14%	F = 0%			F = 11%	
751–775:										
Italy	507	8	(515)	130	19	11	(160)	250	19	(269)
Spain								0	1	(1)
S. Fr.								4	0	(4)
N. Fr.	9	0	(9)	17	0	2	(19)	22	0	(22)
Germ.	20	0	(20)	131	0	20	(151)	1416	196	(1612)
	536	8	(544)	278	19	33	(330)	1692	216	(1908)
		F = 1%			H = 6%	F = 10%			F = 11%	
776–800:										
Italy	385	7	(392)	129	6	11	(146)	197	8	(205)
Spain								3	0	(3)
S. Fr.				2	0	0	(2)	5	0	(5)
N. Fr.	13	1	(14)	7	0	0	(7)	33	10	(43)
Germ.	23	2	(25)	122	4	37	(163)	2196	343	(2539)
	421	10	(431)	260	10	48	(318)	2434	361	(2795)
		F = 2%			H = 3%	F = 15%			F = 13%	
801–825:										
Italy	787	8	(795)	316	26	15	(357)	251	12	(263)
Spain				3	0	1	(4)	6	0	(6)
S. Fr.	1	0	(1)	48	3	12	(63)	34	3	(37)
N. Fr.	3	0	(3)	10	0	1	(11)	19	4	(23)
Germ.	24	0	(24)	54	0	2	(56)	943	113	(1056)
	815	8	(823)	431	29	31	(491)	1253	132	(1385)
		F = 1%			H = 6%	F = 6%			F = 10%	

Table 4 (Cont.)

Master Table

M = Masculine   F = Feminine   H = Heirs   T = Totals

	Patronymics			Boundaries				Donors		
	M	F	T	M	H	F	T	M	F	T
826–850:										
Italy	807	11	(818)	252	39	3	(294)	175	9	(184)
Spain	3	0	(3)	22	0	0	(22)	35	4	(39)
S. Fr.	2	1	(3)	129	6	15	(150)	40	8	(48)
N. Fr.	4	0	(4)	34	0	4	(38)	150	11	(161)
Germ.	6	0	(6)	19	1	0	(20)	443	63	(506)
	822	12	(834)	456	46	22	(524)	843	95	(938)
		F = 1%			H = 9%	F = 4%			F = 10%	
851–875:										
Italy	957	15	(972)	459	66	23	(548)	219	17	(236)
Spain	3	0	(3)	32	1	5	(38)	41	6	(47)
S. Fr.	3	0	(3)	160	0	14	(174)	105	13	(118)
N. Fr.	44	0	(44)	4	0	0	(4)	162	14	(176)
Germ.	7	0	(7)	4	1	0	(5)	466	37	(503)
	1014	15	(1029)	659	68	42	(769)	993	87	(1080)
		F = 1%			H = 9%	F = 5%			F = 8%	
876–900:										
Italy	758	18	(776)	496	48	10	(554)	168	21	(189)
Spain	3	0	(3)	37	9	2	(48)	35	5	(40)
S. Fr.	8	0	(8)	387	1	23	(411)	232	20	(252)
N. Fr.	12	0	(12)	47	0	2	(49)	43	0	(43)
Germ.	6	0	(6)	13	1	0	(14)	244	23	(267)
	787	18	(805)	980	59	37	(1076)	722	69	(791)
		F = 2%			H = 5%	F = 3%			F = 9%	
901–925:										
Italy	922	25	(947)	594	76	18	(688)	168	18	(186)
Spain	104	0	(104)	324	10	48	(382)	142	20	(162)
S. Fr.	8	0	(8)	713	12	62	(787)	405	59	(464)
N. Fr.	2	0	(2)	13 .	0	2	(15)	34	3	(37)
Germ.	2	0	(2)					109	12	(121)
	1038	25	(1063)	1644	98	130	(1872)	858	112	(970)
		F = 2%			H = 5%	F = 7%			F = 12%	

TABLE 4 (Cont.)

Master Table

M = Masculine   F = Feminine   H = Heirs   T = Totals

	Patronymics			Boundaries				Donors		
	M	F	T	M	H	F	T	M	F	T
926–950:										
Italy	1376	80	(1456)	1120	126	61	(1307)	269	24	(293)
Spain	367	0	(367)	404	7	68	(479)	191	33	(224)
S. Fr.	25	1	(26)	1376	17	156	(1549)	945	127	(1072)
N. Fr.	9	0	(9)	26	1	1	(28)	35	4	(39)
Germ.	18	1	(19)					150	8	(158)
	1795	82	(1877)	2926	151	286	(3363)	1590	196	(1786)
		F = 4%		H = 4%		F = 9%			F = 11%	
951–975:										
Italy	2669	123	(2792)	2943	353	94	(3390)	451	74	(525)
Spain	391	1	(392)	437	12	81	(530)	279	36	(315)
S. Fr.	34	2	(36)	2337	55	242	(2634)	1391	223	(1614)
N. Fr.	9	0	(9)	22	0	0	(22)	47	4	(51)
Germ.	3	0	(3)					157	13	(170
	3106	126	(3232)	5739	420	417	(6576)	2325	350	(2675)
		F = 4%		H = 6%		F = 6%			F = 13%	
976–1000:										
Italy	3757	219	(3976)	2925	556	94	(3575)	619	76	(695)
Spain	279	6	(285)	1031	23	259	(1313)	377	80	(457)
S. Fr.	40	8	(48)	1930	21	206	(2157)	1456	211	(1667)
N. Fr.	6	0	(6)	13	0	0	(13)	69	14	(83)
Germ.	2	1	(3)					139	14	(153)
	4084	234	(4318)	5899	600	559	(7058)	2660	395	(3055)
		F = 5%		H = 9%		F = 8%			F = 13%	
1001–1025:										
Italy	5494	532	(6026)	3720	891	113	(4724)	1012	128	(1140)
Spain	375	27	(402)	440	13	95	(548)	225	35	(260)
S. Fr.	167	18	(185)	2029	19	227	(2275)	1579	227	(1806)
N. Fr.	23	2	(25)	8	1	0	(9)	72	13	(85)
Germ.	1	0	(1)					124	17	(141)
	6060	579	(6639)	6197	924	435	(7556)	3012	420	(3432)
		F = 9%		H = 12%		F = 6%			F = 12%	

Table 4 (Cont.)

Master Table

M = Masculine   F = Feminine   H = Heirs   T = Totals

	Patronymics			Boundaries				Donors		
	M	F	T	M	H	F	T	M	F	T
1026–1050:										
Italy	6460	464	(6924)	3938	1012	184	(5134)	1236	186	(1422)
Spain	1058	27	(1085)	256	22	30	(308)	214	43	(257)
S. Fr.	325	69	(394)	539	6	62	(607)	1107	124	(1231)
N. Fr.	186	4	(190)	6	0	0	(6)	192	21	(213)
Germ.	13	0	(13)					201	31	(232)
	8042	564	(8606)	4739	1040	276	(6055)	2950	405	(3355)
		F = 7%			H = 17%	F = 5%			F = 12%	
1051–1075:										
Italy	5892	364	(6256)	3116	853	130	(4099)	1319	214	(1533)
Spain	2229	192	(2421)	520	25	69	(614)	487	115	(602)
S. Fr.	505	87	(592)	371	18	33	(422)	1048	98	(1146)
N. Fr.	935	52	(987)	22	1	1	(24)	454	40	(494)
Germ.	16	1	(17)					199	24	(223)
	9577	696	(10273)	4029	897	233	(5159)	3507	491	(3998)
		F = 7%			H = 17%	F = 5%			F = 12%	
1076–1100:										
Italy	8954	444	(9398)	3461	1007	172	(4640)	1696	229	(1925)
Spain	2668	125	(2793)	440	20	57	(517)	445	112	(557)
S. Fr.	1173	130	(1303)	354	22	27	(403)	2622	304	(2926)
N. Fr.	1710	125	(1835)	10	0	0	(10)	1115	91	(1206)
Germ.	29	0	(29)					176	50	(226)
	14534	824	(15358)	4265	1049	256	(5570)	6054	786	(6840)
		F = 5%			H = 19%	F = 5%			F = 11%	
1101–1125:										
Italy	8685	380	(9065)	3065	832	152	(4049)	1643	225	(1868)
Spain	3386	145	(3531)	360	50	34	(444)	667	184	(851)
S. Fr.	927	142	(1069)	173	7	6	(186)	1512	144	(1656)
N. Fr.	1418	106	(1524)	11	0	0	(11)	824	66	(890)
Germ.	65	3	(68)					457	76	(533)
	14481	776	(15257)	3609	889	192	(4690)	5103	695	(5798)
		F = 5%			H = 19%	F = 4%			F = 12%	

TABLE 4 (Cont.)

Master Table

M = Masculine   F = Feminine   H = Heirs   T = Totals

	Patronymics			Boundaries				Donors		
	M	F	T	M	H	F	T	M	F	T
1126–1150:										
Italy	9830	391	(10221)	4830	1155	267	(6252)	2113	195	(2308)
Spain	3310	119	(3429)	391	12	33	(436)	548	96	(644)
S. Fr.	1711	232	(1943)	416	16	20	(452)	1501	139	(1640)
N. Fr.	836	61	(897)	23	0	1	(24)	725	83	(808)
Germ.	165	12	(177)					1243	151	(1394)
	15852	815	(16667)	5660	1183	321	(7164)	6130	664	(6794)
		F = 5%			H = 17%	F = 4%			F = 10%	
1151–1175:										
Italy	8989	494	(9483)	6789	1166	378	(8333)	2467	244	(2711)
Spain	2196	67	(2263)	811	49	64	(924)	624	144	(768)
S. Fr.	2244	181	(2425)	572	8	33	(613)	1900	164	(2064)
N. Fr.	497	38	(535)	15	0	0	(15)	764	60	(824)
Germ.	147	22	(169)					966	128	(1094)
	14073	802	(14875)	8187	1223	475	(9885)	6721	740	(7461)
		F = 5%			H = 12%	F = 5%			F = 10%	
1176–1200:										
Italy	11731	634	(12365)	11880	1851	572	(14303)	3663	368	(4031)
Spain	2139	46	(2185)	972	125	102	(1199)	694	145	(839)
S. Fr.	1345	142	(1487)	572	6	46	(624)	1259	147	(1406)
N. Fr.	454	61	(515)	26	0	0	(26)	886	97	(983)
Germ.	202	16	(218)					799	110	(909)
	15871	899	(16770)	13450	1982	720	(16152)	7301	867	(8168)
		F = 5%			H = 12%	F = 4%			F =11%	

NOTES

1. Cf. J. Balon, *La Structure et la gestion du domaine de l'église au moyen âge dans l'Europe des Francs,* Ius Medii Aevi 1 (Namur, 1959).

2. J. Gaudemet, "Le statut de la femme dans l'empire romain," *La femme* (Recueils de la Société Jean Bodin 11; Brussels, 1959), pp. 177–89, with bibliography.

3. G. Merschberger, *Die Rechtsstellung der germanischen Frau* (Mannus-Bücherei 57; Leipzig, 1937); K. Weinhold, *Die deutschen Frauen in dem Mittelalter,* 3rd ed. (Vienna, 1897). For Spain see E. de Hinojosa y Naveros, "La comunidad doméstica en España durante la edad media," *Obras* 2 (Madrid, 1955): 329–41, and "Sobre la condición de la mujer casada en la esfera del derecho civil," *ibid.,* 2: 345–88;

C. Sanchez-Albornoz, "La mujer española hace mil años," *España y el Islam* (Buenos Aires, 1943), pp. 83-142; A. García Gallo, *Curso de historia del derecho español* (Madrid, 1950), 2:83-91. For Italy, E. Besta, *La famiglia nella storia del diritto italiano* Padua, 1935); A. Marongiu, *La famiglia nell' Italia meridionale (Milan, 1944);* C. Calisse, *A History of Italian Law,* trans. L. B. Register, (Boston, 1928), pp. 519-22. For France, A. Lehmann,*Le rôle de la femme dans l'histoire de France au moyen âge* (Paris, 1952).

4. *Monumenta Germaniae Historica* (hereinafter *MGH*), *Capitularia regum Francorum* 1, ed. A. Boretius (Hanover, 1883), 8: no. 4.

5. J. Leipoldt, *Die Frau in der antiken Welt und im Urchristentum,* 2nd ed. (Leipzig, 1954).

6. Naples, no. 591 (11 May 1108). References to chartularies and parchment collections are cited in the notes according to their place of provenience. For full bibliographical references, see the explanation given in the bibliographical Appendix.

7. Ordre du Temple, no. 148 (4 March 1138).

8. Vienne—Saint-André-le-Bas, no. 8° (16 Jan. 875), "regnante domno nostro Karolo filium Judit." On Judith's career, see T. Vogelsang, *Die Frau als Herrscherin im hohen Mittelalter* (Göttingen, 1954), pp. 13-15.

9. Amalfi, no. 208 (3 March 1182).

10. Novalesa, no. 2 (5 March 739).

11. Volturno, 1: no. 176 (874) "Nomina servorum de Flaturno." The similar, undated list of "servi" owned by the monastery in the Valle Tritana shows four out of fifty-six bearing a matronymic (*ibid,* 1: 333).

12. Ghent—Saint-Pierre, no. 220 (1137). See also no. 391.

13. ". . . generatio eorum semper ad inferiora declinentur" according to the *Lex Ribuaria* 58.11, ed. A. Eckhardt (Weimar, 1934), p. 174.

14. Children of *colliberti,* serfs widely found in the records of northwestern France, were usually divided between their parents' lords. Cf. Marmoutier—Chartularium vindocinense no. 161 (1071), "Guillelmus calumpniatus est nobis medietatem filiorum, propter colibertam patris sui." Where no formal division was made, each lord could apparently claim half of each *collibertus.* Marmoutier—Livre des serfs, no. 55 (1163), ". . . abbas et monachi asserebant predictos quidem ejusdem Huberti colibertos esse ex matre, monachorum vero ex patre." The frequently divided ownership over these serfs deriving from the marriages of serfs of different lords may be an explanation for their somewhat mysterious name, as the prefix *con-* or *col-* suggests some sort of joint ownership. Cf. Balon, *Domaine de l'église,* 1: 175-81.

15. Capua, no. 11 (Dec. 1109).

16. Above, n. 6.

17. Florence—Santa Maria (Badia), no. 70 (23 March 1070).

18. Cf. Pisa, no. 143 (16 Feb. 1060), in which Ermingarda, "filia bone memorie Vuille," includes among those for whom prayers are requested "Eriti qui fuit genitor suus."

19. Cf. Camaldoli, no. 682 (13 Oct. 1106), "Bernardinus Sidonie filius," and no. 705 (Oct. 1109), where the same man is identified as "Bernardinus filius olim Feralmi." See also nos. 567, 568, 639, 791 and 814. Feralmus, Bernardinus' father, figures in nos. 558-60 (1090), and was apparently not a cleric. See also Gorze, no. 33 (21 Dec. 795), where the same man figures as "Deodatus filius Agliberti" in the text of the charter and "Deodati filii Teudradane" in the subscription.

20. Numerous examples in Aragon—Liber feudorum maior.

21. Maguelone, no. 103, "Eu Raymons de Castrias, filz de Guilhelma, per mandamen de meteissa Guilhelma et de Raymond de Castrias, mon payre. . . ."

22. Cluny, no. 2984 (1049–60) and no. 3031 (1049–1109). Cf. also Vienne—Saint-André-le-Bas, no. 64° (ca. 1090), "ego Vigo comes, filius Gotelenne" (Guigues-le-Gras, son of Guigues-l'Ancien). For Germany, see Lorsch, no. 228 (end March 782), Heimricus comes filius domne nostre Willisuuinde.

23. In order, Eslonza, no. 122 (1199); Liébana, no. 96 (20 Sept. 1067); Reggio—Liber grossus, no. 16 (1 Apr. 1198); Chartres—Saint-Père, no. 54 (1101–15).

24. Montpellier—Guillems. The editor, A. Germain, provides a genealogical table in the introduction.

25. Saint-Maixent, no. 112 (1045–50).

26. La Merci-Dieu, no. 88 (March 1239), "Ludovico rege Francie, filio domine Blanchie, feliciter imperante."

27. Silos, no. 38 (1 Apr. 1126); see also nos. 45 and 46 and Vega, no. 33 (10 May 1125), "Adefonsus rex filius regine domne Urrace." Liber feudorum maior, no. 278 (5 Nov. 1053) for Sicardis and no. 289 (1062) for "Geralli filius Sichardis."

28. Morlaas—Sainte-Foi, no. 8 (1173-1223). Gaston's father was Guillaume de Moncade; this is one of many examples which could be cited in which a son bearing a matronymic has a name different from his father's.

29. Cf. F. L. Ganshof, *Feudalism*, trans. P. Grierson (London-New York, 1952), pp. 119–22; M. Bloch, *La société féodale* (Paris, 1949), 1: 310; P. Guilhermoz, *Essai sur l'origine de la noblesse en France au moyen âge* (Paris, 1902), p. 199.

30. *MGH, Constitutiones* 1, ed. L. Weiland (Hanover, 1903), pp. 89–91, no. 45.

31. Cf. A. Richard, *Histoire des comtes de Poitou 778-1204* (Paris, 1903), 1: 237-65.

32. Cf. J. Barchewitz, *Von der Wirtschaftstätigkeit der Frau in der vorgeschichtlichen Zeit bis zur Entfaltung der Stadtwirtschaft* (Breslau, 1937); E. Grosse, *Die Formen der Familie und die Formen der Wirtschaft* (Freiburg-Leipzig, 1896).

33. *De Germania* 14, 25, ed. C. Halm (Leipzig, 1911), pp. 227–28 and 232.

34. *MGH, Capit.* 2 (Hanover, 1897), pp. 517–30.

35. *Liber apologeticus pro filiis Ludovici pii imperatoris*, PL 104.314A: "Si qua regina semetipsam regere non novit, quomodo de honestate palatii curam habebit . . . ?"

36. *MGH, Capit.* 1: 82–91, especially cap. 16.

37. Aragon—Liber feudorum maior, no. 489 (1056), "Et dono tibi illud mobile quod est in conveniencia dandum castellanis per unumquemque annum."

38. Aragon—Liber feudorum maior, no. 278 (5 Nov. 1053).

39. *Miracula s. Bononii abbatis presb.* AAS 40 (Aug. VI) 633 E: "Non mihi est . . . tantarum copia opum, quae mihi, et omnibus a me petentibus sufficere possit." For the identification, see H. Bresslau, *Jahrbücher des deutschen Reiches unter Konrad II* (Leipzig, 1879), 1: 393.

40. Attonis *Epistula* 9, PL 134.117D.

41. Annalista Saxo, *MGH, Scriptores* 6.608.

42. *Die Briefe des Bischofs Rather von Verona*, ed. F. Weigle (*MGH* Briefe der deutschen Kaiserzeit 1; Weimar, 1949) p. 165 no. 29.

43. According to Liutprand of Cremona, Marozia was the mistress of one pope and the mother of another. *Liudprandi Antapodosis*, ed. J. Becker (*MGH Script.*, in usum schol.; Hanover-Leipzig, 1915), p. 96, but the accuracy of his account is questionable. Cf. M.-L. Portmann, *Die Darstellung der Frau in der Geschichtsschreibung des früheren Mittelalters* (Basel-Stuttgart, 1958), p. 110.

44. Cluny, no. 1535 (July 980).

45. D. Herlihy, "Church Property on the European Continent 701–1200," *Speculum* 36 (1961): 83–84.

46. Lorsch, no. 257 (792–93).

47. See Herlihy, "Church Property."

48. Marmoutier—Chartularium vindocinense, no. 126 (1060–80).

49. Auch—Chapitre cathédrale, no. 64 (*ca.* 1146).

50. *Liudprandi Antapodosis* 67.

51. M. Defourneaux, *Les Français en Espagne aux XI*^{e} *et XII*^{e} *siècles* (Paris, 1949).

52. So Bernard states in a letter to Pope Eugenius, cited by V. Berry in K. M. Setton, *A History of the Crusades,* ed. M. Baldwin (Philadelphia, 1955) 1: 472.

53. Translated by A. Jeanroy, *La poésie lyrique des troubadours* (Toulouse, 1934) 2: 299.

Emily Coleman

···✤ Infanticide in the Early Middle Ages

The last several generations of medieval historians have made great strides in understanding and describing the inventiveness and resourcefulness of early medieval political and agrarian institutions. The battle is being won for the idea of early medieval vitality, and we are learning to recognize and appreciate the difficulties involved in the slow shifting of gears as one civilization becomes another. Yet, in one sense at least, the phrase "dark ages" is as accurate now as it was thought to be a hundred years ago. For despite all the progress historians have made, both in methodology and in perception and perspective, the essence of the social history of the period remains a mystery to us. We know a fair amount about the political factionalism of the aristocracy and an impressive amount about the agricultural organization of the ninth century, but there is very little written on the most basic unit of that society—the peasant family. In this paper, we shall be concerned primarily with only one aspect of peasant family life, hitherto largely neglected by scholars, which apparently played a role of some significance in the social history of the early Middle Ages: the economic and social patterns of family limitation among the servile population.

For this study, I have utilized one of the most magnificent and one of the most justly famous documents of early medieval social and economic history—the polyptych of Saint Germain-des-Prés.[1] The polyptych, which was redacted probably between ca. 801 and cal. 829, is an extraordinary example of a manorial censier or manorial extent, a tax census whose purpose was to record information which was of fiscal importance to the monastery.[2] It included the estates and benefices which belonged to and/or

Published previously as "L'infanticide dans le Haut Moyen Age," *Annales: économies, sociétés, civilisations*, 29 (1974), 315–335. The footnotes have been updated to include some recently published and relevant articles.

47

were dependent upon the abbey, and the people who lived on these lands and/or who were in some less direct way responsible to Saint Germain as their seigneurial lord. This information is categorized by villa, or estate; and a *breve* (or chapter) is devoted to each. Each breve describes in some detail the type and size of the elements of the *demesne* (reserved land of the lord), the amount and types of tenanted land, the number of people on that land, the rents and dues which were owed from it, and any churches, mills, or other appurtenances on the estate or attached to it. Within this larger framework, the redactors recorded the same type of pertinent data by *manse* or family farm.

This polyptych of Saint Germain-des-Prés has been uniquely significant in revealing to the patient scholars who have worked with it much of what is now known about large-scale estate management and organization and the agrarian institutions for the Carolingian era in the north of Europe. It has, in fact, been indefatigably probed from an economic point of view;[3] and yet it has been only cursorily searched from a demographic perspective.[4]

The document is unusually rich in demographic information. The populations on the estates of the monastery were of as much interest to the redactors as the lands, precisely because they paid the dues and taxes levied not only on themselves personally but on the lands they worked as well. The tenures might have been superficially more important to the assessors, but they were well aware that without the peasantry, the unworked villas would have yielded little remuneration; and they were, therefore, closely interested in their people.[5] The manorial extent was more than just a tenurial document, in the sense that it was only concerned with the land. Even a passing glance reveals the attention paid to the dependants of the monastery. Just as the economic information on the serfs was broken down and recorded by manse—land status, types and amounts of land worked, personal and tenurial taxes and responsibilities—so too was the more personal information the peasantry retained. Those on each manse were individually recorded by status and by name, including the children in most instances.[6] The peasants were included, also, even if they belonged personally to other manors but lived on the lands of Saint Germain.[7] And that the assessors were interested in more than an aggregate number, in more than a mere head count, is apparent from the interest that was taken in familial relationships; the population on each manse was recorded by nucleus and, even more, careful mention was made when children were living with women who were not their mothers.[8] The data are readily available on such important subjects as sex ratios, family size, marriage characteristics, and population control.[9]

One might wonder, then, why so little attention has been paid to this facet of the document. Part of this lack of interest in the non-tenurial information it contains is explained by the fact that the polyptych's economic intelligence has been at once more obvious. It is a commonplace to remark that historiography follows fashions and trends in the same way as any other intellectual enterprise. Until relatively recently, historians concentrated on the economic aspects of society, rather than on the demographic, because that is what they were interested in; the study of population and sub-groups within a population has only lately become a solid component of social and economic history.[10] Among medievalists, demography has really just become an important field of inquiry, growing from the historical stepchild of the early fifties to the "favored son" of the seventies. On the other hand, the information on the population characteristics of the polyptych is not as immediately retrievable with the techniques and methodology medievalists have traditionally used. The data are available but require a different, more statistically oriented, type of questioning. So it might be well at this point to pause in order to discuss the types of data that are available and the methodology I have employed in order to discern patterns of population control within the peasantry of the Ile-de-France.[11]

As has been mentioned, the demographic data recorded in the polyptych were registered by the farming unit, the manse. Individuals on these lands were entered by the nucleus: head (by name and status), his wife (by name and status), and their children, if any (quite often by name). If there were two or more nuclei on the farm, they were listed in the same way; and any unmarried adults were noted as well:

> Amalgis, a colona of Saint Germain; Jonam, a colonus and his wife, a colona named Actildis; they have one child with them called Frotgaudus. Martinus a colonus and his wife, a colona named Wandreverta, are people of Saint Germain who have with them . . . children called Gislehardus, Jenesia, and Waldredrudis.[12]

This type of material is repeated quite systematically for some 2,600 nuclei on some 1,700 farms. Simple counting of the population listed in this way gives important results. The average size of the nuclear households and families may be roughly posited;[13] and the size of the average peasant farm and the number of people it supported may be quickly gauged.[14] Moreover, the sex ratios (the number of men per 100 women in a population) can be determined.

The average sex ratio in a normal (modern) population is about 105 at birth and declines with the greater mortality of males until, among the adult population, it becomes approximately equal.[15] On the estates which the polyptych encompasses, this was not the case. In the adult populations of Saint Germain-des-Prés, the sex ratio ranged from 110.3 to 252.9 men for each 100 women; and in the entire population, including children whose sex is determinable, it still went from 115.7 to 156.2.[16] The usual interpretation of these ratios is that women were under-reported; yet if one analyzes these sex ratios, patterns emerge which suggest that when taken at face value they might not reflect some subtleties which exist within these servile populations.

What I have done is to use the relatively simple statistical technique of product-moment correlation. Correlation allows the comparison of one set of data with another; one set is considered the independent variable and the other (the dependent variable) is measured against it. If there is a correlation, then the dependent variable will change proportionately as the independent variable fluctuates; the closer the relationship between the fluctuations of the variables, the higher the degree of correlation. If the correlation coefficient (the number indicating the closeness of the relationship on a +1.0 to a −1.0 scale) is positive, the association between the data sets is a direct ratio (as A goes up, so does B); if the coefficient is negative, the association is an inverse ratio (as A goes up, B goes down).

In order to find the patterns behind the sex ratios of Saint Germain, I used the sex ratios as the dependent variables and compared them to factors which might conceivably have influenced them, such as nuclear household size, the economic potential of the land (in terms of amount of arable), and the population size of the individual family farms. With a note of caution that a correlation does not necessarily imply a cause-effect relationship, it is perhaps time to discuss what patterns this technique has indicated among the peasantry and the possible reasons for them.

One of the significant things about these ninth-century peasants is that they do not necessarily show the characteristics one might expect to find. For instance, there does not appear to be a discernable relationship between the status of the household head and the size of the family he supports. *Coloni, lidi,* and *servi* seem to support the same number of dependents, proportionately.[17] Lidi have nuclear families as large as eight people, servi as large as nine (in one case eleven); and there were only eight coloni families with more than nine members (the largest was twelve).[18] It might have been anticipated that coloni with much less time devoted to the personal call of the lord could afford to support a larger family than servi; yet they did not. It is meaningful as well that the status of the land—in and of itself—makes little difference to family size. By the ninth century, tenurial status is an anachronism in some instances of demography, though it is still greatly important in terms of taxes and inheritance.

On the other hand, the characteristics which the peasantry does have are equally important. For example, the size of the land—measured in units of arable land—significantly influences the number of people working their particular farms. As is perfectly logical, larger manses have more people living on them. The correlation between manse size based on arable and the number of people it supports is a high +0.81 based on aggregate figures; that is, the averages of number of people per manse, identified by size, for all the villas, as may be seen below.

Table 1

Population by Manse Arable[19]

bunuarium (-ia)	individuals/manse	average per manse
less than 1	74/40	1.85
1-2	277/76	3.64
2-3	603/139	4.34
3-4	1055/223	4.73
4-5	845/164	5.15
5-6	873/155	5.63
6-7	482/100	4.82
7-8	538/104	5.17
8-9	324/47	6.89
9-10	449/67	6.70
10-11	300/43	6.98
11-12	618/89	6.94
12-13	250/32	7.81
13-14	293/30	9.77
14-15	138/21	6.57
15-16	276/31	8.90
16-17	186/19	9.79
17-18	235/25	9.40
18-19	46/4	11.50
19-20	167/21	7.95
20-21	76/8	9.50
21-22	46/5	9.20
22-23 and over	153/21	7.29

In more manageable terms, the rather abstract correlation simply means that a large part of the variance of population distribution on these tenanted units is explained in sheer economic terms: richer manses generally supported more peasants than smaller, less economically fruitful ones.[20]

This correlation assumes a general level of fertility on these lands in the Ile-de-France which naturally varies but which—within the broad division of those lands to the south of Paris and those villas on the Beauce plain and in the Perche—may be taken as roughly stable. Generally, these lands are extremely rich with a relatively thick cover of alluvial soil over varying types of limestone rock. This is particularly true for the Beauce, for example, where the alluvial deposits range from 30-40 cm. to a full 2 meters in depth.[21] Moreover, the Paris region is rich in underground water, and it corresponds "parfaitement à une unité climatique régionale;"[22] there is a regularity of temperature and rainfall which favors a productive rural economy.[23]

Manses differed in size, of course, and thereby reflected, in part, changing degrees of soil fertility; but it probably would not be overly dangerous to assume, again within relatively broad (and for the modern historian generally unverifiable) limits, a basic equality of economic potential within the villas. Because of a paucity of information within the polyptych on the kinds and numbers of animals the farms supported, we are forced to rely on arable land as a measure of wealth for the peasants of Saint Germain. Animals are mentioned only when they were due as taxes, and the taxes levied were clearly not differentiated on a basis of ability to pay. Generally, one or two manses of a status had their dues stipulated in detail, and those which followed them in the document were simply reported as paying the same (*solvit similiter, faciunt similiter,* etc.).

The size of the arable land each tenanted farm possessed, then, may be assumed to be, in large part, directly responsible for the wealth of the farm. The larger the unit, the greater the yield that could reasonably be expected from it, fertility being roughly equal; the greater the yield, the more people could be fed. This manifests itself in two ways: not only could the peasant families support more children, but the farms could support more families as well. There is a close relationship among the grain produced, the number of people dependent on it, and the number of draft animals and food animals it

TABLE 2

Sex Ratio by Manse Arable

Arable	Total Sex Ratio	Children's Sex Ratio
less than 1 bunuarium	421.05	200.00
1	145.28	128.26
2 bunuaria	143.46	155.84
3	138.89	166.28
4	125.82	119.88
5	128.10	136.64
6	119.92	116.92
7	127.41	123.53
8	131.73	140.70
9	141.67	167.86
10	141.62	169.44
11	110.71	112.86
12	119.85	142.11
13	129.25	129.63
14	131.62	130.00
15	117.54	112.00
16	128.16	146.34
17	97.33	107.14
18	130.49	150.00
19	100.00	108.33
20	123.08	145.83
21	103.33	86.67
22	170.59	(22 & over) 169.70
23 & over	135.00	

TABLE 3

Sex Ratio by Manse Population

People Per Manse	Adult Sex Ratio	Children's Ratio
2	129.9	200
3	156.6	303.6
4	127.0	136.5
5	119.5	130.2
6	119.2	148.4
7	129.4	145.3
8	109.0	122.2
9	125.0	136.9
10	138.1	149.5
11	115.1	113.8
12	120.7	131.7
13	101.0	107.8
14	94.9	104.9
15	105.9	103.0
16	150.9	165.6
17	131.8	154.6
18	114.3	126.9
19	90.0	(19 & over) 134.0
20	81.8	
21 & over	136.6	

could support.[24] In other words, a large amount of arable land might not only allow more people but, perhaps, an ox to help work the land, making it even more productive. It is also possible that several farms with enough arable land might jointly support a draft animal. Interestingly enough, it is not uniformly true that the largest manses supported the largest number of people for all farms and all *fiscs* (villas).[25] But these are the exceptions which make the norm stand out in clearer relief.

There are tendencies, too, within this overall structure. Careful scrutiny of the polyptych of Saint Germain-des-Prés seems to indicate some of the more elusive population patterns of the ninth-century French peasantry. While sheer size accounts fairly well for the number of people and the number of families per manse, economic potential does not summarize all there is to know. It only partially accounts for the demographic breakdown by sex ratio, although there was a definite relationship between the amount of arable land and the number of men to women on each manse. The sex ratio ran from a high of 421.05 for the land of less than one bunuarium to a low of 97.33 on manses with between seventeen and eighteen bunuaria.

Statistically, the correlation between the size and the sex ratio is negative: −0.39. In other words, there is an inverse relationship between the arable land and the sex ratio; the sex ratio becomes lower as the arable land increases. This is explained in part by the fact that the smallest manses were usually worked by cottars and bachelors.

If we look at the manses from the perspective of the total number of people on each compared to the sex ratio, regardless of the amount of arable land, there is still a decidedly inverse relationship. Here the sex ratios go from 78.6, on the manses with 25 people, to 156.6 on those with three inhabitants, as may be seen below in Table 3.

Again the proportion of men to women is inverse to the total population of the farm. In other words, the proportional difference in the number between the sexes declines as the total population increases; and the correlation is −0.40.[26] The greater the number of tenants on a farm, the greater the relative number of women among them, the less men per woman, or a lower sex ratio. There were more women, proportionately, on the heavily populated lands than on those with a smaller number of people— in the same way larger units of land supported more women than did the smaller farms.

On the other hand, the relationship between the nuclear household size and the sex ratio seems to be entirely different. Here there was a correlation of +0.56 between the number of people per family (we are here using nuclear household and family as synonymous) and the sex ratios in that household. There is a direct ratio between the population of a household and the number of men to women in it, as shown below in Table 4.

TABLE 4

Sex Ratios by Household Size

People per Nucleus	Sex Ratio
2	105.2
3	135.6
4	108.6
5	116.8
6	128.2
7	118.99
8	109.4
9	157.1
10	110.5
11	214.3
12	140.0

The extreme cases of single-person household units are excluded from these calculations since they are composed, for the most part, of bachelors and cottars.

This positive relationship simply means that as the basic family size increases, so does the ratio of men to women. The larger the number of people in the family, the less balanced the sex ratio—the proportion of men to women increases.

The problem, of course, is to interpret these numbers, to determine what they mean within the context of the peasant society of Saint Germain-des-Prés. The pattern which they indicate is relatively simple: a certain proportional balance between the sexes on a moderate, yet still significant scale.

The information in the polyptych indicates that the larger the family, the higher the sex ratio—meaning more males in proportion to females. Conversely, the larger the farm itself and the greater the numbers on it, the smaller the sex ratio; the sexes become, on the whole, more evenly balanced. If we think about it, this is a perfectly logical pattern. In a small household the balance between the amount of work the farm requires and the people available to work it would be in a sort of equilibrium. Women had their place in the medieval household. They would cook, tend the small family garden if there was one, spin cloth, and make clothes, etc. But, in terms of the necessary investment of time and food daughters were a potential financial drain and fiscal loss as well; a point of diminishing returns could soon be reached where there were too few chores to justify too many female mouths. It is also possible that a woman might expect a share in the inheritance of the sons.[27] A man with a large family and a large number of daughters therefore faced a serious problem: could he provide a settlement for each daughter and still leave a tangible inheritance for his sons? A son would pay dividends on the parental investment of time and labor with his work in the fields; he could, in fact, carry the burden of the farming and taxes and dues for the father in his old age. But the investment in the daughter was primarily an investment whose dividends would for the most part accrue to her future husband. She would marry and work her husband's cottage garden, perhaps in his fields, and certainly the cloth and clothes she would make would be for him and their own nuclear family.

Perhaps not all the girls married—a situation not unlikely if there were a number of daughters (and this situation would be reinforced on a basis of status; servi—who often held smaller plots of land and generally had higher taxes in corvée—had a much higher sex ratio, for example, than coloni, as we have discussed elsewhere[28]). There would then be much less given away from the family in terms of dowry, if there was one, or in terms of labor. But the economic utility of women had its limits, and the spinsters were entitled to support, first from their parents and then from their brothers when they inherited the land with its responsibilities. In long-range terms, they would be an economic hindrance to their brothers, too, because they would limit the males' potential family size. This was a period of subsistence agriculture, and the farms could not support an indefinite number of mouths. That unmarried women were entitled to support on the lands of Saint Germain-des-Prés is made clear from the number of unmarried women living in the households of their brothers.[29] A man with many children would pray for sons.

This logic, however, does not persist for the sex ratios compared to the size of the manse and the numbers of people on it. That is why the correlation coefficients mentioned above are negative. The sex ratio is in inverse proportion to the economically productive potential of the arable land of the farm. Logically, a larger, richer manse could simply afford more women than a smaller, poorer one. The same thing is true for a manse with a larger population. Such multiple household units (for these manses with large populations have a larger number of small nuclear families, as we have noted above) can co-operate, work together, and be more productive than individual nuclear families working alone. The land could perhaps be forced to produce enough food for an extra mouth or so. At the same time, women would be more useful because of a proportional increase in their work. In both cases, then, the females present would have been useful and feasible, both economically and in the more obvious social sense.

Yet this describes the effects of the differential sex ratios we have noted more than it explains them. The important and difficult problem here is to isolate the factor, or complex of factors, that caused the unequal proportions of men to women found in the polyptych. There are, in fact, many possible explanations: one should not discount the possibility that women were under-reported or that the redactors simply ignored many female children as essentially unimportant for the purposes of the survey. It is also possible that some numerical masculine superiority was the result of an immigration of men who hoped to find work and protection on the monastery's lands, or that many idigenous women married into other *villae*.[30] Certainly, a high death rate during parturition must have taken its toll on the sex ratio. Perhaps, too, many of the women from the villa were recruited to work in the manor house of each seigneury or were conscripted as servants for the monastery itself. Nor can we omit the possibility of female infanticide. And on a more simply practical level, it is possible that the populations with which we must work are not fully representative: that if we possessed a complete census for the Ile-de-France, the sex ratios would be much closer to what we consider "normal."

It is probably safe to assert that the only sure thing about the question is that there will be as many hypotheses as there are people who are interested in it. Each historian must decide for himself which explanation, or complex of explanations, seems most likely. And it is to this purpose that the remainder of this paper will be devoted: it will simply outline one of the many possible confluences of causes, one which seems to the author to take into account the largest amount of data on the peasantry in the ninth-century Ile-de-France in the most satisfactory way.

Whatever the explanation of the sex ratios found within the polyptych of Saint Germain-des-Prés, the patterns which we have discovered within them are too strong for us to assume that they were achieved by accident. It is probably safe to hazard the guess of human intervention in one form or another. The problem of population control before modern contraceptive devices is a question of lively interest not only to the historian but to anthropologists, demographers, and even economists.[31] The classic statement on the subject was made, of course, by T. R. Malthus in 1798 in his *Essay on the Principle of Population.* He felt the best way to control fertility and population growth was by individual will power and marriage late in life. This apparently was not the medieval solution. Such sources as late Roman imperial legislation, the Salic Law in its redaction under Charlemagne, Frankish penitentials, the canon law compendia, and literature, have left acute observations into the ways and means of population management.

Abortion was probably fairly common. This is witnessed by the number of penitential mentions of it.[32] An eighth-century Frankish penitential decrees two years of bread and water as punishment if a woman takes something in order to prevent conception or to kill an unborn child.[33] In the ninth century, the same clause appears with a ten-year fast, indicating that the practice was still in active use; and some of these documents are concerned specifically with the Parisian area.[34]

Infanticide had been a practice of "civilized" societies long before the medieval era; Greece (probably Sparta rather than Athens) had institutionalized it, and Rome continued it.[35] Roman imperial laws had attempted to outlaw this practice, and as early as 315 Constantine, recognizing the importance of the economic factor, tried to organize a charity for poor parents so that they would not have to expose or sell their children.[36] In 318 he set the penalty at death for infanticide.[37] Infanticide was not unknown among the Germanic tribes either although apparently it did not reach the proportions among them that it did among their more sophisticated neighbors.[38] Naturally, the Church eventually became involved. From the fourth century on, many children were left abandoned at a church's door; and they were accepted in order to prevent their death at the hands of their parents.[39] However, the Church admitted that there was often an economic necessity behind it. Among the lists of punishments in the penitentials for the killing of infants is an illuminating clause indicating that the penance would be reduced by more than half (from 15 to 7 years) if the mother was a poor woman.[40] And the Salic Law deals quite strenuously, in a number of clauses, with the harming of children already born and growing, as do the Decretals.[41]

Moreover, we not only have legal references to the existence of infanticide in the Middle Ages, but literary evidence as well. For example, the life of the English slave girl Balthildis, who rose in society to become the wife of Clovis II and the mother of three kings during the seventh century, records that she attempted to extirpate the practice of abandoning children, common in Gaul, to avoid paying taxes on them.[42] And the life of Saint Liudger is even more enlightening in that it deals with specifically female infanticide. Liudger's mother, Liafburga, was born in Frisia towards the middle of the eighth century to parents who had had several daughters but no son who survived birth; and it was decided she must die. This was permissable by Frisian custom if the child had not tasted "earthly" food. Liafburga was saved only by the intervention of a servant who put some food in Liafburga's mouth.[43]

The Icelandic saga of "Gunnlaug Serpent-Tongue" is even more pointed: it states specifically that if Gunnlaug's mother gave birth to a girl, the girl must be put to death; but a boy might live. The saga goes on to say that "those men who had few possessions, but yet had many dependents on their lands, had their children exposed."[44] This custom is recorded as well in the saga of Ari Thorgilsson ("The Book of the Icelanders") which notes the conversion of Norway to Christianity by St. Olaf. At the time of conversion it was made "law that all people should be Christian and those baptized who still were unbaptized on the land; but as to infanticide the old law should stand. . . ."[45] Later, in "Fresne" (one of the Lais of Marie de France) the whole plot of the story hinges on the survival of a girl who was to have been put to death in infancy.[46] At the very least, it may be said that the idea of infanticide did not shock the sensibilities of the laity in the Middle Ages.

It is this type of demographic administration that is most relevant to the conditions noticed for Saint Germain-des-Prés. Contraception and abortion are effective checks to unwanted children, but they would have only the smallest influence on the sex ratio.[47] And the sex ratios, as has been noted previously, are surprisingly high—for example, higher among servi than coloni and, therefore, influenced by personal status as well as household and manse size.[48]

Many factors undoubtedly enter the problem. As has been suggested, the under-reporting of females might have played some role, although it is questionable whether it is a very large one for the polyptych of Saint Germain-des-Prés. If females were under-reported, they should have been equally under-reported on all the manses. But such is not the case. Adult women, at least, seem to have been recorded rather scrupulously, if for no other reason than that it was they, not the fathers, who passed on their status valuation to their children.[49] The death of many women during parturition would surely have caused some disequilibrium in the sex ratio as would the possibility of the immigration of men who hoped to find work and protection on the monastery's land. But these latter factors, as important within the context of early medieval society as they no doubt were, do not explain the children's overall sex ratio of 136.41 as well as the adult sex ratio of 126.98. Perhaps some little girls were not counted; yet this cannot explain the whole situation either. For if we examine the children's sex ratios in the same way we have looked at the whole and adult populations, we find that very much the same patterns exist.

To begin with, the correlation between the size of the arable land of the farms and the number of children they support is an overwhelming +0.86. In the same way that larger and potentially more productive manses could support a larger population as a whole, it would seem that they could maintain a larger number of young and relatively unproductive mouths to feed. The larger the land, the more children on it. On the other hand, the correlation between the amount of arable land of a farm and the sex ratio of the children on that farm was a −0.33. The ratio is inverse; as the size of the arable land of the farms increased, the children's sex ratios on those farms decreased. The number of boys on these agricultural units came closer to equalling the number of girls; the numerical relationship between the sexes became more balanced. (See Table 2.)

And we find, too, that the sex ratios of the children on the villas of Saint Germain vary according to the total population of the manses themselves. Whereas the correlation between the adult sex ratio and the number of people on the farm was −0.39, the relationship of total population to the proportions of boys to girls was even stronger: −0.47. The sex ratios became lower (more balanced) the more people there were. In other words, as the total number of dependants and workers on the land rose, not only were there more adult females present but, generally, there were even more young girls present in comparison to the boys, as may be seen in Table 3. Moreover, the same type of inverse relationship holds true for the sex ratios of the children when compared to the number of children on the farms, discounting for the moment the adults. The correlation is −0.39; again, the more children altogether, the more girls in proportion to the boys.

If under-reporting were the whole answer, we would be hard pressed to explain the patterns that clearly exist. There is good reason to suppose that some control was being exercised, on the parental level, to the great detriment of girls. Yet on relatively well-managed manorial lands the killing of children of some years, after they had been baptized and known by officials, neighbors, and friends, would surely be difficult to explain. It is unlikely that they would pass unnoticed or unpunished. Conversely, infant mortality at birth and among the first few months of life was notoriously and astoundingly high. It would not be difficult in a community surrounded by harsh and untamed forest for a baby to be exposed, or simply smothered in the home. The death could take place before baptism, and the child announced as stillborn.[50] Conceivably, the priest, the lord, and most of the other peasants need never know. This is not to say, of course, that the deaths of all female babies were due to murder. It is, however, possible that the population patterns we have found among the serfs of Saint Germain-des-Prés might have been achieved, at least in part, by the maxim "Thou shalt not kill, but thou shalt not strive over-zealously to keep alive." In other words, the death of the child might be due to "negative infanticide" rather than "positive infanticide."[51]

Of course, it would probably be unwise to assume than infanticide occurred with regularity in every peasant area and generation. The law codes of the Alamanni, for instance, show unusual care for female children. In one clause it is clearly stated that if someone causes an abortion in a woman, where the sex of the foetus was determinable and male, the punishment was twelve *solidi,* if female twenty-four *solidi:* fully twice as much.[52] The Alamannic Code shows a consistent care for females. One might wonder if this was not at least partially due to the precariousness of a girl's life as well as her sexual value as an adult.

A document of practice, the polyptych of Saint Victor of Marseille shows 106 female children to 99 boys, or a sex ratio of 93.40.[53] This fact, in itself, points out more clearly the significance of the patterns among the peasants of Saint Germain; but this polyptych gives other significant information on the relationship between boys and girls, too. It lists the ages of children between the time they were weaned and the time they reached marriageable age: male children are listed with their ages from two years, females from one year. In other words, male babies were nursed for fully twice as long as females. This would seem to be highly significant in a milieu of ever-present malnutrition. Baby boys, who ordinarily have a much higher rate of infant mortality (which might be mirrored in the sex ratio), were given a nutritive edge over little girls among Saint Victor's peasants. Infanticide was probably a practice governed to a great extent by cycles of famine. It is legitimate to wonder if the children's sex ratio on the lands of Saint Victor might not reflect a period of relatively high yields.

Yet, it is not satisfactory to let the problem rest here. Even if it is conceded that female infanticide was taking place, it would be simplistic to assume that one solution could explain such a complex and difficult demographic dilemma as the differential sex ratios of the polyptych. No one hypothesis could hope to unravel all the nuances of a society which was at once alive and functioning.

It is interesting, for instance, to find that there is a high degree of correlation between the children's sex ratios and the adults': −0.40. (See Table 5) As the sex ratio of the children increases—as the number of boys to girls becomes more and more disproportionate—the sex ratio of the adults decreases, and the number of men to women becomes more balanced.

There appears to be a very subtle, but real, equilibrium between the sexes on the lands of Saint Germain-des-Prés. There were more or less adult women supported on many farms and estates depending upon the number of female babies that were supported on them. Or, conversely, more or less female babies survived depending upon the number of females that already existed on the land.

TABLE 5

Adult and Children's Sex Ratios

Breve	Adult Ratio	Children's Ratio
1.	252.9	88.89
2.	136.6	128.77
3.	150.0	147.37
4.	126.6	200.00
5.	146.9	——*
6.	115.8	93.18**
7.	149.3	——*
8.	140.0	121.88
9.	125.4	129.84
11.	112.5	178.57
13.	119.8	163.79
14.	125.8	121.99**
15.	114.6	161.4
16.	125.8	124.39
17.	125.0	150.00
18.	142.8	75.00
19.	110.3	——*
20.	123.2	148.64
21.	121.5	134.00
22.	112.1	144.2
23.	118.1	140.00
24.	120.2	110.43
25.	145.6	——*
Frag. Duo	133.3	176.4

*Predominantly undeterminable
**Partially undeterminable

In other words, the farms supported a finite number of females. The number of adult women that the men of the land could bring on to it as wives depended upon the number of young girls that it was supporting. On the other hand, the number of baby girls that could be encouraged, or allowed, to survive was closely related also to the number of wives and adult spinsters that already took their sustenance from it. Economically, it was apparently more efficient for a manse to have a dearth of females than a plethora of them.

This fact becomes especially interesting (see Table 5) if we compare the correlations between the sex ratios of the children to the total manse population (−0.47), between their sex ratios to the number of children on the farm (−0.40), and between the children's ratio to the number of youngsters per household (+0.02). The first two correlations would seem to be significant; they explain slightly more than 22% and 16% of the variance in the data. Therefore, as we have discussed above, there apparently was a healthy relationship between the proportion of boys to girls and both the total population of the farming units and the children's population on these units, discounting the adults. Yet there is virtually no affinity between the numbers of boys to girls and the size of their nuclear families; the correlation itself explains less than $\frac{1}{2}$ of 1% of the variance.

It would not appear to be unreasonable to infer from this that the population control involved on a manse involved more than the immediate family of the infant, more than just the parents and the personal problems and idiosyncracies. In fact, it seems that the birth of each new infant on a farm had long-term implications for everyone on that farm, especially the men on it. Each baby was a mouth to feed, the food for which came out of the common store of food and labor. Each baby girl was potential waste from this common supply if she married, and a potential continuing drain to it if she did not; if she did not marry, she economically limited the potential of at least some of the males to take wives, to add females to that manse.

There might then have arisen a subtle but strong group reaction to many of the pregnancies that took place. There may very well have been a strong feeling, especially on the part of the adult and pubescent males on the manse, against the birth of a girl. But since this was not a situation which could have been rectified in the womb, is it not perhaps valid to wonder if there was not group pressure for—or at least the group psychological acceptance of—the private decision not to help a baby girl survive, if there was not a more active suppresion of her existence?

Furthermore, given this psychology, it is not difficult to imagine a complex of factors (although if one studies Table 5, under-reporting is probably not one of them) that acted upon the peasant populations in the Ile-de-France to produce the data with which we must work. The patterns among the children's ratios would seem to indicate some sort of human interference. But there was probably more than that going on in the population as a whole. Might it not be possible to suggest that exogamy and the recruitment of female domestic servants by the lord operated on a selective basis rather than purely at random? That women, on lands which already had a plethora of females, were encouraged to marry away or work in the demesne house? And that the accretion of *hospites* (cottars) to the fringes of the villas, or the small-scale land clearance being done by individuals and small groups of individual peasants from the manor, might indeed even have been encouraged by the indigenous peasantry?

This masculine immigration and expansion could have provided a new economic base for many men who might have become a marital outlet for unmarried adult women on the manor. Many women, despite their sexual attractiveness in a society with such high sex ratios could possibly have faced a problem in finding a husband because many of the farms simply had too many people (and especially women) to support already. This could be an explanation for the number of single women we find in the polyptych despite the fact that there were much greater numbers of unmarried men.[54] If this very tentative suggestion holds, then this basic economic problem could, in fact, be an answer to the obvious question of how a society which valued women as adults could practice female infanticide. It is possible that without this simple form of population control many of the men on many of the manses would not have been economically able to marry and start families of their own until their parents had died and, perhaps, some of their younger brothers left to settle as cottars elsewhere, where not only the economic but marital possibilities might be better.[55]

Moreover, even if we discount the data in Table 5, it is probable that what under-reporting occurred was not systematic; if it were, we could reasonably expect the sex ratios throughout the villas belonging to the monastery—taken as a whole or even only that of the children or adults—to present some greater uniformity. One might even wonder, then, if under-reporting did not often occur with some rationale at times, rather than solely haphazardly—where the balance among produce, labor, and taxes was in a particularly precarious equilibrium. In other words, is it not possible that some female children were quietly suppressed in the census where the extra personal taxes would have created an unbearable burden to the total population on the farm? And if this were so, would it not have been equally rational to suppress the young boys in the census as well?

It might be interesting, too, to investigate those anomalies in the polyptych—those manses and populations on them which had "normal" sex ratios of close to 100–105. It might well be that it is those tenures which had achieved the most efficient balance between population and land; and that a concrete, tangible sign of economic success among the ninth-century Ile-de-France peasantry was, quite simply, the ability to support all the children, regardless of gender, produced by the marriages on these manses.

Clearly, early medieval sex ratios and peasant population control are problems not easily solved. We make no claim to the solutions here. This paper only attempts to suggest a possible approach to them, a possible complex of factors to explain the extremely complicated and difficult data contained in the polyptych of Saint Germain-des-Prés. An underlying assumption in the hypothesis we have outlined is that to discount the sex ratios, and patterns within them, in the document as simple under-reporting, as nothing more or less than the imperfection in the source material, is both to deny the vitality, activity, and subtlety of the early medieval peasantry and to undermine necessary research into the mysteries of the early medieval peasantry's social and economic existence.

Certainly, it should not be argued that infanticide took place in every peasant hut; the purpose of abortion and infanticide was to regulate children, not eliminate them.[56] Yet, the population trends we noted involved a large segment of some 2,600 households.[57] There was too large a portion of society involved for the patterns it exhibits to be strictly coincidental, for there to be more females where they would have been useful and supported and less where they would have been a hindrance to the family's very survival, both in terms of food and what little tangible property there was.

This is as far as our data takes us. Yet, while it is impossible to argue forward from ninth-century data to an eleventh-century situation, one might wonder if the problem of infanticide might not give a possible clue to the extraordinary demographic growth that took place in the central Middle Ages.[58] If one ventures to deal with pure hypothesis for a moment, is it not possible that as the technological innovations of the early Middle Ages—the three-field system, the use of the horse instead of the ox in front of the plow, the increased use of virgin land coming into cultivation—took firmer hold, the yield of the land was increased from a purely subsistence level to where it could support more individuals, more precisely, females?[59] This would help to account for the fact that the sex ratios became more evenly balanced in the documents in this period in a more positive way than the assumption of the under-reporting of women in earlier centuries. And if more females were allowed to achieve maturity, then they, in turn, could bear more children and the population of Europe would increase. This, naturally, is conjecture; yet it might suggest an avenue of approach for future investigation. Within the context of medieval society, moreover, it helps fill in a gap in the standard theory of "demographic transition," which holds that population increase is due to declining mortality rather than a rise in fertility, in that it suggests one possible reason for this declining mortality.[60]

At the very least, however, one thing seems clear: the peasantry on the lands of Saint Germain probably maintained internal controls on itself as a population. It is, in fact, probably fair to wonder if the answer to many a hard-pressed peasant's prayer came in the form of death, primarily of female babies.

NOTES

1. The document has been edited twice, first by Benjamin Guérard [*Polyptyque de l'Abbé Irminon . . . avec Prolégomènes*, 2 vols. (Paris, 1844)] whose detailed introduction provides a fundamental starting point for all who have and will follow in studying the document. The second edition was by Auguste Longnon [*Polyptyque de l'abbaye de Saint Germain-des-Prés rédigé au temps de l'abbé Irminon*, 2 vols. (Paris, 1886–95)] who reduced the introduction to more immediately manageable proportions, amended some of Guérard's paleographical and geographical interpretations, and added a significant section on the names within the document. The original manuscript is preserved today in the Bibliothèque Nationale (*Fonds latin*, #12832).

2. For a history of the monastery, one should consult J. Bouillart, *Histoire de l'Abbaye Royale de Saint Germain-des-Prés, contenant La Vie des abbez qui l'ont*

gouvernée depuis la fondation (Paris, 1724). The article "Saint Germain-des-Prés" in the *Dictionnaire d'archéologie chrétienne et de liturgie*, vol. 6, part 1 (1924) by H. Leclerq is useful not only in its text but for a select bibliography. The best bibliography for the history of the monastery is still L. H. Cottineau, *Répertoire topo-bibliographique des abbayes et prieures*, 2 vols. (1939–40) listed under the monastery of Sainte Croix et Saint Vincent. The most recent general work is *Mémorial du XIVe Centenaire de l'Abbaye de Saint Germain-des-Prés* (Paris, 1959); also see L.-R. Ménager, "Considérations sociologiques sur la démographie des grands domaines ecclésiastiques carolingians," in *Etudes d'histoire du droit canonique dédiées à Gabriel Le Bras*, vol. 2 (Sirey, 1965). Unfortunately, these works do not contain a bibliography of recently published books or articles of related interest. For additional bibliography, see the *Cambridge Economic History* 2nd ed., vol. 1, (Cambridge, 1966) or the concluding bibliography in G. Duby, *Rural Economy and Country Life in the Medieval West* (Columbia, S. C., 1968).

3. Polyptychs, especially that of Saint Germain-des-Prés, are mentioned as a prime source of information in any economic survey of the early Middle Ages: one need only mention as a basic beginning G. Duby, *Rural Economy;* M. Bloch, *French Rural History* (Berkeley and Los Angeles, 1966); B. H. Slicher van Bath, *The Agrarian History of Western Europe, A. D. 500–1850* (London, 1966); R. Latouche, *The Birth of Western Economy* (New York, 1966). An obvious and excellent example of the more detailed type of work which has been done with our polyptych is Ch.-E. Perrin, "Observations sur le manse dans la région parisienne au début du IXe siècle," *Annales d'histoire sociale* 7(1945): 39–52.

4. The most ambitious attempt at a demographic analysis was by Ferdinand Lot, "Conjectures démographiques sur la France au IXe siècle," *Le Moyen Age* 32 (1921): 1–27 and 107–37. This study has been variously criticized by Henri Sée, "Peut-on évaluer la population de l'ancienne France," *Revue d'économie politique* 38 (1924): 647–55; Charles-Edmund Perrin, "Note sur la population de Villeneuve-Saint-Georges au IXe siècle," *Le Moyen Age* 69 (1963): 75–86; L.-R. Ménager, "Considérations sociologiques."

5. See, for example, Perrin, "Note sur la population," 80–81.

6. A. Longnon, *Polyptyque*, Brevia I, II, III, IV, V, *passim.* The edition of the polyptych which will be referred to throughout is that of Longnon.

7. For instance, *Polyptyque*, IX: 145, 157, 289, 290; XXI: 1, 3, 81, 82, 86; XXII: 53, 72, 84. These are only a few examples; many others could easily be found.

8. See *Polyptyque*, XXI: 25, 27, 33; XXIV: 25; etc.

9. See E. R. Coleman, "Medieval Marriage Characteristics: A Neglected Factor in the History of Medieval Serfdom," *Journal of Interdisciplinary History* 2 (1971): 205–19.

10. For a survey of the historical background to the study of historical demography see D. V. Glass, "Introduction," and D. E. C. Eversley, "Population, Economy and Society," in D. V. Glass and D. E. C. Eversley, *Population in History* (Chicago, 1965), pp. 1–22 and 23–69. These essays concentrate especially on the eighteenth century and more modern periods. Also see N. Keyfitz, "Population Theory and Doctrine: A Historical Survey," in W. Petersen, *Readings in Population* (New York, 1972), pp. 41–69. For medieval demography, see J. C. Russell, *Late Ancient and Medieval Population*, Transactions of the American Philosophical Society, 48, part 3 (Philadelphia, 1958) and "Recent Advances in Mediaeval Demography," *Speculum* 40 (1965): 84–101; and J. Heers, "Les limites des méthodes statistiques pour les recherches de démographie médiévale," *Annales de démographie historique* (1968), pp. 43–72. The latter surveys deal, naturally, with the later Middle Ages for the most part.

11. A more detailed description of the methodology used may be found in E. R. Coleman, "A Note on Medieval Peasant Demography," *Historical Methods Newsletter* 5, no. 2 (1972): 53–58.

12. *Polyptyque*, XV: 20, "Amalgis, colona sancti Germani; Jonam colonus et uxor colona, nomine Actildis, habent secum infantem I, nomine Frotgaudus; Martinus colonus et uxor ejus colona, nomine Wandreverta, homines sancti Germani, habent secum infantes . . . , his nominibus, Gislehardus, Jenesia, Waldedrudis."

13. For a study of the average peasant household and family size and structure see my forthcoming book, *A Peasant Society and Social Changes: The Serfs of Saint Germain-des-Prés*.

14. See Perrin, "Observations sur le manse."

15. Russell, *Late Ancient and Medieval Population*, pp. 13–14.

16. See Coleman, "Medieval Marriage Characteristics," Table One, p. 211.

17. The *coloni* were originally, for the most part, the descendants of Roman peasants who were tied to the land they worked by the late imperial legislation of Diocletian and Constantine. The origin of the *lidi* is a matter of mystery. Some historians believe them to have originally been *laeti*—the barbarians introduced into Gaul as auxiliaries during Diocletian's reign; they came as both farmers and soldiers, but, during the decline of the Roman world with the barbarian invasions, they became servile laborers. On the other hand, the word may simply be a form of the common Germanic term for freemen. (I am grateful to Walter Goffart for information on this point.) The *servi* were simply the descendants of slaves. For more on these groups and the redevances owed by them, see Guérard, *Polyptyque . . . Prolégomènes;* Longnon, Polyptyque, "Introduction," pp. 31ff; H. Sée, *Les classes rurales et le regime domanial en France au moyen âge* (Paris, 1901); and Coleman, "Medieval Marriage Characteristics."

18. *Polyptyque*, II: 30; V: 25; IX: 43; XIII: 62, 84; etc. This count only includes families with male household unit heads and those groups in which the entire nucleus was determinable; families listed as wife and an unspecified number of children not belonging to Saint Germain are not counted since the total size is undecided.

19. If, however, we use the figures for the manse size categories on each fisc separately, we get a correlation of +0.47 for 288 observations. The trend is still clear even though the correlation coefficient, being very sensitive to individual idiosyncracies in the data, is not as strong on this level as in the aggregate.

For sources on the use of land measures such as *aripenna* (arpents) and *bunuaria* (bonniers), see Guérard, *Polyptyque . . . Prolégomènes;* P. Guilhiermoz, "De l'équivalence des anciennes mesures à propos d'une publication récente," *Bibliothèque de l'Ecole des Chartes* 74 (1913): 267–328; Lucien Musset, "Observations historiques sur une mesure agraire: le bonnier," *Mélanges d'histoire du moyen âge dédiés à Louis Halphen* (Paris, 1951), pp. 535–41.

20. This not unsuspected finding agrees with information being derived from the study of other peasant societies. See, for example, W. Stys, "The Influence of Economic Conditions on the Fertility of Peasant Women," *Population Studies* 11 (1957–58): 136–48.

21. O. Tulippe, *L'habitat rural en Seine-et-Oise. Essai de géographie du peuplement* (Liège, 1934), p. 37.

22. J. Beaujeu-Garnier and J. Basté, eds., *Atlas de Paris et de la région parisienne* (Paris, 1967), pp. 32, 42.

23. J.-M. Sourdillat, *Géographie agricole de la France* (Paris, 1959), pp. 13–14.

24. See Slicher van Bath, *Agrarian History*, pp. 7–18.

25. Fertility, as we noted, seems to account in part for some of the variation in manse sizes. O. Tulippe, "De l'importance des exploitations agricoles au IXe siècle dans L'Ile-de-France," *Annales de géographie* 40 (1931): 310.

26. This explains 16 percent of the variance, or why the relationship is not uniform, excluding the extremes of the data (the farms with only one person on them, for example, or farms with more than 23 people on them which—having only one case of each—were not representative).

27. In *Polyptyque*, IX: 247, it seems that a woman has an inheritance of her own over which she was in control: "Euthari mater, libera femina, dedit infantibus de propria sue hereditate jornales VIII." G. C. Homans, *English Villagers in the Thirteenth Century* (New York, 1970), discusses some of the implications of these problems

28. Coleman, "Medieval Marriage Characteristics."

29. *Polyptyque*, II: 101; VI: 14; VIII: 17; IX: 49; XIV: 15, 18, 38, 40; XV: 5, 7, 68; etc. Also see Homans, *English Villagers*, p. 142, for some of the implications of this.

30. L.-R. Ménager, "Considérations sociologiques," pp. 1334-35.

31. See, for instance, D. M. Heer, "Economic Development and the Fertility Transition," *Daedalus* 97, no. 2 (1968): 447-68; E. Van de Walle, "Marriage and Marriage Fertility," *Daedalus* 97, no. 2 (1968): 486-501; J. Blake, "Demographic Science and the Redirection of Population Policy," in K. C. W. Kammeyer, *Population Studies: Selected Essays and Research* (Chicago, 1969), pp. 378-400; P. M. Hauser, "Population Control: More than Family Planning," in W. Petersen, *Readings in Population* (New York, 1972), pp. 413-23; D. Davis and J. Blake, "Social Structure and Fertility: An Analytic Framework," *Economic Development and Social Change* 4 (1956): 211-35; A. J. Coale, "The Voluntary Control of Human Fertility," *Proceedings of the American Philosophical Society* 3 (1967): 164-69; J. Bourgeois-Pichat, "Social and Biological Determinants of Human Fertility in Nonindustrial Societies," *Proceedings of the American Philosophical Society* 3 (1967): 160-63; S. Kuznets, "Population and Economic Growth," *Proceedings of the American Philosophical Society* 3 (1967): 170-93; M. Douglas, "Population Control in Primitive Groups," *British Journal of Sociology* 17 (1966): 263-73.

For an historical treatment of contraception and population control, see for example, N. E. Himes, *A Medical History of Contraception* (Baltimore, 1936); J. T. Noonan, *Contraception* (New York, 1967); Hélène Bergues et al., *Prévention des naissances dans la famille: ses origines dans les temps modèrnes*, Institut national d'études démographiques: Travaux et Documents 25 (Paris, 1960); P. Ariès, "Sur les origines de la contraception en France," *Population* 8 (1953): 465-72; J. Dupâquier and M. Lachiver, "Sur les débuts de la contraception en France ou les deux malthusianismes," *Annales: économies, sociétés, civilisations* 24 (1969): 1391-1406; J.-L. Flandrin, "Contraception, mariage, et relations amoureuses dans l'Occident chrétien," *Annales: ESC* 24 (1969): 1370-90; E. Patlagen, "Sur la limitation de la fécondité dans la haute époque byzantine," *Annales: ESC* 24 (1969): 1353-69; K. Hopkins, "Contraception in the Roman Empire," *Comparative Studies in Society and History* 8 (1965-66): 124-51; Y.-B. Brissaud, "L'infanticide à la fin du moyen âge, ses motivations psychologiques et sa répression," *Revue historique de droit français et étranger* 50 (1972): 229-56; R. Trexler, "Infanticide in Florence: New Sources and First Results," *History of Childhood Quarterly* 1 (1973): 98-116; S. X. Radbill, "A History of Child Abuse and Infanticide," *Violence in the Family*, eds. S. L. Steinmentz and M. A. Strauss (New York, 1974), pp. 173-79; J. Manuel Perez Prendes, "Neomalthusianismo Hispano-Visigodo," *Anuario de Historia Económica y Social* 1 (1968): 581-83.

Also see L. deMause, "The Evolution of Childhood"; R. B. Lyman, Jr., "Barbarism and Religion: Late Roman and Early Medieval Childhood"; and M. M. McLaughlin, "Survivors and Surrogates: Children and Parents from the Ninth to the Thirteenth Century," in L. deMause, ed., *The History of Childhood* (New York, 1974), pp. 1-74, 75-100, 101-83, for childhood in general.

32. See, for example, F. W. H. Wasserschleben, *Die Bussordnungen der Abendländischen Kirche* (Halle, 1851), pp. 364, I, clause 5; 380, XIX; 393, XVIII; 413, XI; 507, III, clauses 1 and 2; etc.

33. *Ibid.*, p. 432, XXIX. Hopkins, "Roman Empire," points out that the Romans apparently could not differentiate between contraceptive and abortive practices. In our sources, we find the two linked in description and penance.

34. Wasserschleben, *Die Bussornungen*, p. 380, XIX. On the Parisian area, *Ibid.*, p. 413, XI; and H. J. Schmitz, *Die Bussbücher und die Bussdisciplin. Der Kirche.* (Mainz, 1883), 1: 687, clause 58.

35. For a survey of the practice see L. Godefroy, "Infanticide," *Dictionnaire de théologie catholique*, vol. 7, part 2 (Paris, 1923): 1717–26. A relatively recent book by W. K. Lacey, *The Family in Classical Greece* (Ithaca, 1968) has dealt with the subject for Greece. For Rome, see P. A. Brunt, *Italian Manpower, 225 B.C.–A.D. 14* (Oxford, 1971). The practice was apparently quite common in "primitive" societies as well. See, for example, Douglas, *Population Control*, and J. V. Neel, "Lessons from a 'Primitive' People," *Science* 170 (1970): 815–22. Also see N. Miller, *The Child in Primitive Society* (New York, 1928), pp. 36–37. The problem of infanticide continued in post-medieval periods as well; see the article by W. Langer, "Checks on Population Growth," *Scientific American* (February, 1972), pp. 92–99. (See note 32 for further bibliography.)

36. P. Krueger, ed., *Corpus Iuris Civilis*, vol. 1, *Institutiones et Digesta* (Berlin, 1963), *Digest*, "De Agnoscendis et Alendis Liberis," XXV, III, 4, for example. Many other instances of this type of legislation could easily be found. On Constantine, see Godefroy, "Infanticide," 1720.

37. J. T. Noonan, *Contraception*, p. 113 and Bergues, *Prévention*, pp. 165–66.

38. Godefroy, "Infanticide," 1722; Tacitus, *Germania, The Complete Works of Tacitus* (New York, 1942), XIX.

39. L. Lallemand, *Histoire des enfants abandonnés et délaissés. Etudes sur la protection de l'enfance aux diverse époques de la civilisation* (Paris, 1885), p. 99.

40. Schmitz, *Die Bussbücher*, 1: 687, clause 56.

41. *Monumenta Germaniae Historica* (hereinafter *MGH*), *Legum Sectio* 1, ed. A. Boretius (Hanover, 1962), 4: part 1, no. 24, 1–4, pp. 89–90.

In the canon law literature, one should see *Corpus iuris canonici*, editio Lipsiensis secunda, ed. E. Friedberg (reprinted., Leipzig, 1959), Lib. V, Tit. X; or *Decretales D. Gregorii Papae IX suae integritati una cum glossis restitutae* (Venice, 1591), Lib. V, Tit X. At this point, one might also cite Innocent III's "De Miseria humane conditionis," Book I, cap. XXX in *PL*, 217: col. 716—although Innocent closely follows Josephus (*The Jewish War*, Book VI, pp. 3–4) here. Many other references to the problem are easily found.

42. J. Bollandus, *Acta Sanctorum* (Paris, 1863), 3: 358. "Ordinavit etiam, imo per eam Dominus, ut et alia pessima consuetudo cessaret, pro qua multo plures homines filios suos magis mori quam nutrire optabant, dum de eis videbant exactiones fieri, publicaque, ex antiqua consuetudine, mala urgebantur accipere, unde gravissimum rerum suarum patiebantur damnum. Quam nequissimae cupiditatis averitiam, ipsa pietate plena pro mercede aeternae retributionis prohibuit, et ut in perpetuum servaretur legibus tradidit, ex quo copiosa merces calde a Domine reddita ei manet."

43. *MGH, Scriptores* 2, ed. G. H. Pertz (Hanover, 1829), p. 406, #6; ". . . quia sic mos erat paganorum, ut si filium aut filiam necare voluissent, absque cibo terreno necarentur."

44. M. H. Scargill and M. Schlauch, *Three Icelandic Sagas* (Princeton, 1950), pp. 11–12. "In the course of the summer Thorstein got ready to go to the meeting of the Assembly. Before he left home, he said to his wife, Jófrid, 'It so happens that you are

with child. If you bear a girl, you must expose it; but if the child is a boy, you shall rear him.'"

According to P. du Chaillu, *The Viking Age* (New York, 1889), 2:39, "The exposure of the child depended so entirely upon the will of the father, that not even the mother dared to oppose it. . . ." Also on the barbarian male's power over his children see N. Belmont, "Levana, ou comment 'élever' les enfants," *Annales: ESC* 38 (1973): 77–89. For a more detailed discussion of female infanticide in Scandinavia, see J. Pentikäien, *The Nordic Dead-Child Tradition: Nordic Dead-Child Beings: A Study in Compatative Religion* (Helsinki, 1968), pp. 68–76.

45. H. Hermannsson, *The Book of the Icelanders*, Icelandica Series, 15 (Ithaca, 1930), p. 66.

46. J. Rychner, *Les Lais de Marie de France* (Paris, 1966), pp. 47ff. While the child was abandoned, it was the mother's original intention to have the child killed.

47. Both R. P. Riquet, "Christianism et population," *Population* 4 (1949): 616–30 and P. Ariès, "Sur les origines de la contraception en France," *Population* 8 (1953): 465–72, agree that there was no contraception in the Middle Ages, though they differ as to the reasons for this. If they are correct, this would remove a possible population control from the psychology and milieu of the peasants of Saint Germain.

48. J. V. Neel, "Lessons," has found infanticide among the primitive groups he has studied and has also found the sex ratios among them to be 128 during the age interval of 0 to 14 years, a situation not greatly unlike that of Saint Germain. Moreover, he believes that "the infanticide is directed primarily at infants whose older sibling is not thought ready for weaning . . ." (p. 810). The fact that the ratio is higher among the lower statuses would argue against the thesis presented by Douglas, *Population Control*, that population control takes place more on a basis of prestige than economics.

49. Coleman, "Medieval Marriage Characteristics," 209–10, 214.

50. Wasserschleben, *Die Bussordnungen*, p. 507, III, clause 2 deals with this.

51. L. Godefroy, "Infanticide," p. 1718.

52. *MGH, Legum Sectio* 1, vol. 5, part I, ed., K. Lehmann (Hanover, 1888), cap. xci, p. 150 and cap. li, clause 2, p. 109; the same attitude is implied in the *Pactus legis Salicae. Kapitularien und 70-Titel Text*, ed. K. A. Eckhardt (Berlin and Frankfurt, 1956), cap. CIV, 8, p. 422. (The *Pactus* is to be distinguished from the *Lex Salica*.)

53. "Descriptio mancipiorum ecclesie massiliensis," in B. Guérard, *Cartulaire de l'abbaye de Saint Victor de Marseilles* (Paris, 1857), 2: 633–56, and D. Herlihy, "Life Expectancies for Women in Medieval Society," *The Role of Woman in the Middle Ages*, ed., R. T. Morewedge (Albany, 1975), p. 5.

54. *Polyptyque*, I: 25, 33; II: 81, 94; IV: 7, 23; V: 77; VI: 8; and so on.

55. The polyptych seems to indicate that adult sons could control the land jointly with their fathers. *Polyptyque*, XXIV: 4: "Furdoldus colonus et filius ejus Frotlandus colonus, homines sancti Germani, tenent mansus I ingenuilem. . . ." I intend to discuss this question in more detail at a later date.

56. E. A. Wrigley has noted, too, that: "Viewed coldbloodedly, indeed, infanticide is an efficient method limiting fertility in that it endangers the health of the mother less than an abortion procured in unhygienic surroundings and need be much less often carried out since a child unfortunate enough to die in this way will have gone to full term, whereas an abortion takes up only a few months of a woman's fertile period." *Population and History* (New York, 1969), p. 126.

57. This also coincides fairly well with what Neel, "Lessons," p. 816, found among his "primitive" people: "we calculate that it involves 15 to 20 percent of all live births." If we assume that in some of our approximately 20 percent of the households

we have in fact some coincidence in the data, then we are still faced with a significant, but perhaps not singular, number of cases in which this happened.

58. This hypothesis came out of a conversation with Emmanuel LeRoy Ladurie.

59. If this hypothesis is correct, it would run against that presented by E. Boserup, *Conditions of Agricultural Growth* (Chicago, 1965) which argues that agricultural innovation is the result of population pressure rather than population increase being the result of technological innovation. For some criticism of this exciting book see F. Dovring, *Journal of Economic History* 26 (1966): 380–81 and T. W. Schultz, *Journal of Farm Economics* 48 (1966): 486–87. For an interesting symposium on the book and the controversy, see the *Peasant Studies Newsletter* 1, no. 2 (1972).

60. For the theory of demographic transition and some of its problems see, for example, Wrigley, *Population and History*, and R. G. Tabbarah, "Toward a Theory of Demographic Development," *Economic Development and Cultural Change* 19 (1971): 257–76.

Heath Dillard

⁕ Women in Reconquest Castile: The Fueros of Sepúlveda and Cuenca

How does the legal and social position of women reflect the objectives and values of medieval Spanish society? The earliest documents which reveal the status of women in the Reconquest and repopulation of Christian Spain are the land charters (eighth to eleventh centuries) of the northern kingdoms of León, Castile, Navarre, and Aragon-Catalonia and the settlement charters (*cartas pueblas* or short *fueros* of the tenth and eleventh centuries) which confer legal, political, fiscal, economic, and social privileges upon the present and future populations of the small fortified settlements near the fluctuating frontiers between Christian and Muslim Spain. These texts date from the first major stage of Reconquest and repopulation, that centered on the basin of the Duero River and characterized by the settlement of unpopulated empty lands (*despoblado*) by large numbers of small landowners side by side with the larger holdings of lay and ecclesiastical, primarily monastic, lords.[1] Asturo-Leonese land charters, for example, show women as well as men inheriting, buying, selling, alienating land; making wills; serving as guardians of minor children; and acting with a husband or children, or alone as unmarried women and widows, in the large number of legal capacities allowed by the Roman and Visigothic traditions of the *Law Book of the Judges (Forum Judiciorum)* which provides for equal division of family property among male and female heirs.[2]

The settlement charters, drawn up by king or count to attract settlers who would defend the frontier outposts and raid into Muslim territory, illustrate less the legal independence of and privileges granted specifically to women than their importance as wives of colonizers (*pobladores*) and mothers of future citizens (*vecinos*): women are the necessary guarantors of permanent settlement through a second generation. The frontier settlements were subject to attack, destruction, and even repossession by Muslim forces, and it is understandable that under such precarious circumstances women would be reluctant participants, in the enterprise of colonization. To encourage them, two concessions might be made: servile women were given juridical freedom and could thereby enjoy the legal privileges of free women in the regions governed by the lord of the town;[3] women might also be exempted from the payment of *ossas* or *huesas*, a common seigneurial tax paid to a lord at the time of marriage.[4] Given the necessities of colonization and the more elaborate inducements offered male settlers, privileges granted to free women and to those freed by settlement are, however, much less prominent in these municipal charters than one would expect. All male colonizers were routinely granted exemption from a multitude of seigneurial obligations (*malos feuros*), the right to choose local officials in open assembly (the *concejo*), and equal justice regardless of social status. Indeed, many of the inducements which refer to women seem designed to accomodate the interests of the male soldier-colonizers rather than to encourage women to come on their own, perhaps in part because pressures were brought to bear by lords elsewhere when their female serfs sought mobility in other ways, as by marrying a man from outside the lord's estates.[5] Frequently the charters affirm that any able-bodied thief, murderer, rapist, or other criminal will be welcomed with impunity—often with total immunity—especially if he brings along a woman, a girl, or a wife abducted from some other place.[6] The abduction of women is not forced, however, and represents a way of obtaining a wife without the consent of her lord if she is a serf, or of her family if she is a free woman. In order to assure stable families and growing population in a society scarce of women, a wife who deserted her husband might be fined in the amount of the murder fine, whereas a husband would be let off quite lightly for abandoning his wife.[7] This is a reflection of the more immediately essential role of the male soldier-colonists on the frontier. The marriage tax, a mark of servile status, was eventually levied only on widows who married within a year of a husband's death, an offense widely considered a threat to legitimate paternity and patrimonial inheritance. It is but another example of the kind of regulation of women's actions designed primarily to protect the interests of male colonizers.

   In short, the early settlement charters give some indication that an unfree woman could improve her status by settling in a new frontier fortress-town or by being abducted by a male colonizer, but they do not contain any evidence that a free woman might improve her status by coming to the frontier from the parts of northern Spain where her legal independence was a matter of record. Municipal charters of the eighth to the eleventh centuries clearly reveal two of the most important and conflicting characteristics of the status of medieval Spanish women, characteristics which will appear in all of the later medieval codes of customary and statute law: considerable legal independence, particularly in regard to property, but an independence often restricted by or conditional upon an assigned role in the major enterprises of Reconquest and repopulation. The right of women to own property will be preserved throughout the Middle Ages, but their legal capacities will be regulated and modified by the family structure and the customary laws of medieval Spain which develop in the context of continuous warfare against the Muslims and the slow and often interrupted process of recovery and colonization.

The persistence of women's ambiguous position is, in part, based on the continuity of certain demographic factors which persist throughout the whole process of expansion and colonization. While Spanish demographic studies of the Middle Ages are in their infancy, it is now thought that at no time from the eighth through the fourteenth century was there sufficient overpopulation in Christian Spain to meet the demand for colonists in the territory conquered from the Muslims.

During the Middle Ages, competition for colonists, reflected in the broadening privileges granted in the charters of new towns, is a result of growth in population in northern Spain which is less than adequate for the colonization requirements. This is due not only to low birth rates, but also to the high mortality rate of young women in childbirth. The statistics, shadowy at best, indicate that marriages lasted about ten years; that while there was a high proportion of second and third marriages throughout the Middle Ages, half the population as a whole never married, and over 60 percent of men never married. Families were often "incomplete" rather than nuclear; that is, one parent was dead when there were young children. In short, there was insufficient population for the political and military objectives of repopulation—a result primarily of short marriages which were usually dissolved by the early death of the wife, not, as one would expect in this society, by the death in war of the husband.[8] This pattern persists from the tenth to the mid-fourteenth century, and it is reflected in the inheritance laws and in the social organization of the family. It is the particular purpose of this study to examine the status of women in respect to property law and family organization in two municipal law codes (*fueros extensos*), those of Sepúlveda and Cuenca, and to show how the rights and privileges of this apparently demographically valuable sex were shaped to serve the interests of the Reconquest and repopulation. This is the period during which the frontiers between Christian and Muslim Spain flowed and ebbed, a period of successive conquests, losses, and reconquests of the same territory. The unstable frontier conditions produced the varied customary law of the *fueros extensos*. This rich body of common law thus precedes the final stage of the Reconquest which resulted in the incorporation into Castile of large parts of Andalucía (Córdoba, Jaén, and Sevilla). And it precedes the Reception of Roman law embodied in the *Siete Partidas* and other important royal codes by means of which the kings of Castile sought to standardize the divergent practices of their greatly expanded kingdom.

The *fueros extensos* embody the municipal customary law which grew up during the period from the end of the caliphate of Córdoba (1031) to the final defeat of the Almohads at Las Nava de Tolosa (1212), a stage of the reconquest which comprises the geographical extension of León-Castile southward into the tablelands stretching, roughly, from the Duero River into the basin of the Tagus. The kings of León, and Castile attempted to consolidate their conquests and colonize the central Meseta in the face of African invasions by Berber Muslims (Almoravids, 1086, and Almohads, 1147), and to populate this area with Christian colonists from the north and Mozarabs (Christians living under Muslim rule), Jews, and Muslims who remained in the newly conquered territories or who sought refuge from Muslim Al-Andalus.[9] The *fueros*, granted to the colonizers of important towns, are considerably more complex than the earlier settlement charters and were designed not only to encourage settlement but also to organize political and economic life, provide for defensive and offensive military forces, and regulate contact between the Christian majority and the Jews and Muslims who also lived there. The municipal law of these long *fueros*, often known only in late thirteenth-century redactions, came to embody much customary law based on earlier charters, territorial law (in places, the Visigothic law of the *Forum Judiciorum*), the precedents of judicial decisons (*fazañas*), royal privileges and decrees, religious law, and social habit. Effective in the core settlement (*población* or *villa*) and its surrounding territory (*término* or *alfoz*) of agricultural and grazing lands and small hamlets (*aldeas*), the customary law of the *fueros* differed widely or slightly from town to town. This law is applicable to the free and nonnoble townsmen and townswomen. Some *fueros*, including those of Sepúlveda and Cuenca, were more influential than others, their provisions being extended to other settlements as the Reconquest progressed.[10]

These two *fueros* are products of the same customary legal tradition and display many similarities in respect to political privileges, military organization, and economic regulations. The *Fuero* of Sepúlveda (hereafter, F. Sepúlveda) embodies the tenth- to thirteenth-century legal traditions of the Castilian Extremadura, the region lying east of Toledo between the Duero and the Central Cordillera. Some of these traditions were incorporated into the great *Fuero* of Cuenca (hereafter, F. Cuenca) at the time Alfonso VIII authorized its redaction following the town's conquest in the late twelfth century. F. Sepúlveda, compiled in its presently known form late in the thirteenth century, contains some laws copied or adapted from the text of F. Cuenca, as do a large number of other *fueros* elsewhere in Castile and in parts of Aragon.[11] The manner of electing town officials, the organization of agricultural and livestock production, and criminal procedure are among those matters which the two *fueros* treat in similar fashion, but they differ at some points in their regulation of property and family law as these relate to women. Comparison of these differences illustrates the ways in which the status of women in law was being shaped to meet the exigencies of Castilian society in the period of the Reconquest.

This process is well illustrated by the rules of inheritance. Succession, as it is regulated in the customary law of Extremadura embodied in these two *fueros,* follows three general principles: inheritance is bilateral; inherited property is equally partible among the "the closest blood relatives"; and where there are no legitimate descendants, property reverts, through a system of inheritance by lineage (*troncalidad*) to the collateral or ascendant kin of the family of origin traced through the common ancestors, male or female, who have owned the property. This is a rule which stipulates that when a person dies intestate without legitimate descendants, his property is distributed exclusively to the relatives of that side of the family from which it came. A corollary of this system is a distinction, appearing first in late Visigothic law, between inherited property (*bienes de abolengo* or *raíz*) governed by inheritance by lineage and the acquired goods of an individual or a man and wife (*ganancia*) which are, with some limitations, fully disposable by will. [12] These general rules, more explicit in F. Cuenca than in F. Sepúlveda, result in equal inheritance from both parents by all legitimate descendants; no child can be favored over another by either parent, and none can be disinherited; half brothers and half sisters are all claimants against a natural parent's estate. [13] Inheritance by lineage governs succession of family property when there are no legitimate descendants: "la raíz se torne onde vienne el heredamiento"; "alia radix redeat ad radicem." [14] By this rule inherited property reverts to the branch of the family, either male or female, from which it came to a parent, nieces and nephews, uncles and aunts, or grandparents, per stirpes and not per capita. [15]

A number of consequences follow from these rules of inheritance. Property tends to be fractioned, particularly when there are no direct descendants, but in such a way as to give all heirs an equal share of patrimonial land. It is a system particularly well designed to give all residents of a place a piece of land, the major requirement for citizenship (*vezindad*) and rights in consequence thereof: to communal pasturage, in the election of officials, and to equal justice before the town judge (*juez*) and elected judicial officials (*alcaldes*). By prescribing equal shares for all heirs of the same degree, friction within families is minimized, and all brothers and sisters have equal resources for beginning a new family, the primary economic unit. The provisions for collateral and ascendant succession provide a legal basis for powerful family control over property, and inheritance by lineage assures the interest of all blood kin (the *parentela*) in the partition of any estate and in the marriages, births, and deaths of all actual or potential heirs. Coupled with the private justice exercised by kinsmen as oath helpers and avengers, the system of inheritance assures a powerful voice to collaterals and ascendants in any matter affecting a blood relative. For purposes of vengeance, the kinsmen (*parientes*) in Sepúlveda are defined as father, son, brothers; first, second, and third cousins; and the husband of a living sister, thus adding an affinal relation.[16] But in matters of inheritance the kin group is much larger (including uncles, aunts, cousins, grandparents), and, for any individual, is bilateral.[17] Thus, succession by lineage, the equal sharing of all children, male and female, in the patrimonies of both parents, and private vengeance in a number of areas reflect a social organization in which a daughter and heiress has at her disposal the same recources and family support as her brother, and they assure that this girl will, after marriage, maintain contact with her family of origin through its lively interest in her patrimony and its devolution.

An important distinction exists between the two *fueros* in the regulation of the inheritance of military arms: in F. Sepúlveda they are inherited by preference through the male line and are subject to the rules of inheritance by lineage. Arms descend to sons, going to daughters only when there are no sons. When there are no children half go to the males in a man's lineage, half to males in his wife's; if, however, a wife predeceases her husband, all arms are inherited by the husband, this last provision appearing also in F. Cuenca.[18] This may seem eminently practical, but the possession of arms (hauberks, swords, lances, etc.) has a social significance which outweighs mere military utility: the quantity and quality of arms and horses of a mounted soldier of the town militia, the nonnoble urban knight of León and Castile (*cabellero villano*), determine the number of retainers in his household who will be excused from military service (*excusados*) and from payment of the tax (*fonsaders*) levied to maintain the town defenses.[19] This means that the better the quality of the arms provided by the urban knight who serves the king in the town militia, the more retainers he will be allowed to employ—servants who will tend to his property, and livestock—without themselves having to serve in the militia. Arms are thus a measure of status and wealth, comparable in effect to the possession of real property. Ownership of a good horse and fine arms is the primary means of becoming an urban knight and thereby rising into the class of nonnoble urban horsemen who in this period are coming to constitute the urban patriciate of Castilian towns. That arms can descend or ascend according to the rule of inheritance by lineage is further evidence of a concern to maintain family wealth and status through control of the means to land and arms. Preference by sex gives important advantages to males who inherit arms or to any man who marries the daughter of an urban knight who has no sons. Thus, while males are preferred in the direct succession of arms, inheritance of these goods remains cognatic by virtue of the application of inheritance by lineage in F. Sepúlveda, and a woman's importance is enhanced to the extent that she can determine their succession. This importance is reflected in the increasingly hereditary nature of the status of *caballero villano:* while women do not serve in the militia, the privileges acquired by the knight will be enjoyed by his widow and his children. The possibility of upward mobility thus exists for both men and women through marriage to a man or a woman who possesses the required house and arms.[20]

Marriage in Cuenca produces a civil community of property consisting of three parts: the separate *raíces* of each spouse (family property subject to inheritance by lineage) and the property owned jointly by husband and wife. This community property includes moveables given either spouse as a wedding gift; whatever is given or promised to either on or after the marriage; and all goods and debts acquired in the course of the marriage— land and moveables (money, furnishings, livestock, and additions or improvements to the *raíz* of either spouse). Half of this belongs to the husband and half to the wife, but the husband represents in court and in any transactions all the property: his own family property, that of his wife, and the community property. The resulting civil incapacity of the wife places her, in effect, in the power of her husband ("in potestate mariti").[21] The concept of community property is not as well developed in F. Sepúlveda, representing a stage in the development of community property which precedes that found in F. Cuenca. The integrity of each household as an economic unit is implicit in F. Sepúlveda's stipulation regarding brothers who live together and exploit conjointly an undivided inheritance: "the eldest enjoys citizenship (*vezindad*) for all."[22] The exploitation by heirs of a common undivided inheritance, and the community property of husband and wife, are both products of the family domination of property characteristic of Spanish history from the early Middle Ages.[23]

Marriage marks the beginning of a man's full responsibilities as an adult citizen in Sepúlveda and Cuenca; until this time he lives as a dependent with his parents or a lord. During the first year of marriage an urban knight enjoys exemption from military service and taxes (notably the *fonsadera*)— privileges granted to increase the population, particularly of the fighting class.[24] When a girl marries, she leaves her father's house and, like her husband, takes into the new patrimonial community created by the marriage any inheritance that might have come to her or whatever part of it a parent might give her as a marriage gift. This marriage gift is later deducted from her share of inheritance at the time her parents' estates are distributed.[25] The Germanic dower (*dos* or *arras*) survives in F. Cuenca, a gift "in dotem uel apreciaturam" which is given to the wife at the time the marriage is negotiated between the bridegroom and her father and mother, and which can never be reclaimed by the husband or his creditors. For a girl from the town (*villa*) this is twenty gold *moravedís*, twice that for a widow or a girl from the surrounding territory (*término*) and indicative of the added privileges and prestige which were being acquired by the residents within the town walls in this period. Dower contributed by the groom usually took the form of clothing rather than money; the bride customarily provided household furnishings for the new household.[26]

The property of the new couple is dominated by the husband. Any advantages gained by the wife depend entirely on her husband's wise management and on his control of the means of access to wealth: land and arms. In Sepúlveda a woman's power over her own *raíz* and her half share of wealth acquired during marriage is no greater than were she living at home with her father, and unlike her husband, she is expressly prevented from devaluing the property of the couple. Married women, like their single adult or widowed sisters who live in the house of a parent or kinsman, cannot sell any personal possessions or contract any debt of more than one *moravedí* without the express consent of the husband or the relative in whose house the woman lives. The husband can mortgage his own or her *raíz*, an indebtedness which, like any others that he incurs, is incumbent upon his wife as well. The wife's major protection against a profligate husband is the requirement that he obtain her consent before selling her family inheritance (*raíz*), a consent her kinsmen (those relatives with a potential claim on the inheritance of the property) would surely view with alarm, if they do not prevent it. A greater measure of constraint exists in regard to debt, for, like the gains of marriage, this is shared equally rather than conjointly, and if the husband should die having sold all his patrimony and leaving many debts, the wife is liable for only half the debts incurred by him as head of the household, and the creditor cannot take from her property more than her half of the amount of the debt.[27]

A wife's liability for her husband's debts is considerably broader in F. Cuenca. There, she is first given the opportunity to locate him, if he has fled the town's territory, and bring him to court, but if she refuses to swear that she will do so, the creditor can immediately go to the house and seize whatever is owed. If she does produce him, but he then flees without payment, the wife must pay double the debt or be put in chains in his stead, although, like children under twelve, she is spared the jail, shackles, stocks, foot irons, and manacles with which creditors were allowed to confine their male debtors. When a husband dies, the jointly contracted debt falls entirely on the widow.[28] The wife's and widow's greater responsibility for debt is a result of F. Cuenca's more well-developed concept of community property.

The legal burdens of women in F. Cuenca appear notably greater than in F. Sepúlveda, a conclusion that is suggested by the considerable responsibility of a wife for a husband's delicts, which extends fully to pecuniary fines for the serious crimes of theft and murder, on the grounds that "it is only proper that she who shares in his good fortune, should also share in his troubles."[29] In F. Sepúlveda, however, the wife of an urban knight or squire is permitted but not required to pay the fines of a husband.[30] This is one of a number of privileges noticeably more common in F. Sepúlveda than in

F. Cuenca, guaranteed to citizens of this class, and many of these privileges are enjoyed by the wives (*duennas*), widows, and daughters (*donzellas*) of knights. That this class is singled out in this respect may imply that wives of other citizens did have pecuniary responsibility for their husbands' crimes, but the language of F. Cuenca, expressly instituting this liability or order to reform customs elsewhere, probably indicates that it is an innovation in practice.

F. Cuenca represents a further development and crystalization of custom not only with community property, as discussed above, but also by the wider mutual responsibilities of parents and children. This seems to indicate a weakening of the kin group (more prominent in N. Sepúlveda) and a strengthening of ties among members of nuclear families and single households (including the servants and employees of the townsman).[31] In F. Cuenca both parents are responsible for the property (debts excepted) and delicts of all children until they marry and for their pecuniary fines until they receive an inheritance, that is, until the death of one parent.[32] These parental responsibilities are attributed to parental power (*potestas parentum*), a mistaken distortion by the redactor of F. Cuenca of the Roman *patria potestas*, which institution it resembles in name only.[33] The only reference to an institution comparable to this in F. Sepúlveda is to a father's (but not a mother's) responsibility not to shelter a son who, while living at home (*fijo emparentado*), has killed a man; there is no joint parental power, and the *fuero* merely seeks to prevent protection of a fugitive, just as it penalizes villagers who conceal thieves in the town's territory.[34]

The substitution in F. Cuenca of parental power for the authority of the kin group, retained in F. Sepúlveda, is illustrated by the manner in which consent is given to the marriages of women. Both *fueros* make provision for marriage only by consent, and comparison of their provisions illustrates the differing family organization in the two towns. The system of partible inheritance explains, in part, the necessity for consent. Where it must be obtained, it can also be withheld, and family property can be kept together by limiting the number of marriages and thus the number of descendants who have a claim in the property. That this was an effective mechanism is borne out by the large numbers of unmarried men and women in medieval Spain. That the marriages of women and not of men are controlled is a reflection of the dominance of the male sex in matters of property, a dominance exercised by fathers of unmarried women, succeeded to by a husband, and eliminated only when the wife becomes a widow.

F. Cuenca provides that the father and mother of the bride, under the joint parental power, give consent to a daughter's marriage; when one parent is dead, the survivor gives consent. F. Sepúlveda, acknowledging no community property or parental power, gives the decision to the father alone, but when either parent is dead the surviving parent (mother or father) gives consent; the survivor must, however, upon pain of a fine and exile and liability to vengeance (*enemistad*) consult the relatives of the deceased parent on the choice of bridegroom.[35] This represents an earlier form of family organization, and Rafael Gibert sees in this shared authority of a widow or widower with the relatives of the deceased parent the origins of the joint parental power which the redactor of F. Cuenca confuses with *patria potestas*.[36] The consultation with the relatives is absent in F. Cuenca, and other sections of this *fuero* point to a deliberate attempt to check the powers of the kin group found in F. Sepúlveda and to an evolution of family organization from one in which all blood kin are consulted in important family matters to one in which the mother and father represent the kin groups.

In both towns marriage, when consent has not been given, is treated as abduction: a valid marriage may result, but penalties are levied for failure to obtain consent. At Cuenca, the girl who marries without the consent of her parents is declared an *enemiga* (that is, she is outlawed and must leave the town territory), and she is disinherited.[37] F. Sepúlveda continues the tradition of its eleventh-century Latin *fuero* in allowing urban knights and squires of other towns to be admitted to citizenship despite the fact that they bring in a woman abducted from elsewhere, but it treats the abduction of its own women with considerably less equanimity.[38] The girl and her alleged abductor are called to a parley of all her kinsmen, which takes place only after the girl is safely in their custody. If the abductor can prove that she went with him of her own volition, he is let go, and she is disinherited. If, however, he cannot establish this, she retains her inheritance but remains unmarried, while the man becomes an outlaw subject to vengeance by her kinsmen.[39] In both *fueros* the purpose of the restrictions is the same: to prevent the marriage of a female heiress against the wishes of parents or kinsmen. Partible inheritance and family control of property lie at the root of these provisions. The more powerful voice given the kinsmen in F. Sepúl-veda, both for orphans and abducted girls, multiplies the number of relatives who can choose the bridegroom or even prevent the marriage, and it is less than likely that they will regard the bride's interests with greater attention than their own. Such laws could well have contributed to the high incidence of celibacy and to a lively exchange of disinherited abducted brides from one town to another.

Similarly, in cases of rape the kinsmen intervene in F. Sepúlveda whereas they do not in F. Cuenca. Like murder, theft, and arson, rape is one of the most serious offenses in Castilian customary law. If a woman of Sepúlveda is raped, she must walk around the walls of the town and call out her complaints and the name of the rapist as she makes her way up to the gate of the castle, there summoning forth the town's elected officials to hear her grievances. The following Sunday she issues a complaint against the man with two kinsmen and two other citizens; the man can prove his innocence with twelve witnesses: five kinsmen, six citizens, and the tithe collector. If he is unable to do so, he pays fifty *moravedís* and becomes the personal enemy of the woman's kinsmen, pending appeal to the king if he chooses.[40] At Cuenca a woman has three days to make her complaint and show her injuries to the town officials, a somewhat less public and spectacular, but equally degrading, accusatory process. Here, too, the man can absolve himself with twelve witnesses (citizens not kinsmen); if he cannot, he is fined three hundred *solidos* and exiled, any accomplices being fined and exiled for a year.[41] In both *fueros* rape is treated with the same gravity as regards penalties and follows similar procedure. The important difference is the presence in F. Sepúlveda of the kinsmen, both as witnesses supporting the woman and oath helpers supporting the man; these are not found in F. Cuenca.

The same difference appears in the laws governing adultery. In both *fueros* an offended husband has the right to kill without penalty both his wife and the man, if discovered *in flagrante delicto,* but only in F. Sepúlveda are the kinsmen given the same prerogative: there, adultery is as much a shameful blot on the honor of the woman's relatives as on that of her husband.[42] It should be noted that neither *fuero* permits killing the man and not the wife, that is, forgiving her after the fact. It is the dishonor brought on the woman's husband and kinsmen which makes the crime, and both offenders must be punished.

Whereas in F. Sepúlveda kinsmen intervene in a large number of matters regarding women, they are deliberately restrained from doing so in F. Cuenca. There, for example, only wives are permitted without penalty to come to the aid of husbands in a public quarrel, and only husbands to the aid of their wives; anyone who aids another's wife is subject to a fine of three hundred *solidos,* the same penalty as for murder, rape, and arson.[43] This extreme measure represents a conscious attempt to restrict the customary interference of large numbers of relatives in interfamily strife and is a deliberate restriction on the range of a kin group's action. Also, in Sepúlveda the illegitimate son of a common-law wife (*barragana*) can be legitimized and inherit from his father only by act of the town officials and with the consent of the relatives who might otherwise inherit from the father. F. Cuenca, however, again ignores the kinsmen, acknowledging the right of the illegitimate child to inherit from his father; it further provides that the common-law wife will control the father's possessions, including his *raíz,* in the name of the child until he reaches maturity (age twelve).[44] What are the implications of these differences between the two *fueros* for the status of women in law?

In the later thirteenth century, individual responsibility for delicts and crimes will become law in Cuenca, thus weakening the effects of the twelfth-century *fuero*'s requirements that husbands and wives and parents and children are responsible for one another's transgressions and fines.[45] These modifications continue the weakening of the kin group begun in F. Cuenca's limitations on the actions of the kinsmen whose earlier authority in customary law is retained in F. Sepúlveda. It has been suggested, regarding the absence of provision for a wife's imprisonment for debt in F. Sepúlveda, that the thirteenth-century redactor of that *fuero* adopted only those provisions of F. Cuenca which were still in force following the modifications made by Pedro IV in 1285, modifications which put responsibility for fines on individuals rather than on husbands and wives, parents and children.[46] But this explanation seems inadequate to account for the absence in F. Sepúlveda of the provisions of F. Cuenca which tend to strengthen the authority of husband and wife and which deliberately restrict the intervention of kinsmen, a change which can only have come about through the increasing effectiveness of law and justice represented by the elected officials of the town. On the contrary, retention in F. Sepúlveda of earlier forms of private justice, exemplified by vengeance and other types of intervention by blood relatives, perpetuates a form of social organization which reinforces the kin group's control of its members, its property, and of justice. By elaborating explicitly the joint parental power and restricting the actions of kinsmen, F. Cuenca limits the participation of numerous blood relatives in the maintenance of peace and order and weakens the legal effectiveness of the kin group. These changes, apparently rejected by the redactor of F. Sepúlveda as contrary to local custom in this town, suggest that a married woman would receive less support from her own kin in matters affecting herself and her children.

Does a wife actually lose family support for actions independent of her husband as a result of this change in family and social structure, which diminishes the role of her kinsmen in her life preceding and after marriage? Such does not appear to be the case. The joint power of a man and wife over their children and their children's property would certainly raise the status of a married woman in Cuenca above that of a married woman in Sepúlveda, or any woman living with a relative, who can neither sell anything nor transact any business of substance without the consent of the husband or kinsman. The actions of the kinsmen in F. Sepúlveda in regard to a woman's marriage, whether legitimate or by abduction, and in the vengeance of rape, adultery, and other crimes relating to her honor, indicate that this intervention is exercised more in the interests of the kinsmen than of the woman. To the extent that the husband in F. Cuenca succeeds to the joint power of a girl's parents in the affairs of his wife, and can act as head of the household without interference from her male kinsmen, the wife rids herself of the claims of the larger number of men who control her actions and to whom she is responsible for her behavior. On the other hand, if she becomes a widow, she may well find that the support of her male kinsmen will be of considerable advantage to her, both in relation to the kinsmen of her former husband and in respect to her economic interests in the town.

Although marriage comes to an end solely by the death of husband or wife, the patrimonial community of husband and wife is dissolved only when partition is made among the heirs of either spouse. There is one exception to this in F. Cuenca. Just as common-law marriage is recognized as a form of uncanonical but civil and legal marriage, there is also a form of civil, if uncanonical, divorce. When a husband and wife wish, for any reason, to separate from one another, they simply divide whatever increased wealth they have acquired and renounce all claims on one another's goods which would be made by a widow or widower. [47] When the marriage ends by death, F. Cuenca institutes survivor's rights for both: these constitute that part of the marriage property which can properly be said to belong to each, the perquisites of widowhood rather than an inheritance, for they belong to the survivor only so long as he or she intends to, and in fact does, remain widowed and chaste. A widow's property consists of the marriage bed, one small field, a yoke of oxen, and a small piece of vineyard. [48] This is intended to sustain her during widowhood, and if she remarries, everything is partitioned by the heirs, at which time she will retain her half of the couple's acquired wealth, her own *raiz*, and her dower of ten or twenty *moravedis*. F. Cuenca specifically prohibits both gifts and testamentary legacies between husband and wife unless the other heirs give consent. It also permits usufructory rights to all the community property (but not the husband's *raiz*) when there has been a public ceremony creating *unitas*, at which all heirs must be present and give their consent. *Unitas* thus delays the division of community property until the death of both spouses. [49]

F. Sepúlveda, however, allows testamentary succession of any or all moveables as well as the privilege of remaining in the residence of the deceased spouse, a usufructory right which may postpone the disposition of *raiz*, as well as community property, until the survivor's death. [50] Moveables can include all household possessions, money, livestock, and slaves, and represent a large proportion of a man's estate. A widow might become quite wealthy in her own right by inheriting these as well as usufruct of the husband's *raiz*. Thus, children might have to await the death of the mother in order to come into any inheritance, a fact which might well prevent early or any marriage and encourage emigration. If the husband has been a provident manager of their joint property and has acquired wealth, particularly in the spoils of war, half of this would in any case belong to the widow in either town, and with the husband's death, the widow becomes the administrator of all this wealth and whatever widow's rights (in Cuenca) or legacy (in Sepúlveda) she receives. In Cuenca she will also control the property of any surviving child under the age of twelve. As tutor, her responsibilities are to protect the child but also to conserve and, if possible, increase the value of his inheritance, making an accounting to the child's agnatic kinsmen; if she is negligent, one of them will succeed her as tutor.[51] Thus, she does not succeed to the joint parental power over unmarried children, which ceases at the death of either parent. The widow of an urban knight in Sepúlveda is further advantaged in succeeding to the rights of her husband: she and her children inherit the same fiscal privileges and exemptions as the knight, an inheritance of status (independent of the inheritance of property or arms) which is a major factor in the perpetuation of the *caballero villano* class as a privileged one.[52]

If a widow in Sepúlveda goes to live with a relative or remarries, she loses the independence of property and person which she has gained as a widow. The relative would have to give his consent in any property transactions; she would lose usufruct of the first husband's *raíz*. While a second husband would not acquire any additional wealth (with the possible exception of arms) by marrying a widow, he would nonetheless manage her property, and she would thereby lose what independence she had gained as a widow. The economic consequences of widowhood could, then, vary considerably. As a minimum, a widow will have the security of subsistence, and as a maximum, weath and the independent capacity in her economic affairs equivalent to that of any man.

The major advantage which women do not gain in widowhood is citizenship (*vezindad*). Whereas a man who is in possession of land in the town or its territory for a year and a day and who pays his tithes and taxes is a citizen, there is no indication in either *fuero* that women, fulfilling all these requirements, ever gain the political rights which are the consequence of citizenship: to elect town officials or to become a town official. In the early days of the emergent municipality, it is thought that all inhabitants were theoretically citizens, irrespective of rank, age, or sex. Gradually, in the course of the twelfth century, nobles, clerics, and women were excluded from the political (as well as military) processes of town life as these came to be controlled by the men of probity (*boni homines*) who lived in the town or its territory or, later, only by those who lived in a house within the town walls and fought with horse and arms in the king's name as members of the town militia.[53] It seems doubtful that even the widow of an urban knight would possess any political privileges in the town, and if she had a grown son, it would be he, like the eldest of brothers living together, who would represent her interests in the political affairs of the town. If she lives with a male relative, or if she remarries, it is the relative or new husband who is the citizen of the household. Whatever economic power she might retain or gain as a widow, through the possession of land and livestock, would not be reflected in any political power except insofar as she is able to exercise this through a subsequent husband, son, or other kinsman. In this way, however, a woman could acquire considerable control, as distinct from power, a control which a widow might well exercise through her male kinsmen who are citizens.

If the widow gains in widowhood an independence which she does not possess before or during marriage, the married woman remains in medieval Spain more honored and esteemed. In Sepúlveda, fines for dishonoring a woman's body are scaled according to status: for a widow, double that of molesting a virgin, but for a married woman four times as high.[54] The married woman's honor and sexual shame reflect not only on herself but on her husband and, in Sepúlveda, her kinsmen, as is clearly set out in the adultery statutes discussed above. *Cornutum,* or cuckolded, is among the gravest insults which can be given a man, and if a husband even suspects that his wife is deceiving him, he can demand that she establish her innocence (proveable by the testimony of twelve female witnesses) under pain of justified repudiation.[55] A man who merely boasts that he has seduced a married woman must pay the murder fine.[56] The *fueros,* particularly F. Cuenca, demonstrate their preoccupation with the honor and shame of women both by protecting them from physical and verbal abuse and by prescribing severe penalties for delictual behavior which is chiefly sexual. These laws provide the social and criminal sanctions and judgments necessary for protecting and vindicating the honor and reputation of Christian women. To be declared an outlaw is not merely a penalty. *Enemistad* is said to be a state of dishonor.[57] Thus, a woman who marries without consent is dishonored. Behavior which is considered dishonorable often requires that women, unlike men, invoke the divine in the form of the hot iron ordeal in order to establish innocence and restore reputation; such is the burden of proof in cases of induced abortion, establishing paternity, procuring or pandering, casting spells, or preparing potions.[58] There is a connection, in the mind of the redactor of F. Cuenca, between female sexuality, magic, and religion.

Of all the possible crimes which a woman can commit, interracial (more accurately, interfaith) sexual intercourse is the most severely punished. For Christian men this is not an offense in either *fuero*: clearly a double standard is in force. In both towns an offending Christian woman and her Jewish or Muslim lover are executed if discovered *in flagrante.* In Sepúlveda the woman is burned, the man thrown from a precipice (the usual manner of execution for men in that town); in Cuenca both are burned.[59] F. Sepúlveda provides, further, that a Christian woman who lives with or has a child by a Moor or Jew shall be judged shameless, publicly flogged, and thrown out of the town; she is given no opportunity to prove that the father is a Christian, and the town officials are completely within their rights to judge her guilty on whatever evidence they think convincing. While that *fuero* does not raise, as a problem, the child produced by a Christian father and Jewish or Muslim woman, F. Cuenca dismisses this as no problem at all by merely requiring the man to pay the woman a dower and allowing him to redeem the child from the mother's lord, at which time the child becomes eligible to inherit from the father along with other legitimate children. [60] It seems inescapable that a double standard of sexual conduct is operable in both towns.

One explanation for the severe penalties given to Christian women but not to Christian men is that the child remains with the mother in either case, and the child of a Christian father and Jewish or Muslim mother would, in the Christian community, enjoy greater anonymity and could be ignored more easily than the child of mixed heritage living with its Christian mother. Fathers in Cuenca are required to support a child and its mother only for the first three years (the normal nursing period). The father can then decide whether to redeem (in Cuenca) or legitimize (with the consent of his kinsmen in the presence of the town officials in Sepúlveda) and raise the child as a member of the Christian community. A further explanation of the discrepancy between the sexes in this matter is the growing confidence and sense of identity in the Christian community, particularly after the mid-twelfth century, which asserts its superior values by setting apart those who follow different law: the Jewish and Muslim minorities. With the persistence of opposition from Muslim Al-Andalus, intensified by the invasions in 1086 and 1147 of fanatical Berbers from North Africa, the Reconquest develops more and more the attributes of a Christian crusade against the infidel. This leads to the establishment of desirable norms for members of the Christian community and to provisions for protecting them from the verbal and physical abuse of those who are thought inferior or lacking in esteem. Thus, Christian women who sleep with Muslims or Jews are sullied by this contact and the whole Christian community is thereby disgraced. Sexual intercourse between Christian men and Jewish or Muslim women would, then, be considered or justified as a form of insulting inferiors and demonstrating prowess. The sexual conquest of Muslim and Jewish women can be regarded as a legitimate form of aggression and an expression of superiority which, consequently, brings no civil penalty.

Women who ignore expected norms of behavior lose the protections the law provides for women who adhere to standards set by the society. Thus, it is lawful to strike the shameless woman (*muger mala*) who insults or dishonors verbally any person of repute, and it is permitted to kill her without penalty if it is discovered that she has slept with two or three men. [61] Public prostitutes are totally without honor and may be defamed or raped with impunity, but many fines result when an honorable woman is physically or verbally abused. [62] The private and personal, as opposed to civil, nature of these offenses is reflected in the retributive penalties of F. Sepúlveda where private justice generally retains more force. A husband or male relative of the victim is allowed to select a kinswoman of the offender and dishonor her

with the same offense committed against his kinswoman.[63] Thus, it is men
who avenge the honor of their women, while the women who bring dishonor
upon husband or kinsmen are punished severely, as are the kinswomen of
men who dishonor other women.

The protective and punitive provisions regarding a woman's honor are a
result, in part, of her significance in the property structure. The importance
of women in the society is institutionalized in the provisions for partible and
bilateral inheritance. But restrictions are placed on women's control of
property to promote the wider interests of her family, and these restrictions
contribute to the high incidence of celibacy in the society. While it would be
a parachronism to fault medieval Spanish society for a rational demographic
policy, the discrepancy between a recognized need to colonize and the
existence of a population large enough to accomplish this objective must be
explained: demographic growth is a limiting rather than a causative factor in
the expansion of medieval Spain. And the low marriage and birth rates are a
result of the family structure and rules devised to perpetuate a family's
control of property.

Family control of property is effected by partible inheritance, inheritance by lineage, and the necessity for women to obtain consent to marry.
Partible inheritance strengthens ties within a family and gives each child
who survives to adulthood a stake in society, but it also threatens the
economic base from which large families can emerge. If there are many
heirs, some will not be able to marry. Inheritance by lineage assures the
continuance of a family's control of property regardless of the sex of
children. When there are no children, it results in succession by collateral and
ascendant kin, thus preventing the transfer of and from one family to
another through marriage. It is no accident that the marriage of women
without consent is an offense for which disinheritance is a penalty. This
provision serves to discourage or prevent the first marriages of women when
the wider interests of her family oppose the marriage, and it epitomizes the
control of property by the family and, in particular, by its male members.
Thus, partible inheritance, inheritance by lineage, and the marriage of
women only with consent work to hold down marriage and birth rates. The
family and property structures restrict the demographic growth required for
rapid reconquest and colonization while preserving the interests and prestige of existing structures and the limited objectives of two or three generations. The whole system is oriented toward the maintenance of the status
quo, and the broad royal objective of repopulation is thereby violated.

By forbidding the participation of women in warfare and its profits, and
by preference given males in the inheritance of arms, women are directly
excluded from a major source of riches, unless their husbands or fathers are
valorous and successful in the town militia. A wife profits indirectly from
booty, however, because this is considered a part of the accrued wealth of

the marriage community of property; half of this is hers and could revert to her family of origin if she has no children, a further example of the molding of women's property rights to serve the interests of her family. Technically, the Christian woman's legal capacites to own and determine the fate of land and money are considerable, but they will vary according to her status within her family; her ability to influence the decisions of parents, husband, and kinsmen; and the extent to which she is able to extricate her decisions from the dominance of consanguineal or civil male connections. What autonomy a widow gains is conditional upon her remaining widowed in Cuenca and upon her living alone in Sepúlveda. The independence of the widow may be seen as a compromise between the conflicting claims of her own kin group and that of her deceased husband. Where testamentary succession between spouses is permitted, a widow's opportunity for acquiring and controlling considerable wealth increases, and the absence in either *fuero* of any requirement that she obtain consent from her father or kinsmen to remarry is undoubtedly a result of her greater economic independence and symbolizes social recognition of her personal autonomy.

While limitations on women's freedom to marry and restrictions on their freedom to manage property represent an important element in the Spanish family's control of property, bilateral inheritance and inheritance by lineage point to a significantly important role for women in the family and social structure, an importance reflected elsewhere in Spanish society by the inheritance of nobility from either parent and by the Spanish tradition which preserves the names of both lineages in a child's name. The role of the kinsmen in vengeance and the social sanctions for maintaining the honor of Christian men by dictating the behavior of their women are reflections of women's important role not only as mates and possessions but also as elements in the property structure. The Spanish woman's assigned role as a symbol of Christian virtue and honor is a result of her importance in the property structure and is intensified by the military and social circumstances of the Reconquest. Honorable women are symbols of the superiority of Christian society and of a family's wealth and prestige won by men in wars against the Moors.

The preoccupation with affronts to honor, which must be avenged by men in order to regain prestige, is aristocratic in origin, but it flourishes in the context of the medieval Spanish town where all inhabitants are known to one another and where valor and courage mean more than birth and titles in the measure of a man's worth. The acquisition by the wives, widows, and daughters of urban knights of privileges and status won by force of arms reflects the importance of women in the preservation of acquired prestige. The honorable Christian woman is, indeed, an object of pride and esteem. The honor code elevates her to a position analogous to that of the lady on a pedestal celebrated by the poets of courtly love. It represents the social, as opposed to literary, response to woman's importance in society.[64] But unlike the real or imagined etiquette of courtly love, the honor code reserves its highest pinnacle for one's own wife, not for elusive and unattainable goddesses (the wives of other men), and it harshly condemns adultery. It reflects, more realistically than the anguished rituals of courtly love, woman's importance in the social structure and the mentality of medieval Spain, shaped by its preoccupation with the Reconquest. It is in the context of the continuous warfare against the Muslims, in which the honor, prestige, and wealth of men are won in battle against an enemy who comes to be considered religiously, morally, and socially corrupt, that the male redactor of F. Cuenca pays tribute to the Christian woman held captive in Muslim Spain: "As wise men confirm, the Moors would never attack the Christians were it not for the daring of the Christians who are with them and of the daughters of Christians who are their wives."[65]

NOTES

1. C. Sánchez-Albornoz, *Despoblación y repoblación del valle del Duero* (Buenos Aires, 1966).

2. J. Guallart, "Documentos para el estudio de la condición jurídica de la muger leonesa hace mil años," *Cuadernos de historia de España* (henceforth *CHE*) 6 (1946): 154–71; A. C. Floriano, *Diplomática española del periodo astur, 718–910,* 2 vols. (Oviedo, 1949–51). See also E. Hinojosa y Naveros, "Sobre la condición de la mujer casada en la esfera del Derecho civil," *Obras,* 2 vols. (Madrid, 1948–55), 1: 345–85; Sánchez-Albornoz, "La mujer en España hace mil años," in *España y el Islam* (Buenos Aires, 1943), pp. 83–141, reprinted in *Del ayer de España, tripticos históricos* (Madrid, 1973), pp. 91–117; A. Lewis, *The Development of Southern French and Catalan Society, 718–1050* (Austin, 1965), pp. 212–24, 170–71, 210–12, 275–76, 391–92.

3. E.g., *Carta puebla* of Cardona (986), in *Colección de fueros municipales y cartas pueblas de los reinos de Castilla, León, Corona de Aragón y Navarr,* ed. T. Muñoz y Romero (Madrid, 1847), 1 [*unicum*]: 52.

4. This privilege usually appears in its later form as a tax on widows who marry within a year of a husband's death: e.g., *fuero* of Melgar de Suso (950), *ibid.,* p. 28; *fuero* of Santa Cristina (1062), *ibid.,* p. 223; cf. L. Garcia de Valdeavellano, *Curso de historia de las instituciones españoles de los origines al final de la edad media,* 2nd ed. rev. (Madrid, 1970), p. 253.

5. E.g., a charter of Fernando II of León (1169) granted to a monastery which seeks relief from the injustice of the emigration of its female serfs through marriage, in Muñoz y Romero, *Colección,* p. 164.

6. ["Et siquis homo de aliqua t]erra mulier, aut filia aliena, aut aliquam rem de suis facinoribus quod contingerit adduxerit, et ubieret se mittere in Sepuluega, nullus tangat eum," *Fuero latino* of Sepúlveda 17 (1076), in *Los fueros de Sepúlveda, edición crítica y apéndice documental,* ed. E. Sáez, et al. (Segovia, 1953), p. 37; "et si servus aut ancilla venisset inter eos, aut aliquis homo cum alienum uxorem aut sponsa aut latio inieniosus, aut aliquis falsator vel criminosus, securus stesisset inter omnes alios abitatores sine aliqua dubitatione," *carta puebla* of Cardona, in Muñoz y Romero, *Colección,* p. 52; "et homo qui rauso aut homicidium fecerit, et in villa se ubiar, intrare quomodo non habeat quem timet, sed gardetse de suos inimicos," *fuero* of Santa Cristina, *ibid.,* p. 222.

7. "Si aliqua mulier laxauerit uirem suum, CCC solidos pectet; et si uir laxauerit uxorem suam, uno arienzo deuerit," *Fuero latino* of Sepúlveda 16, in Sáez, *Los fueros de Sepúlveda,* p. 47.

8. R. Pastor de Tognieri, "Historia de las familias en Castilla y León (siglos X-XIV) y su relación con la formación de los grandes dominios eclesiásticos," *CHE* 43-44 (1966): 88-118; L. C. Kofman de Guarrochena and M. I. Carzolio de Rossi, "Acerca de la demografía astur-leonesa y castellana en la alta edad media," *CHE* 47-48 (1968): 136-64.

9. The best study is still J. González, "Reconquista y repoblación de Castilla, León, Extremadura y Andalucia (siglos XI a XIII)," in *La Reconquista española y la repoblación del país,* ed. J. M. Lacarra (Zaragoza, 1951), pp. 163-206.

10. Hinojosa, "Origen del régimen municipal de León y Castilla," *Estudios sobre la historia del derecho español* (Madrid, 1903), pp. 5-70; A. García Gallo, "Aportación al estudio de los fueros," *Anuario de la historia del derecho español* (henceforth *AHDE*) 26 (1956): 387-446; R. Gibert, "El derecho municipal de León y Castilla," *ibid.,* 31 (1961), 695-753; R. Gilbert "Estudio histórico-juridico," in Sáez, *Los fueros de Sepúlveda,* pp. 358-62; J. M. Font y Rius, *Origen del régimen municipal de Cataluña* (Madrid, 1946), also in AHDE 16 (1945): 389-529; M. del Carmen Carlé, *Del consejo medieval castellano-leonés* (Buenos Aires, 1968).

11. *Fuero de Cuenca (Formas primativa y systemática: texto latino, castellano y adaptación del fuero de Iznatoraf, edición critica, con introducción, notas y apéndice,* ed. R. de Ureña y Smenjaud (Madrid, 1935); "Fuero romanceado," in Sáez, *Los fueros de Sepúlveda,* pp. 59-166. The Latin text of F. Cuenca (abbreviated in the notes as "FC") is divided into chapters and titles; the Romance text of F. Sepúlveda (abbreviated in the notes as "FS") is divided into titles only.

12. The restrictions (FS 62, 23, 24) are attempts to limit donations to religious orders and for the soul, but result (as in FC x, 28) in preventing the dissipation of the heirs' inheritance. The donation of small inheritances to monasteries, a consequence of the fractionalizing resulting from partible inheritance, is thought to have contributed to the increasing size of ecclesiastical estates in the older settled regions of Asturias, Galicia, León, and Old Castile: Pastor de Tognieri, "Historia de las familias," pp. 110-18.

13. FC x, 1, 2, 3, 11, 16-24, 27, 41. *Mejoría,* the practice of favoring one child over another, will be allowed in 1285: "Carta del RRey Don Sancho [IV] en majoria sobre el fuero de Cuenca," In Ureña, *Fuero de Cuenca,* p. 841; this practice, permitted in late Visigothic law, will subsequently have a long history.

14. FS 61; FC x, 1. In French law and English Common Law, *paterna paternis, materna maternis;* German *Fallrecht.* On the whole question, see G. Braga da Cruz, *O direito de troncalidade e o regime jurídico de patrimônio familiar,* 2 vols. (Braga, 1941-47), 1: 1-20; cf. García de Valdeavellano, *La comunidad patrimonial de la familia en el derecho español medieval* (Salamanca, 1956), pp. 12-29, where he stresses the contemporary evidence of joint ownership of land, a normally temporary condition preceding the partition of an estate; cf. Gibert, "Estudio histórico-jurídico," pp. 490-97.

15. FS 61; FC x, 1. The act of partition among brothers and sisters (or other heirs) formalizes inheritance, and if a childless son predeceases one parent, that parent inherits his moveables, while "la raíz torne a la raíz," that is, to his brothers and sisters; they also inherit his moveables if partition has been made at the time of his death (FS 67). At Cuenca, however, the surviving parent of an orphaned child who has lived at least nine days retains usufruct during the parent's lifetime; thereafter "la raíz torne a la raíz" (FC x, 13).

16. "Por segudar enemigo, qui oviere de segudar, assí segude: padre, o fijo, o hermanos, o primo, o segundo, o terçero, todos estos maten por su cabo, o todos en uno comol' fallaren, sin calonna ninguna; Et cunnado, de tanto parentesco como esto es, aviendo la parenta biva, mate con ellos, mas non en su cabo; y si la parienta finare, non segude más" (FS 50).

17. F. Uclés (1179), derived from the *Fuero latino* and customary law of Sepúlveda, defines the claims as extending to the seventh generation. Sáez, *Los fueros de Sepúlveda*, Apéndice 5, p. 179.

18. FS 66; FC x, 15 and 21. Women and children are specifically prohibited from fighting and sharing in the spoils of war, but by the rules of inheritance, a wife would share half of a husband's *ganancia* acquired as a result of his portion of the booty due the militia.

19. FS 74 and 42c.

20. On the whole question, see C. Pescador del Hoyo, "La caballería popular en León y Castilla," *CHE* 33–34 (1961): 101–238; *CHE* 35–36 (1962): 56–201; *CHE* 37–38 (1963): 88–199; *CHE* 39–40 (1964): 169–260; cf. E. Lourie, "A Society Organized for War," *Past and Present* 35 (1966): 54–76.

21. FC x, 14, 21, 22, 28; FC xix, 4.

22. "Los hermanos que moraren en uno, si partido non ovieren en uno, el mayor faga vezindat por todos" (FS 237).

23. García de Valdeavellano, *Historia de España*, 4th ed., 1 vol. in 2 parts (Madrid, 1968), 2: 207–9; García de Valdeavellano, *La comunidad patrimonial*, pp. 19–36.

24. "Todo sobrino de cavallero, o parente, que con él morare, non peche fonsadera ninguna, salvo ende si fuero casado" (FS 239a); "Todo cavallero o escudero, el anno que casare non vaya en hueste nin peche fonsadera" (FS 237a); "Filii sint in potestate parentum donec contrahant matrimonium. . ." (FC x, 4).

25. FC x, 22.

26. FC ix, 1, 6, 7. If either repudiates the other after betrothal, he or she is fined one hundred gold *moravedís*, and if he repudiates her after consummation of the marriage he becomes the *enemigo* of her kinsmen (FC ix, 4); cf. J. García González, "El incumplimiento de las promesas de matrimonio en la historia del derecho español," *AHDE* 23 (1953): 612–42.

27. "Todo mujer casada, o mançeba en cabello, o bibda, que morare con padre, o con madre, o con pariente, en su casa, non aya poder de adebdar debda ninguna más de fata I moravedí, nin de vender seyendo de seso [age 18 for a girl] si non fuer con plazentería del pariente con qui morare; y qui quier que más le manlevare ol' comprare lo suyo a menos de como sobredicho es, piérdalo el que lo comprare" (FS 64); "Todo empennamiento que fiziere el marido, seyendo con su muger, quier sea d'él quier sea d'ella, vala" (FS 65b); "Todo omne que muger oviere, non aya poder el marido de vender raíz de su muger, si a ella non ploguiere" (FS 64b); "Toda debda que marido con su muger fiziere, si alguno d'ellos muriere, échenlo por meetad; y si amos murieren, páguenlo aquellos que ovieren de heredar su heredamiento, como dicho es" (FS 64a).

28. FC x, 15.

29. "Qui sunt loca et sunt gentes, quibus est consuetudo adque forum, cum maritus homicidium perpetrauerit, aut latrocinium, aut tale scelus, pro quo omnia bona habent perdere, tunc uxor prius extrahet omnem medietatem tocius subere, que contigit ei et alia medietas capitur pro calumpnia, ad istam consuetudinem extirpandam, mandamus quod . . . iudex intret omnia bona tam uiri quem uxoris. . . . Dignum utique est, ut qui uno gaudio solent participare, tristicia cum uenerit, participentur" (FC xv, 10).

30. "Todo cavallero o escudero [de] Sepúlveda que malhetría, y non diere fiadores pora complir la malhetría, échel' el rey de la tierra, y lo suyo sea a mercet del rey. Et su muger non pierda del su algo ninguna cosa por malhetría que su marido faga. Et si la malhetría oviere fecha pechare, o otri por él, sea perdonado, y de lo suyo non pierda nada" (FS 65).

31. The responsibilities of the *dominus domus* extend to fines incurred by any member of his household: *mancipiis, proselitis* (Moors whom he has caused to be converted), and their children (FC x, 13, 14); FS 18a has a similar intent.

32. "Filii sint in potestate parentis donec contrahant matrimonium et sint filii familias. . . . Quidque filii adquiserint . . . totum sit parentum suorum. . . . Post diuisionem non habet [that parent who survives] utique respondere" (FC x, 5).

33. The *potestas parentum* of FC will be explained at length in an article on family organization, now in preparation. For the controversial literature on the survival of *patria potestas* in medieval Spanish law see A. Otero, "La patria potestad en el derecho histórico español," *AHDE* 26 (1956): 209–41, with extensive bibliographical notes. See also the comments of S. M. Belmartino, "Estructura de la familia y 'edades sociales' en la aristocracía de León y Castilla según los fuentes literarias y historiográficas (siglos X–XIII)," *CHE* 47–48 (1968): 278–82. Cf. A. M. Guilarte, "Cinco textos del fuero de Cuenca a proposito de la 'potestas parentum,'" in *Homenaje a Don Ramon Carande*, 2 vols. (Madrid, 1963), 2: 195–218.

34. FS 34, FC x, 32, 37, 38, 40. A child, because he or she is in *potestas parentum*, cannot acquire property or make a will before marriage.

35. "De los casamientos: Otrossi, toda muger virgen que a casar oviere, assi case: si padre non oviere, la madre non aya poder de casarla a menos de los parientes del padre que la avríen de heredar. Et si non oviere madre, el padre non aya poder de casarla a menos de parientes de la madre . . ." (FS 55).

36. Gibert, "Estudio histórico-jurídico," p. 487.

37. "Mulier que parentibus inuitis nupserit, sit exheredata, atque parentum suorum inimico"(FC xiii, 9). Disinheritance is also allowed for striking a parent (FC x, 41). With these two exceptions, inheritance by descendants is mandatory.

38. FS 63.

39. "Todo omme que demandaren que levó muger a fuerça, si lo negare, salvesse con doze; y si él dixiere que se fué ella de su grado, adugan la muger a medianedo y fablen los parientes con ella, y ella seyendo segura d'ellos . . ." (FS, 35).

40. FS 51 and 33.

41. FC xi, 26. If she is a nun, the fine is five hundred *solidos* (FC xi, 27). Abduction and rape have been called the earliest forms of marriage; here there is no marriage by rape, only by abduction, but the penalties are closely related; cf. Gibert, "El consentimiento familiar en el matrimonio según el derecho medieval español," *AHDE* 18 (1947): 706–61.

42. FS 73. If the raped woman is married, F. Cuenca requires that the man be burned if caught, a penalty commonly reserved for women who commit sexual offenses; she is also burned if she consents; if he is not caught, all his possessions are confiscated by the woman's husband (FC xi, 25).

43. "Quicumque in bandum uenerit ad auxilium alicui prebendum, pectet quamcumque calumpniam fecerit duplatam, licet [sit] filius uel consanguineus excepta uxore; vxor enim licet in bandum ueniat sui mariti, aut maritus in bandum sue uxoris, neuter eorum proinde habet aliquid pectare, qui una eret calumpnia anborum. . . . Siquis uxorem alienum defenderit, pectet trecentos soldos et exeat inimicus" (FC xiii, 2, 3).

44. FS 61; FC x, 30, 31; FC xxiii, 18. *Barraganas* (called *concubinas* in the Latin version of FC) are, in effect, common-law wives; they are strictly forbidden to married men on penalty of flogging for both (FC xi, 37).

45. "A los que me enbiastes dezir que manda el vuestro fuero que por las culpas de [1] marido que lazaran la muger, y por las culpas del fijo que lazdra el padre y por las culpas del mal fechor que muera su sobre leuador; a esto vos digo que non es derecho y tengo por bien que se libre por derecho y non por ese fuero." "Carta del RRey Don Sancho," in Ureña, *Fuero de Cuenca*, p. 837; this same modification also allows unmarried children to acquire property and make wills. *Ibid.*, p. 841.

46. F. Tomás Valiante, "La prisión por deudas en los Derechos castellanos y aragonés," *AHDE* 30 (1960): 324-25.

47. "Cum maritus et uxor aliquo occasione abinuicem uolerint separari . . ." (FC x, 8).

48. "Hoc habent uidui de iure iuditatis, et non aliud . . ." (FC x, 43, 44). A widower retains a horse, arms, the marriage bed, and the hunting birds.

49. FC x, 28; FC ix, 11; FC x, 36.

50. FS 66.

51. FC x, 34. Tutelage of minors is absent in FS; cf. J. Martínez Gijón, "Los sistemas de tutela y administración de los bienes de los menores en el derecho local de Castilla y León," *AHDE* 41 (1971): 9-31.

52. "Otorgo a todo cavallero de Sepúlvega, o biuda, muger que fué de cavallero, o escudero, o donzella de tiempo de XVIII annos, que ayan todos sus aportellados, yuveros, medieros, pastor, ortelano, colmenero, quantos ovieren d'estos a sacar, sáquelos de todo pecho, fuera moneda" (FS 198).

53. ". . . Ecce nos omnes qui sumus de concilio de Berbeia et de Barrio, et de Sancti Saturnino, varones et mulieres, senices et iuuenes, maximos et minimos, totos una pariter qui sumus habitantes, villanos et infanzones. . . ." *Fueros* of S. Zadornin, Berbeja y Barrio (955), in Muñoz y Romero, *Colección*, p. 31; cf. Carmen Carlé, *Del concejo medieval*, pp. 33-35 and 81-90.

54. FS 186.

55. FC xi, 50 and 51. On the significance of this symbolism, and for the discussion which follows, see J. Pitt-Rivers, "Honour and Social Status," in J. G. Peristiany, ed., *Honour and Shame, the Values of Mediterranean Society* (Chicago, 1966), pp. 19-77; cf. J. Caro Baroja, "Honour and Shame: a Historical Account of Several Conflicts," in *ibid.*, pp. 79-137, where he discusses the meaning of honor in the *Siete Partidas* of Alfonso X (late thirteenth century). The municipal *fueros* raise the issue in the negative sense, *desonra*.

56. FC xiii, 8.

57. "Enemigo, de los desafiados, a desonra . . ." (FS 32).

58. FC xi, 39-44.

59. FC xi, 48; FS 68 and 71.

60. "Toda christiana que criare fijo de moro o de iudíio, o que morare con ellos, sea dada por mala, y sea fostigada y echada de la villa; y los alcaldes fagan esta iusticia doquier que lo sepan, y sea sobre sus iuras" (FS 215; FC xi, 22, 23); the language of FS indicates that cohabitation was not unknown.

61. "Toda muger mala que denostare a bon ombre o a bona muger, o bona mançeba denostare o desondrare . . ." (FS 235).

62. FC xi, 29. The offenses include stealing her clothes from the public baths (reserved to women on Mondays and Wednesdays; to men three days a week; to Jews once; to Moors never: FS 111; FC ii, 32), pulling her hair, knocking her down, kissing her, touching her breasts, and cutting off her petticoats "without authorization of the alcaldes" (FC xi), 29-34. The title of FS which describes these offenses is, modestly, the only one in Latin (FS 186).

63. FS 235.

64. See the remarks in Lewis, *The Development of Southern French and Catalan Society*, pp. 391-92, 275-76; see also H. Moller, "The Social Causation of the

Jo-Ann McNamara
Suzanne F. Wemple

⁕ Marriage and Divorce in the Frankish Kingdom

The organization of the family—the rights and duties of the husband, the wife, their descendants and dependents—has always had a profound effect on the entire body politic, in primitive societies as well as in highly developed states. The management and distribution of property necessitated extensive marital regulation in the ancient world, and with the establishment of the Christian church, a growing effort was made to legislate the moral aspects of marriage. Yet for centuries the most basic questions remained unresolved. What persons can marry one another? What are the privileges and obligations of the partners to a marriage? Under what, if any, conditions can a marriage be dissolved?

Legislators and theologians alike strove to solve these problems. We have their texts and they illustrate a history of the efforts of church and state to regulate the most intimate tangles life can create. But laws and theories can only tell us what their authors desired to accomplish and not what was, in fact, the truth of everyday life. To be sure, legal codes may be supposed to derive from actual cases brought before tribunals. However, we have no means of judging the extent to which such laws were obeyed by men of the early middle ages. Nor were secular and ecclesiastical laws in harmony. We cannot estimate with certainty which set of rules the ordinary man chose to obey at any given instance.

We have sought to supplement the general picture presented in the Germanic law codes and formulae and the records of ecclesiastical councils with illustrative material from chronicles, letter, and treatises. But such material for this early period tends to be confined to the more scandalous entanglements of the ruling class rather than to the more ordinary marital arrangements of the majority. Therefore, though we cannot speak with assurance of the practical effects of the legislative efforts of the church and state, we can delineate the history of their development, which followed two separate lines until the advent of the Carolingian kings. Thereafter, the leaders of both church and state began to collaborate on creating a more uniform body of regulations. Previously, secular customs in the Germanic kingdoms, influenced to some extent by the traditions of the Roman law, were primarily concerned with the social and economic aspects of marriage, a union legalized by the account of the bride's parents and the payment of a dowry. Such unions could be dissolved with relative ease if either party transgressed certain laws or by mutual consent if suitable economic arrangements were made. The church, on the other hand, had been traditionally concerned with the moral aspects of marriage. In particular, the Latin church had tried consistently to restrict divorce and subsequent remarriage, and by the middle of the ninth century it adopted Augustine's uncompromising position that marriages could not be dissolved even if one party had committed adultery or wished to enter the monastery. The reconciliation of these two concepts: marriage as a social and economic fact and marriage as an indissoluble spiritual bond, was the great problem facing the Frankish church. Our aim is to trace marriage from its genesis in the two opposing systems of law to the success of Hincmor of Rheims in imposing church law in the ninth century.[1]

Christian attitudes toward marriage and its regulation were, of course, formed within the existing framework of the Roman state where property arrangements and questions concerning the guardianship or tutelage of women remained the province of the civil law. Though the fathers did not dispute that these powers were proper to the secular society, Christian doctrine differed radically from Roman law on the fundamental question of divorce and remarriage.[2] Divorce among the Romans was easily obtained. If one party were taken into captivity or reduced to servitude, the marriage was automatically dissolved. Despite some efforts of the emperors to discourage the practice, divorce by mutual consent was allowed in Roman Law, and the *Lex Julia* required the husband to divorce his adulterous wife.[3] Jewish law, from which the Christians drew most of their precepts, similarly made divorce readily available to men, and by Roman times, the trend was toward equal rights for women in this respect.[4] At the time of Christ, Jewish doctors were debating the whole question of divorce. Despite the objections of the Pharisees and the dismay of his own followers, Christ himself established the Christian position, enunciating on several occasions the principle of marital indissolubility though he appeared to leave an opening for a man to divorce an adulterous wife.[5]

From the outset, Christian thinkers made radical departures from both Jewish and Roman traditions in conceiving the idea of Christian marriage within the larger context of the Christian way of life. Though some early Christians, following Paul, regarded marriage as necessary for the containment of lust or a limited good for the fulfillment of God's commandment, "Be fruitful and multiply," Christianity as a whole was developing the innovative concept of marriage as a spiritual bond which might, in its highest form, eliminate sexual relations altogether.[6] The principle of spiritual equality between man and woman was basic to Christian thought, and accordingly the fathers came to glorify marriage as a divine gift and a symbol of the union of Christ and his church which sanctified husband and wife joined by mutual love. Being primarily concerned with the spiritual aspects of marriage and its value as a model of Christian virtue in a pagan world, the early fathers were little concerned with its legal aspects.[7] They preached that marriage constituted an indissoluble bond and those who allowed divorce did so only in case of adultery.[8] In contrast to the eastern fathers, who did not oppose too strenuously the double standard of divorce inherent in civil law, the later western fathers almost unanimously declared that what was not allowed to women in Christian law was equally illicit for men.[9] Ambrosiaster stands alone in sanctioning double standards, allowing divorce and remarriage to the husbands of adulterous wives on the basis of Matthew 19, while denying the same right to women.[10] St. Ambrose's prohibition against the remarriage of men during their wives' lifetimes, and St. Jerome's specific command that husbands who had dismissed their adulterous wives could not remarry culminated in St. Augustine's teaching that even adulterous marriages were indissoluble: the partners could separate but neither could remarry while the other was alive.[11]

Ecclesiastical legislation, however, was considerably more ambiguous than the moral writings of the Latin fathers. The early councils were frequently unclear on the question of indissolubility. They specifically opposed themselves to secular law by prohibiting divorce.[12] But, with some misgivings, they followed Paul in allowing divorce to Christians married to Jews, heretics, and pagans, though they generally preferred to prohibit such marriages in the first place.[13]

The greatest problem was whether adultery justified divorce and remarriage and here the councils occasionally wavered over Christ's apparent exemption for husbands of adulterous wives. Though willing to recognize the possibility of separation from adulterous partners, most of the fourth and fifth century western councils tended to apply their rules of indissolubility to both men and women. Only the Council of Angers, held in 453, limited its prohibition of remarriage to women.[14] The Council of Arles, in 314, advised against the remarriage of a man who had repudiated his adulterous wife.[15] Without entering into a discussion of adultery, Canon 8 of the ninth synod of Carthage (convened in 404) which was incorporated into the *Codex Canonum Ecclesiae Africanae*, prohibited remarriage to either partner on pain of penance.[16] There were, however, earlier canons softening this rule, such as canon 10 of the Council of Elvira which stated that a woman contracting marriage in good faith with a man who had repudiated his wife without reason should not be excommunicated.[17] The Council of Vannes (465) appears to have recognized the dilemma posed by Matthew 19 and allowed remarriage if adultery could be proved.[18] This council may have been mindful that, despite ecclesiastical prohibitions, divorce continued to be allowed by the secular codes. The fathers at the ninth synod of Carthage apparently meant to get to the root of the problem by recommending the promulgation of an imperial law to support their prohibition of divorce and remarriage, but there is no evidence that such legislation was ever considered by the emperor.[19] The popes were equally ineffective in condemning the remarriage of both men and women as adulterous unions.[20]

The Christian emperors never made any discernible effort to bring their marriage legislation into conformity with conciliar decrees. Their divorce laws continued to be less strict and maintained the double standard. Constantine allowed women to repudiate their husbands unilaterally if they had committed homicide, sorcery, or tomb desecration whereas husbands were allowed a divorce if their wives were guilty of adultery, acted as procuresses, or were proved to be sorceresses. If a wife could not prove her charges, she was deported but in a similar situation the husband had only to restore the wife's dowry and was not allowed to remarry. To this, Honorius and Theodosius added that a woman who had succeeded in obtaining a divorce could remarry only after five years and could not remarry at all if she had left her husband for a less serious crime. The husband, however, could remarry immediately if he had repudiated his wife for a serious crime and after two years if he repudiated her for a defect of character. Only if he had dissolved the marriage for a trivial disagreement was he required to live in perpetual celibacy.[21]

This divergence between secular and ecclesiastical law is apparent in other areas of sexual regulation as well. For example, concubinage was never prohibited by Roman Law and in some instances it was specifically allowed.[22] The church, on the other hand, insisted that the concubine must either be relinquished or married, depending on her status.[23] Incest regulations in Roman Law conformed only partially to Christian principles, and were never extended to include the prohibitions against spiritual affinity which the Christians had derived largely from Jewish Law and incorporated in their own legislation.[24]

The problem of accommodating Christian precepts to secular law was further complicated by the eruption of Germanic tribes into the shattered Roman Empire. Their laws, codified from the fifth to the ninth century, show occasional Roman influences in the regulation of divorce and Christian influences in the incest prohibitions. We know little about their original marital practices. Tacitus noted that they paid for their wives, which he took to be indicative of the esteem in which they held women, but the practice is capable of less flattering interpretations. Likewise, he praised the fidelity of married couples, though he admitted that the royal families were polyga-mous.[25] Gregory of Tours attested the continuation of polygamy among the Franks through their first century as Christians and, surprisingly, the bishop did not appear to be disturbed by the practice. For example, he calmly related the story of Chlotar's marriage to Guntheaca, the widow of a murdered rival, followed by his marriage to the daughter of another slain enemy, Radegunda. Lest it be supposed that Chlotar was in the habit of repudiating one wife before taking another, we must further cite the king's virtually simultaneous marriage to the sisters, Ingunda and Aregunda. Moreover, Gregory carefully distinguished all these wives from Chlotar's concubines.[26]

Apparently, the Franks abandoned polygamy during the seventh cen-tury, for Gregory's continuator, writing in the eighth century, felt he needed some other explanation for the multiple marriages of Chilperic and sug-gested that he had repudiated his first wife because she had been tricked into standing as godmother to her own child. This solution, however, depended on incest prohibitions introduced only in the eighth century.[27] In contrast, Chlotar presumably knew that under Christian law he was committing incest as well as polygamy when he married the two sisters. Gregory of Tours must have known it too. Their indifference, complemented by the widespread discussion of the problem in other sources, suggests that the incest prohibition was so far opposed to Germanic custom that it was only uprooted with the greatest difficulty after several centuries of effort.[28]

Beginning in 511, and through all the councils of the sixth century, the Frankish bishops repeatedly condemned incest in all its forms.[29] Marriage with a brother or sister, nephew or niece, sister-in-law, mother-in-law, cousins to various degrees of kinship, and so forth, was absolutely forbid-den. Yet the frequency of the reservation that those who had contracted such marriages in ignorance could gain pardon by separation suggests that they remained common among the people, and the same conclusion is supported by papal pronouncements for other areas.[30] By the late sixth century, the Frankish kings were willing to incorporate the church's incest prohibitions into their own legislation. Such marriages became a secular crime in the Salic law as they were in the Bavarian, Alemannic, Visigothic, and Lombard codes.[31] In 596, Childebert II decreed the death penalty for a man who married his father's wife or his wife's sister or a woman who married her dead husband's brother.[32] Fredegar said that Chlotar II (584–629) ordered the execution of a son of a major domus because he had married his stepmother, indicating that the grandson of Aregunda had come quite a distance from his pagan forebears.[33]

But on the all-important question of indissolubility, the variance be-tween the church and the Germanic law was almost total. Again, we know little of Germanic custom before the conversion, but Gregory of Tours cited a unique example of unilateral divorce by a woman, the mother of Clovis, who left her husband to marry Childeric because she thought him a better man.[34] The codes issued by Clovis and his successors do not reflect this freedom. While under Frankish law a husband could repudiate his wife for just cause, particularly for adultery and the inability to bear children, a woman could not initiate separation.[35] Only the Roman codes issued by the Visigoths and Burgundians allowed women to divorce their husbands for homicide, sorcery or violation of graves with the possibility of remarriage.[36] But under Visigothic law, women were allowed to repudiate their husbands only for homosexuality or for having been forced to fornicate with another.[37] If an unfortunate Burgundian woman attempted to divorce her husband she was to be smothered in mire.[38] On the other hand, in addition to adultery, husbands could divorce their wives for sorcery and violation of tombs under the Burgundian code.[39] Moreover, all the codes recognized that a man could repudiate his wife for very slender reasons by requiring some monetary consolation for the unoffending wife thus left with her children.[40]

Where there was no question of unilateral repudiation, divorce was even easier, and divorce by mutual consent was generally recognized in the Germanic world, as it had been in Roman Empire.[41] In the sixth century, even the church showed signs of weakening on the subject. The Council of Agde, in 506, forbade divorce without prior presentation of the causes to the bishop's court.[42] This was a rare effort to achieve some control over the problem. In general, the Merovingian councils were ineffective in their meager attempts to restrict divorce. The Council of Orléans held in 533 forbade repudiation of a partner who was too ill to fulfill the conjugal duty, but this rule was not incorporated into the secular codes and, lacking the support of the Merovingian Kings, the church could not enforce it.[43] Apart from incest regulations, secular laws, whether incorporating the customs of the Roman or Germanic inhabitants of the Frankish kingdom, confined themselves to the social element: the protection of the family interest and the disposition of property between the bride and groom.[44]

The one area in which secular law appeared to give weight to the wishes of the woman concerned was in the area of abduction but here again the codes were primarily concerned with the protection of the family's financial interests. A woman might occasionally succeed in marrying the man of her choice or repudiating an unwanted husband and marrying another by cooperating in her own abduction. In such cases the laws were primarily concerned with compensating the family involved and repairing the pride of the injured husband or betrothed.[45] The laws, however, varied on the subject. Many were more relaxed in cases where the girl had consented to the abduction but others punished the girl severely.[46] Among the Saxons, for example, the family had to be paid a bride price of three hundred solidi if

57052

she had consented to the abduction. If she had not consented, she was to be restored to the family.[47] The Thuringians and the Visigoths punished the girl who married without her family's consent by exclusion from the inheritance.[48] Burgundian and Ripuarian laws stipulated that if a girl had fornicated with a man on her own volition, the union was not to be regarded as valid and the man could return her to her parents upon payment of a fine of fifteen solidi.[49] Further, where the family had not received satisfaction, the formulae of the seventh and eighth centuries show that marriages resulting from abduction were not validated and the children were regarded as illegitimate.[50]

Churchmen of the seventh century made no apparent effort to interfere with these secular practices. In the seventh century, few councils were called and the legislation passed was not concerned with marriage. Furthermore, the papacy was too distracted by its effort to protect itself from the encroaching Lombards to interest itself in this problem. The new energy and creativity in both church and state in the eighth century therefore introduced a new period in the history of both institutions that was reflected in the laws regulating marriage and divorce. The pontificate of Gregory II marked a general resurgence of legislative activity in Rome while, in the north, the Carolingian family relied heavily upon ecclesiastical approval to justify their rise to power. Foundations for papal cooperation in the transfer of the Frankish kingship were laid as early as 741, when Pepin and Carloman interested themselves in the question of church reform, inviting the great English missionary Saint Boniface to undertake the resuscitation of Frankish conciliar activity.[51]

Germanic marital customs had troubled Boniface in his earlier apostolate and he had sought the advice of Gregory II in dealing with incestuous practices among the pagans.[52] The pope answered with a series of pronouncements on incest which strengthened the older tradition and extended it in some directions. In 721, the Council of Rome added to the usual prohibitions against marriage with a brother's wife, a niece, stepmother, daughter-in-law, and cousins, placing the godparent of one's child, cognates, and the spouses of cognates within the forbidden degrees.[53] These prohibitions were introduced into the Frankish church by Boniface. Cooperating with the missionary, Pepin included the further papal legislation on the subject at the Council of Rome (743) into his own capitularies.[54] At this time, the incest prohibition received its last extension with the interesting addition of "nuns, priestesses and deaconesses" to the forbidden list, which suggests a certain degree of confusion in the mind of the pope on the definition of incest and consanguinity.

In keeping with the religious aspect of their governance, the Carolingians continued the Merovingian effort to bring secular legislation on incest into conformity with church decrees. They extended their concern even to such moral problems as incest arising from extramarital fornication.[55] Sexual relations, before or after marriage, with a relative of the spouse was held to constitute a bond of affinity similar to those rising from betrothal, marriage, and baptism or confirmation.[56] Disregard for such bonds was regarded as a serious offence which disqualified the transgressors from marriage for life, with the single exception of consanguineous marriages of cousins in the sixth degree.[57] Although such marriages were also prohibited, the offenders were subjected to penance without being obliged to separate if the marriage had already been concluded.[58]

Under Charlemagne, cooperation between church and state was intensified. In 774, at the king's request, Pope Hadrian sent him the *Dionysio-Hadriana* collection, which served as the basis for a sweeping series of instructions on illicit and incestuous unions.[59] Though he added nothing new to the incest legislation of his predecessors, Charlemagne provided for their enforcement throughout his vast realm.[60] The bishops were given the power to judge such cases, while confiscated property or fines were to go to the royal fisc, and the possibility of appeal to the king himself remained open.[61]

This work virtually completed the incest legislation. Thereafter, both church and state addressed themselves to the problem of enforcing these laws. Apparently, they were so well understood and generally accepted that by 813 they were being used for purposes never anticipated by the legislators. The bishops assembled at the Council of Châlons were obliged to prohibit women from standing as godmothers to their own children or as sponsors to their confirmation in order to have an excuse for separating from their husbands. Persons seeking divorce by that route were to submit to lifelong penance, not the least of which was to live together henceforward in chastity.[62]

The question of divorce saw dramatic changes in the eighth century, with the initiative for strict rules coming from the princes rather than the pope. In 726, there is evidence that the papacy was moving in the direction of relaxing the rigorous prohibitions of the past. Gregory II, in one case, allowed a man to remarry if he could not persevere in continence with an infirm wife, though he added that abstinence was more virtuous and that the man must, in any event, continue to support the repudiated invalid.[63] But two decades later, Pepin demonstrated an altogether unprecedented desire to abolish most secular causes for divorce. One of his earliest acts as Mayor of the Palace was to undertake the enforcement of the decree of the Council of Soissons (744) prohibiting remarriage during a spouse's lifetime, with allowance made only for the man who had repudiated an adulterous wife.[64] At the same time, Pepin wrote Pope Zachary for clarification of the church's position. The pope answered with extracts from the *Dionysiana* including some of the most uncompromising decrees of the early church.[65]

Since Pepin continued to treat questions of sexual irregularity as matters for secular jurisdiction, this move in the direction of including church laws in secular legislation was an important step. In practice, however, the effect appears to have been minimal. The formulas of the period amply demonstrate that the practice of divorce by mutual consent was as popular as ever.[66] The later Frankish councils of the 750s reflect this trend in their canons mitigating church law on divorce and remarriage. Perhaps Pepin had come to recognize his inability to uproot such vernerable customs. Or he may have recalled his own unsuccessful attempt to repudiate his wife, Bertrade, to marry another woman.[67] In any case, the Council of Compiègne (757) allowed a man to remarry if he had to leave his home in order to follow his lord, or if his wife entered a nunnery, or if illness prevented her from fulfilling her marital duties. A woman was allowed to remarry if her husband had ceased to cohabit with her. The Council of Verberie allowed a man to remarry if his wife tried to kill him or if she refused to follow him, though the woman was not allowed to remarry. The same council stipulated—perhaps to protect wives from being forced into the nunnery—that a man "qui uxorem dimiserit velare," could not remarry.[68]

This tendency of the church to relax its earlier strictures appears to reflect the actual practice through Charlemagne's reign. Even as the emperor was following his father's example in strengthening the marriage laws, the penitentials of the period reflect considerable laxity in their application.[69] Their provisions seem to relate to older secular laws rather than to papal decretals, conciliar decrees, or Charlemagne's own legislation. The solution to this apparent contradiction may be that, like the *Formulae*, penitentials dealt more closely with actual practice than with the ideals of the law. Pseudo-Egbert allowed men to repudiate adulterous wives and then remarry. Even if the repudiation had been for some other reason, he allowed a man to remarry after five years if the bishops consented. Ignoring the consistent church policy of holding men and women to the same standard, Pseudo-Egbert allowed a woman to repudiate a promiscuous husband and remarry only if he entered a monastery. If her husband were reduced to servitude for fornication or theft she could remarry after two years, and after one year if he were taken into captivity. If her husband were impotent, she could remarry immediately.[70] These concession may have reflected an awareness of the pressures that always affect a priest in his daily work. But the general tendency of papal legislation was also towards relaxation: the Roman synod convoked by Pope Eugenius in 826 allowed the innocent party to divorce and remarry in cases of adultery.[71]

It appears, therefore, that the opposition between secular and ecclesiastical marriage laws was on the way to being settled by the church's acknowledgment of the principle of dissolubility in cases of adultery. However, it was the pope who was out of step with the times by 826. In 789, Charlemagne cited the ninth synod of Carthage prohibiting the remarriage of any husband or wife who had repudiated their spouse in his *Admonitio generalis*.[72] This instruction appears to have been directed against the prevailing custom of remarriage after a union was dissolved for reasons other than adultery. But Charles did not stop at this point. In 796 the bishops whom he had gathered at Friuli went even further than the generality of earlier councils and decreed unequivocally that adultery could not dissolve the marriage bond. Even though a husband could separate from his adulterous wife, and even though she might be subjected to severe punishment and penitence, he could not remarry while she lived.[73] This legislation was later incorporated into the Capitulary to the Missi in 802 extending it to the entire empire.[74] For three hundred years, after Augustine had enunciated the absolute indissolubility of marriages, the church had hesitated on the question, but now a secular law upheld it for all Christians.

To be sure, Charlemagne's concern for ordering the world on Christian principles was not always expressed by his own example. His marital and extramarital arrangements were far less flamboyant than those of his Merovingian predecessors but he was hardly a model of propriety. According to his admiring biographer, Einhard, he had four wives and when the last of these had died he took four concubines. This list of the wives of Charlemagne omitted the first alliance of his youth with Himiltrude, the mother of Pepin the Hunchback.[75] Tact may have compelled Einhard's silence concerning the lady's position and her unknown fate, but Pope Stephen III certainly thought they were married. When he heard that the Frankish king was negotiating a union with the daughter of the Lombard King, he sought to persuade him not to enter into an alliance so revolting to the pope. Not knowing whether the intended groom was Charles or his brother Carloman, he wrote to both of them.[76] The letter is an important document for the historian of Christian marriage because it indicates that in the late eighth century impediments to marriage and divorce were still vague principles lacking precise legal definitions.

To the pope, the proposed marriage could only be considered "a consortium of the most evil intention." Yet he expressed his opposition as violently as possible without recourse to the standard prohibitions:

> Indeed mildest and most beneficent of the kings instituted by God, you are presently joined as befits illustrious and noble kings, in lawful wedlock with beautiful wives of your own noble Frankish race. It becomes you to cleave to them in love. Surely it cannot be allowed that you should dismiss them to take other wives or that you should mingle consanguineously with a foreign race.[77]

The pope went on to supply biblical citations against marriage with foreign women and to remind the kings that their father had obeyed his predecessor when he had been forbidden to put aside their mother. Surely the pope was aware of the canons enforcing the indissolubility of marriage. But he did not cite them. He must have believed that they would carry no weight with the

Frankish kings. Equally the pope must have known the meaning of consanguinity and yet he applied it in this farfetched context.

For his part, Charlemagne ignored the pope's efforts. All his biographers agree that he married the Lombard princess. A year later he repudiated her to marry the Swabian Hildigard. Einhard baldly stated that no one knew why he had put her aside.[78] Nearly a century later the gossipy monk of Sankt Gallen supplied the apologetic explanation that "since she was bedridden and unable to bear a child, she was by the advice of his devout clergy put on one side as if already dead."[79] We do know that at least one of the devout clergy did not give such advice but "mourned that the Franks would be perjured thereby and that the king would be involved in unlawful marriage, since his proper wife had been driven away without any reason."[80] This was Adelard of Bath, Charlemagne's own cousin and a forerunner of the Frankish bishops of a later generation. Rather than serve the unlawful queen, Adelard left the palace and entered a monastery. The event may have served as a warning to the King for he never reverted to this youthful behavior. Henceforth, not counting his concubines, Charlemagne lived with each wife until her death and, indeed, firmly refused the demands of many of his nobles that he repudiate his fourth wife, the unpopular Fastrada.

Thus Charlemagne's later life, like his later legislation, contributed the vital thrust in the direction of harmony between church and secular law regulating marriage. The introduction of the principle of indissolubility into secular law and the concommitant advancement of the principle that men and women were equally subject to moral laws produced complications which would only be clarified by the practical experience of the next two generations.

Under the more relaxed control of Louis the Pious, energetic prelates were able to secure the initiative in ecclesiastical affairs, working to eliminate conflicting canons, eradicate secular customs, and arrive at a clear set of synodal regulations regarding impediments to marriage and divorce. In 829 four great councils held in various parts of the Frankish kingdom set the seal on this effort.[81] Under the leadership of Jonas of Orléans, the bishops assembled at Paris declared that, since marriage was instituted by God, a man could separate from an adulterous wife but would himself be guilty of adultery should he marry again.[82] The bishops enjoined the emperor to admonish the people accordingly, and that year Louis incorporated the precept into his own capitularies.[83] Other synods and capitularies followed this pattern, devising ever more precise and subtle formulations which extended even to abduction with ecclesiastical penalties being added to the customary requirements for compensation.[84]

The bishops were not unaware of the contradictions inherent in the earlier church legislation, but they did not turn to Rome for elucidation. Hrabanus Maurus (784–856), at the request of the bishop of Wuerzburg, undertook the reconciliation of the *majorum dicta* with what he found in the *sacrorum librorum volumina*. In the course of this study he took issue with papal strictures on incest, urging a more temperate application of the laws prohibiting marriages to the sixth and seventh degrees. To Hrabanus, the overriding need was to apply severe punishment for adultery and fornication, which were prohibited by both divine law and evangelical authority, while the incest impediments appeared only in sacred canons. According to Hrabanus, the practice of annulling consanguineous marriages relaxed the sanctions on fornication and adultery.[85]

While the Frankish bishops were thus taking a legislative lead, they were also addressing themselves to the problem of jurisdiction. In 829 Louis the Pious subjected men who had repudiated or killed their innocent wives to public penance meted out by the church. The role of the state was confined to the stipulation that the count would arrest and imprison contumacious offenders until the emperor could render judgment.[86] Similarly, after the abolition of monetary penalties by the reforming Synod of Châlons, in 813, the church had the sole right to punish incest, though they looked to secular arms for assistance in enforcement.[87] However, the bishops did not claim sole jurisdiction over illicit marriages or separations. It remained customary to hold such trials in general assemblies where both bishops and lay nobles were present, and Daudet has argued convincingly that the bishops still acknowledged the competence of the laity in marital cases.[88] For example, at the general *placitum* and synod held by lay nobles and bishops at Attigny in 822, a lady named Northilda presented the emperor with a complaint against the shameful practices of her husband. The bishops refused jurisdiction on the grounds that the laymen, being more familiar with marriage and with secular laws, were better qualified to handle the case. They did, however, add that if the lay judges found that a crime had been committed, they were prepared to impose penance according to the canons.[89] But when the emperor's second wife, Judith, was accused of adultery, she purged herself by taking a public oath before a synod of bishops.[90] These two conflicting procedures show that at this period there was considerable confusion even in the minds of the bishops as to the competence of ecclesiastical courts.

Judith's story provides further elucidation of the practice of repudiation by the 830s. The fact that Louis was obliged to promise to enter a monastery when Judith's enemies forced him to judge her guilty of adultery in 830 seems to demonstrate that by this time the indissolubility even of adulterous marriages became generally accepted, and a man could not rid himself of one wife to marry another on the grounds of adultery. Moreover, their efforts to prove the empress guilty of some grave crime, adultery or witchcraft if necessary, seems to show that the powerful coalition of nobles and bishops who backed the sons of Louis' first wife, Ermengard, were conscious of the need to create very compelling reasons to justify separating a man from his lawful wife.

Ultimately, of course, the case was determined by the emperor's desire to keep his wife. But the failure of the coalition to procure her repudiation depended on their failure to prove her adultery. The entire story illustrates the legal confusion that still governed the question of marriage and divorce: with bishops seeking to dissolve a marriage despite the church's principle of indissolubility, and laymen seeking to prove adultery rather than rest upon the long tradition of repudiation in secular law. Thus, much still remained to be done by the generation of active and learned bishops who took the leadership of the Frankish church during the middle of the ninth century.

These bishops were inspired by the concept of a dual government of church and state, governed respectively by bishops and princes working in practical harmony. The ministerial duties of the princes would be undertaken with the guidance of the bishops, and the work of the bishops would be enforced by the princes. In matters concerning marriage and divorce, as in other aspects of life, they sought to complete the process of welding secular and ecclesiastical practice into a uniform code. In this effort they were largely successful, though the whole matter was frequently obscured and complicated by the interaction between the popes of the period, bishops, and princes, all seeking to assert their claims to leadership of this society.[91]

In pursuit of this goal, bishops at the Council of Meaux-Paris (845-46) enjoined Charles the Bald to give them power to require the cooperation of secular officials in securing the presence of the contumacious in court.[92] They required this assistance frequently in ensuing years, especially for incest cases which were now customarily tried in episcopal courts.[93] On the other side, where cases would normally be expected to be referred to lay courts (as were affairs involving rape and adultery), the bishops sought to impose conformity with ecclesiastical laws and to extend ecclesiastical jurisdiction.[94] Thus the Council of Meaux-Paris passed legislation designed to match secular penalties with canonical requirements for penance and absolution to both types of cases. This in turn necessitated complementary procedures in ecclesiastical courts.[95]

One of the participants in the Council of Meaux-Paris was Hincmar, the newly elected Archbishop of Rheims, who was to prove a master in using the complex techniques designed by the council. During the course of his strenuous career (842-82) Hincmar was to hear a variety of cases involving marriage and divorce. Historians have special reason to be grateful to the meticulous prelate for his legacy of detailed records in these cases, which at last gives us a concrete base for our conclusions. To be sure, the complaints brought before Hincmar concerned only affairs of the greatest moment and persons of the highest consequence. It is doubtful whether so much time and attention was ever expended on the marital difficulties of lesser people. But the decisions made in his court set the judicial pattern to which they were expected to conform. Hincmar sought to reconcile the ecclesiastical law with secular customs and to use both secular and ecclesiastical courts to enforce a unified doctrine which included a precise definition of marriage and an absolute prohibition against its dissolution.

The archbishop was introduced to the most fundamental aspect of the problem in the rudest possible fashion. In 846 a vassal of the Emperor Lothar, Fulrich, was accused of having summarily repudiated his wife and marrying another woman. The case was referred to Hincmar, who based himself on the firm principle of indissolubility established in the contemporary legal compilations of Benedictus Leviat and Pseudo-Isodore.[96] Relying on that principle, the archbishop excommunicated Fulrich, who then appealed to Pope Leo IV.[97] Fulrich based his appeal on an argument which received support, in 852, from the decision of the Council of Mainz that a woman was a concubine if she had no formal contract of *desponsatio* and could therefore be simply abandoned if her partner decided to contract a legal marriage.[98] Thus in 853 Fulrich was freed from Hincmar's sentence on the grounds that he had never been married, a decision which caused much rancor between prelate and pope.[99] Hincmar's embarrassment at having failed to make this fundamental distinction was probably not relieved by the confusion in church law regarding concubinage.[100] In 860, when four different marriage cases were referred to him for judgment, as he was careful to begin by defining all the elements which constituted a legitimate marriage, using both secular and ecclesiastical requirements.

> We learn from the fathers and find it handed down to us by holy apostles and their successors that a marriage is lawful only when the wife's hand was requested from those who appear to have power over her and who are acting as her guardians and when she had been betrothed by her parents or relatives and when she was given a sacerdotal benediction with prayers and oblations from a priest and at the appropriate time established by custom was solemnly received by her husband, guarded and attended by bridal attendants requested from her nearest kin and provided with a dowry. For two or three days, they should then take time out for prayers, guarding their chastity, so that they may beget good offspring and please the Lord. Then their children will not be spurious but legitimate and eligible to be their heirs.[101]

The first of the cases he took up in 860 had been in progress for two years before Hincmar was brought in. Lothar II, king of Lotharingia, had been married to the politically desirable Tetberga probably since 854 but had begun proceedings in 858 to dissolve the marriage in order to marry his concubine Waldrada.[102] Unlike his great grandfather Charlemagne, Lothar was no longer in a position simply to put aside one wife and substitute another. First he tried to rid himself of his queen by accusing her of incest before her marriage, but in 858 she had successfully purged herself by ordeal.[103] Then he imprisoned her until she declared herself desirous of exchanging the married state for the life of the convent.[104] This request was conveyed to the Lotharingian bishops at the synod of Aix in January 860. When, however, the queen refused to confess her guilt publicly, the bishops were not willing to proceed further than a suspension of marital relations between the couple. This sentence they based on the queen's private confession submitted to them by the emperor's chaplain, Gunther, Archbishop of Cologne. The assembly was dissolved and the queen was probably threatened with torture while a new assembly augmented by non-Lotharingian bishops and lay magnates was being gathered.[105] There, on 15 February, the queen confessed to the incest and was sentenced to public penance. But the king's request for remarriage, though received with sympathy, was deferred until still more dignitaries could be consulted.[106]

The report of these councils seems to demonstrate that the bishops felt themselves to be on uncertain ground. In addition to their suspicion that the queen might have been coerced and their fear that Lothar's failure to act earlier constituted a tacit admission of her virginity upon marriage, their queries to Hincmar evidence confusion regarding the laws and the nature of the procedure which ought to be followed.[107] Hincmar, who had not attended the February meeting, apparently shared their doubts.[108] Although he did not oppose the use of general synods in such cases, his examination of the report convinced him that the specific proceedings at both synods had been illegal.[109] He listed many objections against the validity of the bishops' sentence and concluded that the queen's guilt had not been established according to legal proceedings prescribed by the canons. If the case were to be further pursued, it had to be tried by a lay court since the queen had placed her deposition into the king's hands. Only if a lay court convicted her, might an episcopal tribunal be called to impose conditions of penance.[110]

The reasons for Hincmar's support of a secular tribunal in this case have been hotly debated. Sdralek accused him of acting in the interests of Charles the Bald by seeking to perpetuate Lothar's childless marriage, a view that is supported also by Brühl.[111] Daudet defended him on this point because Hincmar did acknowledge the possibility of annulment if the fact of incest before the marriage could be established, for a woman who had committed incest was forever unworthy to be called a wife.[112] However, Daudet still considered Hincmar's preference for the secular court to be inconsistent with his principles.[113]

In fact, the choice of court was irrelevant to the principle that Hincmar was trying to establish. He was simply indifferent to the persons of the judges, though he thought custom supported a secular tribunal in this case. His concern was with the law to be applied. He wanted to ensure that in this case, and in other cases where Christian principles were applicable, Christian law would be enforced by all courts and that secular law and human custom would never be used to excuse an unchristian act. Accordingly, he stated:

> As Christians, they must know that on the day of judgment they will be judged, not by Roman, Salic or Burgundian law, but by divine and apostolic law. It is only fitting, therefore, that public law in a Christian kingdom, be consistent and consonant with Christianity.[114]

On the legal points involved he was inflexible. Except in cases of incest, marriage was indissoluble and the incest must be manifestly proved in a legal trial. In all other cases, separation was permissible only where one or both parties wished to enter a monastery or where fornication had been proved by clear confession or open conviction. But in neither case could either party remarry:

> For a man and woman, as sacred authority says, are no longer twain, but one in the flesh . . . and if for manifest fornication they are separated, they must remain so or may be mutually reconciled. Nor can they be disjoined so that only one part of the body, either that which is in the man or that which is in the woman, observes continence while the other part is polluted. They may, however, separate by common consent and abstain from uxorious acts so that in perpetual continence they may serve God.[115]

In the matter of jurisdiction, Hincmar insisted only that proper legal proceedings be observed in all courts and that the sentences of lay magnates be corroborated by sacerdotal pronouncement. For the dissolution of any marriage, the bishop's sanction must be received.[116] Despite Hincmar's clear instructions the case was not referred back to a lay court. The question of jurisdiction became further complicated when Pope Nicholas entered the case, following Tetberga's appeal and Lothar's request of a papal review.[117] By the time Nicholas responded and sent two legates in 862, a third synod had been convened by Lothar's supporters. On the ground of the queen's incest, this synod had dissolved the marriage and Lothar had married Waldrada. The pope was furious and became further exacerbated when the Synod of Metz in 863 upheld the sentence with the support of the legates who had been bribed. Nicholas pursued the affair on the principle that once the case had been appealed to his court, it could not be recalled to an inferior court. Accordingly, he held his own Lateran council, denouncing the Synod of Metz, heaping invective upon Lothar for his treatment of Tetberga and enlisting the emperor's uncles and the Frankish bishops to force the restoration of the queen.[118] For years, the pope steadfastly resisted further attempts by Lothar to escape his marriage.[119] The case was closed only in 869 when Lothar appeared as a penitent in Rome and Nicholas' successor Hadrian II absolved him. Lothar's death on the way from Rome was regarded by contemporary chroniclers as a providential end to the affair.[120]

The only real difference between the pope and Hincmar in this affair turned on Nicholas' opinion that the case, having been taken to a higher court could not be concluded in a lower court, though Nicholas accepted Hincmar's basic argument that defendants could purge themselves through ordeal in secular courts and had the right to choose their own judges.[121] Of the two, Hincmar was perhpas more of a realist in insisting on the complementary proceedings in secular and ecclesiastical courts in matters of sexual transgressions. The pope was pursuing a more exalted goal in seeking to establish the superiority of the papal court, but Hincmar was prepared only to insist on conformity in the observance of church law in all courts and work for cooperation in sentencing that would balance secular and spiritual penalties.[122]

On the vital principle of indissolubility Hincmar and Nicholas were in complete agreement also over a case brought before the Synod of Tusey in 860. Engeltrud, the wife of an Italian count, Boso, had run away from her husband with one of his vassals, Wanger, and was living with him openly. Boso had tried to bring her back unsuccessfully and finally sought to dissolve his marriage by taking the case to a secular court which according to civil law allowed him to repudiate or kill her. This move was opposed by both the pope and Hincmar.[123] The archbishop reiterated his opinion that adultery could not dissolve a marriage: Engeltrud had to return and her husband had to take her back.[124]

At the same synod, the problem of defining a valid marriage was introduced in the case of Stephen, a vassal of Charles the Bald. Stephen's father-in-law complained that although all due formality had been observed in uniting his daughter with Stephen, the groom had failed to consummate the marriage.[125] Stephen testified that fear of his father-in-law had obliged him to go through with the ceremonies but he could not consummate the marriage because prior sexual relations with a relative of the bride would then make him guilty of incest.[126] In considering the case, Hincmar introduced a new and final element into the definition of marriage. He agreed that the young man was right in refraining from consummation. But instead of reiterating earlier decrees which would have required him to live henceforth in chastity because the *desponsatio* had taken place, Hincmar declared that an unconsummated union did not constitute a valid marriage.[127] Stephen, therefore, was free to marry again though he would have to be sentenced by an episcopal court for fornication and also had to answer a lay court for breaking his engagement. The girl's family, Hincmar advised, should be recompensed by being allowed to keep the bridegift.[128]

The case of Stephen turned upon the sexual aspect of marriage. Another case, that of Charles the Bald's daughter Judith, turned on the social aspect of parental consent.[129] The widowed Judith had eloped with Baldwin of Flanders and married him despite her father's opposition.[130] Following the procedures laid out by Hincmar in other cases, Charles turned to the secular court to have his daughter returned under the abduction laws and to an ecclesiastical court to have the couple excommunicated.[131] Hincmar approved the dual action. He appears to have been anxious to accord recognition for secular customs when they did not conflict with ecclesiastical laws and thereby to prove that harmony between the two jurisdictions could indeed be achieved. Baldwin, however, appealed to the pope who interceded for the pair.[132] Against the pope's urging, Hincmar upheld the first pronouncements of the two courts and stubbornly continued to do so for some time after the pope had succeeded in winning the king's consent to the union, though he was forced to yield in the end.[133]

Hincmar maintained the same position in the case of Louis the Stammerer. He accepted Louis' remarriage because his first union was concluded without paternal consent.[134] The papacy, following the precedent set by Nicholas, refused to acknowledge the relevance of secular customs, and Pope John VIII would not crown the Stammerer's second wife, Adelheid.[135] But the whole problem of defining legal marriage seemed at this point to become secondary to the question of ecclesiastical competence and the greater question of papal authority. Pope John's aggressive assertion that all matrimonial cases were to be judged by the church opened a new era in the history of marriage and divorce. Although in the late ninth and tenth centuries his less energetic successors did not enforce the notion that the pope was the supreme judge in all matrimonial cases, episcopal competence came to be generally accepted by the middle of the tenth century. Apart from the precedent set by ninth-century popes, the weakening of princely power contributed to the disappearance of dual jurisdiction.[136]

Nine hundred years had passed before the church began to move in the direction of claiming sole competence in marital cases. The movement was to be completed with the Gregorian period and the great flowering of canon law in that period. Throughout the middle ages and into modern times there continued to be confusion and debate over the concrete facts of individual marriages, but a firm foundation in law had been laid by the legislators and theologians of the Frankish kingdom. The Carolingian kings and their bishops had moved a great distance in the effort to reconcile secular and ecclesiastical interests in a social institution which must always be compounded of both elements. They had established the Christian principle of marital indissolubility but, at the same time, they had shown a necessary capacity to be flexible in judging complex and dubious cases. The emperors had given way to the jurisdictional claims of a church in which they were themselves active members. But the prelates had shown themselves ready and able to accommodate the realities of a society in which they, too, must live.

NOTES

1. For this investigation, we are greatly indebted to past research in various aspects of the problem from both the fields of canon and civil law, in particular, Esmein's synthesis on marriage in the canon law: *Le mariage en droit canonique,* ed. R. Genestal and J. Dauvillier, 2nd ed. (Paris, 1935); Ignaz Fahrner's *Geschichte des Unauflöslichkeitsprinzips und der vollkommenen Scheidung der Ehe im kanonischen Recht* (Freiburg, 1903); Pierre Daudet's *Etudes sur l'histoire de la juridiction matrimoniale* (Paris, 1933); and the articles by François L. Ganshof, "Le statut de la femme dans la monarchie franque," and by René Metz, "Le statut de la femme en droit canonique médiévale," in Société Jean Bodin, *Recueils* 12 (1962): 5–58, 59–113.

2. Geneviève Serrier, *De quelques recherches concernant le mariage contrat-sacrement et plus particulièrement de la doctrine augustinienne des biens du mariage* (Paris, 1928), Introduction, recounts this history.

3. H. Jelowicz, *Historical Introduction to the Study of Roman Law* (Cambridge, 1932), p. 241; Edoardo Volterra, "La conception du mariage à Rome," *Revue internationale des droits de l'antiquité,* 3rd ser., 2 (1955): 373; Biondo Biondi, *Il diritto romano cristiano* (Milan, 1959), 3:156–62. According to Volterra, "La conception du mariage" p. 378, marriage in postclassical law was no longer founded on the continuing will but on the initial will of the partners, a view that was reflected in imperial legislation against divorce and bigamy. On divorce in Roman law, see *Ad legem Iuliam de adulteriis et de stupro, Codex Iustinianus,* 9.9, ed. P. Krueger (Berlin, 1954), 2: 374.

4. Deuteronomy 21, 23, 24. Cf. Reuven Yaron, "On Divorce in Old Testament Times," *Revue Internationale des droits de l'antiquité,* 3rd ser., 4 (1957): 117–28. On late Jewish law, Serrier, *De quelques recherches,* p. 12. Herbert Preisker, *Christentum und Ehe in der ersten drei Jahrhunderten,* Neuen Studien zur Geschichte der Theologie, ed. R. Seeberg, vol. 23 (Berlin, 1927), pp. 67–99.

5. Matthew 5:31–35, 19:3–12; Mark 10:2–12; Luke 16:18; Matthew 19:9. According to G. H. Joyce, *Christian Marriage,* 2nd ed. rev. (London, 1948), p. 288, the passage could be interpreted as an "exceptive clause" allowing "of a divorce *a mensa et thoro* but not of divorce *a vinculo,*" and also as "an interpolation devoid of authenticity."

6. Paul, I Corinthians, 7.

7. Paul, Ephesians 5:21. The western fathers supported the idea of mutual teaching of husband and wife: Tertullian, *Ad uxorem* 2, 9, in J.-P. Migne, ed. *Patrologiae cursus completus* (Latin Series), vols. 1–222 (Paris, 1844–1864), I: 141B (henceforth cited as *PL*) and in *Corpus Christianorum Series Latina, Tertullian* (henceforth cited as *CCSL*), 1: 393. Ambrose insisted that husband and wife share their religious duties, *De Abraham* 1, 5, 37, in *Corpus Scriptorum Ecclesiasticorum Latinorum* (henceforth cited as *CSEL*), 32, pt. 1: 530.

Tertullian, *Ad uxorem* 2, 6–7 in *CCSL Tertullian,* 1: 393; Ambrose, *Epistola* 42, 3, in *PL*, 16: 1172. On Ambrose's teaching of marriage as a way to salvation, see W. J. Dooley, *Marriage According to St. Ambrose,* Catholic University of America, Studies in Christian Antiquity, vol. 11 (Washington D.C., 1948), pp. 16–30. On patristic teaching, in general, of marriage as a means of sanctification, see L. Godefroy "Mariage dans les pères. Le sacrement." *Dictionnaire de théologie catholique*, ed. A. Vacant *et al.*, (1927), 9: 2105–9; on the application of the term "sacrament" to marriage by the fathers, see Joyce, *Christian Marriage*, 158–68. St. Justin in *Apologia* 1, 29, in Migne, *Patrologia Graeca* (henceforth cited as *PG*), 6: 373, contrasted Christian marriage for the sake of children and Christian continence with pagan corruption. In a similar vein, Minucius Felix, *Octavius*, 31 in *PL*, 3: 351.

8. Victor J. Pospishil, *Divorce and Remarriage* (New York, 1967), pp. 141ff., has assembled patristic texts relevant to this problem to support his argument that the early church allowed divorce and remarriage. In most cases, he admits that he is obliged to argue from silence, so difficult is it to find explicit texts approving remarriage.

9. Basil, *Epistola 188 ad Amphilochium*, 9 in *PG*, 32: 677, acknowledged the legal inequality of sexes as accepted by custom, although he argued that Matthew 19 should logically hold good equally in regard to women and men. Ambrose, *De Abraham* 1, 25 in *CSEL*, 32: 519; Jerome, *Epistola 77 ad Oceanum*, 3, in *PL*, 22: 691; Augustine, *De conjugiis adulterinis*, 1, 8 in *PL*, 40: 456.

10. Ambrosiaster, *Comm. in Epist. ad Cor.* 7, in *PL*, 17: 230.

11. *De Abraham*, 1, 7, 59 in *CSEL*, 32, pt. 1: 541. Ambrose acknowledged that women could divorce their adulterous husbands, *De Abraham* 1, 4, 25, in *CSEL*, 32, pt. 1: 519. That he disapproved of remarriage is evident from *Expositio evangelii Lucae* 8, 6 in *CSEL*, 32, pt. 3: 394. *Commentarium in evangelium Matthei* 3, 19, 9 in *CCSL*, 77: 167. *De nuptiis et concupiscentia*, 1, 10, in *CSEL*, 42: 222. As Fahrner, *Geschichte*, has pointed out, Augustine perceived the difficulty posed by Matthew 19 and solved it by the use of more emphatic passages from Mark 10, 11 and Luke 16, 18 with a strict interpretation of Paul, I Corinthians 7:12. See also Nicholas Ladomersky, *Saint Augustin, docteur du mariage chrétien*, Urbaniana, 5 (Rome, 1942).

12. S. Laeuchli, *Power and Sexuality: the Emergence of Canon Law at the Synod of Elvira* (Philadelphia, 1972), chapter one, has provided an interesting insight into this ambiguity by applying linguistic analysis to the canons. See also *infra*, notes 14–19.

13. I Corinthians 7:15. Grappling with this dispensation, Ambrose argued that Paul did not allow the dissolution of marriages sealed by God, but that he recognized that not all marriages were made by God and those that were not could be dissolved, at least if the unbeliever took the initiative. *Expositio evangelii Lucae*, 8, 2 in *CSEL*, 32, pt. 3: 394. *Concilium Eliberitanum*, canons 10, 15, 16, in *Sacrorum conciliorum nova et amplissima collectio*, ed. G. D. Mansi (henceforth cited as Mansi), 53 vols. (Florence, 1759–1927), 2: 7–8. Canons 15 and 16 prohibit marriages with non-Christians, and canon 10 appears to admit that marriages with non-Christians may be dissolved. For a discussion of this canon, see Joyce, *Christian Marriage*, pp. 505–6. For a comprehensive bibliography on the councils, see J. T. Sawicki, *Bibliographia synodorum particularium*, Monumenta iuris canonici, Ser. C, vol. 2 (Vatican City, 1967.)

14. *Concilium Andegavense*, 6, in *Concilia Galliae A. 314–A. 506*, ed. C. Munier, *CCSL*, 148 (Turnholt, 1963): 138.

15. *Concilium Arelatense*, 10, in *CCSL*, 148: 11.

16. *Codex canonum ecclesiae africanae*, 102, in Mansi 3: 806; and *Canones apostolorum et conciliorum*, ed. H. T. Bruns (Berlin, 1839), 1: 156. On the history of this collection and on the connection of canon 102 with canon 8 of the ninth Carthaginian synod, held in June, 404, see C. H. Hefele, *A History of the Councils*, trans. H. N. Oxenham (Edinburgh, 1896), 2: 440–41, 458–68, 474. This canon came to

be associated with the decrees of the Council of Milevis held in 416, canon 17, in Mansi, 4: 331. For a discussion of the problem and bibliography see *Dictionnaire de théologie catholique* 10, pt. 2 (1928): 1752–58.

17. *Concilium Eliberitanum*, 10, in Mansi, 2: 7. Although the fathers assembled at Elvira were cautious in not prescribing punishments they could not enforce, they tended to support the principle of indissolubility in case of adultery. Canon 70 required men to cast off their adulterous wives, but canon 69 provided equal penalties for men and women caught in adultery. Canon 8 prohibited women leaving their husbands without "preceding cause" and canon 9 prohibited a woman who had left an adulterous baptized husband from marrying another.

18. *Concilium Vernerticum*, 2, in *CCSL*, 148: 152.

19. *Codex canonum ecclesiae africanae*, 102, in Mansi, 3: 806, see note 16 *supra*.

20. See, for example, Innocent I, *Ad Exuperium Episcopum* 4 and 6, in Mansi 3: 1040.

21. *Theodosiani libri XVI*, 3, 16, 1–2, ed. Th. Mommsen and P. Meyer (Berlin, 1905).

22. Provincial governors could take concubines in the provinces where they served, *ibid.*, 25, 7, 5, 2.

23. *Constitutiones sanctorum apostolorum*, 8, 32, in Mansi 1: 579. Although the same admonition was issued by Pope Leo I, he did not exclude a man from communion if he lived with a concubine, *Epistola* 167, in *PL*, 11: 493.

24. Though impediments because of blood relationships were gradually extended under Christian influence, Justinian allowed the marriage of cousins, *Codex Iustinianus, Institutiones*, 1, 10, 4. For an extensive discussion of methods of computation, see Jean Fleury, *Recherches historiques sur les empêchements de parenté dans le mariage canonique des origines aux Fausses Decrétales* (Paris, 1933). The concept of relationship by marriage derived from Leviticus 18: 6–19. The early church extended the definition of incest to include some relatives by marriage on the basis that marriage united the partners in one flesh.

25. Tacitus, *On Britain and Germany*, trans. H. Mattingly (Penguin, 1965), p. 115. On the question of royal polygamy, Tacitus distinguished "his" Germans from other groups as "almost unique among barbarians."

26. Gregory of Tours, *History of the Franks*, 4, 3, trans. E. Brehaut (New York, 1969), p. 75.

27. *Liber historiae francorum*, 31, in *Monumenta Germaniae Historica* (henceforth *MGH*), *Scriptores rerum merovingicarum*, 2: 292. Fleury, *Recherches historiques*, p. 154, specifically discusses the problem of interpreting the Frankish chronicler.

28. The same problem was the subject of a series of queries addressed by St. Augustine of Canterbury to Gregory the Great in the course of the conversion of England. Bede, *Historia ecclesiastica gentes anglorum*, 1, 27. William Chaney, *The Cult of Kingship in Anglo-Saxon England* (Manchester, 1970), pp. 26–27, has amply demonstrated that marriages with relatives by marriage was a common practice among the Germanic tribes, possibly related to ancient laws of inheritance which, in Bede's day, survived only among the Picts.

29. The Council of Orléans (511), canon 18, in *Concilia Galliae, A. 511–A. 695*, ed. C. de Clercq, *CCSL* 148A (Turnholt, 1963): 9–10, prohibited the marriage of the dead brother's wife or the dead wife's sister, but no penalty was listed which Fleury (*Recherches*, p. 56) thought resulted from the bishops' awareness that they could not enforce the law. The Council of Tours (567) canon 22, prohibited marriages of near kin in strong terms, *CCSL*, 148A: 184. The Council of Epaone (517), canon 30, in *CCSL*, 148A: 31–32, included the same relationships and added the mother-in-law

and cousins german to the sixth degree. The canon penalized such marriages only by nullification, allowing the partners to marry again. The same prohibitions were repeated by the Council of Orléans (533), canon 10, in *CCSL*, 148A: 100, called jointly by Clovis' three sons, and by the Council of Clermont (535), canon 12, in *CCSL* 148A: 107–8.

30. Fleury, *Recherches*, p. 110.

31. *Dec. Childeberti*, 1, 2, ed. K. A. Eckhardt, *Lex salica*, in *MGH, Legum Sectio* 1, 4, pt. 2: 176–77; *Lex baiuariorum*, 7, 1, in *MGH, Legum Sectio* 1, 5, pt. 2: 347–48; *Lex alamannorum*, 39, in *MGH, Legum Sectio* 1, 5, pt. 1: 98–99; *Lex visigothorum* 3, 5, 1, in *MGH, Legum Sectio* 1, 1: 159. *Edictus Rothari* 153, in *MGH, Legum Sectio* 1, 4: 35 and also p. 44, art. 185 prohibited marriage with the mother-in-law, the stepmother, the daughter-in-law, and sister-in-law under penalty of separation and loss of half the wife's goods to the king.

32. *MGH, Capitularia regum francorum*, 1: 15.

33. Fredegarius, *Chronica*, 4, 54, in *MGH, Scriptores rerum merovingicarum*, 2: 147.

34. *History of the Franks*, 2, 12, p. 33.

35. Ganshof, "Le statut de la femme," p. 31.

36. *Lex romana visigothorum* 3, 16, 1, ed. G. Haenel (Leipzig, 1849), pp. 92–94. *Leges burgundionum: Lex romana* 31, 3, in *MGH, Legum Sectio* 1, 2: 144.

37. *Lex visigothorum*, 3, 6, 2, in *MGH, Legum Sectio* 1, 1: 169.

38. *Leges burgundionum: Liber constitutionum*, 34, 1, in *MGH, Legum Sectio* 1, 2: 68.

39. *Leges burgundionum: Liber constitutionum*, 34, 3, in *MGH, Legum Sectio* 1, 2: 68.

40. *Leges burgundionum: Liber constitutionum*, 34, 2, in *MGH, Legum Sectio* 1, 2: 68; *Pactus legum alamannorum*, 52, ed. K. A. Eckhardt (Göttingen, 1958), p. 142; *Lex alamannorum*, 52, in *MGH, Legum Sectio* 1, 5, pt. 1: 110–11; *Lex visigothorum*, 3, 6, 1, in *MGH Legum Sectio*, 1, 1: 166–67; *Lex baiuariorum*, 8, 14, in *MGH, Legum Sectio* 1, 5 pt. 2: 359.

41. *Leges burgundionum: Lex romana*, 21, 1, in *MGH, Legum Sectio* 1, 2: 143, acknowledged divorce by mutual consent; its source is *Theodosiani libri XVI*, 3, 16, 1. For the inhabitants of the Merovingian kingdom living under Germanic laws the formulae bear out the practice of divorce by mutual consent: *Formulae Marculfi*, 30 in *MGH, Formulae*, p. 94; reiterated in *Formulae Senonenses*, 47, in *MGH, Formulae*, p. 206; *Formulae Turonenses*, 19, in *MGH, Formulae*, pp. 145–46; *Formulae salicae Merkelianae*, 18, in *MGH, Formulae*, p. 248. Divorce by mutual consent also appeared in *Pactus legum alamannorum*, 3, 2, in *MGH, Legum Sectio* 1, 3: 38; The subject is more extensively discussed by V. Hubert Richardot, *Les pactes de séparation amiable des époux* (Paris, 1930).

42. *Concilium Agathense* (506), canon 25, in *CCSL*, 148: 204. But an instance of restriction which may have been influenced by the church was introduced by Chindaswinth who prohibited a person from remarrying if the spouse entered a monastery, K. Zeumer, *Neues Archiv* 24 (1899): 627.

43. *Concilium Aurelianense*, 13, in *MGH, Concilia*, 1:63 and *CCSL*, 148A: 8. The twenty canons attributed to the Council of Nantes (658) have been shown to date from the ninth century by E. Seckel, "Studien zu Benediktus Levita I," *Neues Archiv* 26 (1901): 39f. The conclusion of Joyce, *Christian Marriage*, p. 337, that we do not have sufficient evidence to believe that the Merovingian bishops did not raise protest against divorce seems to rest on tenuous ground.

44. The permutation in the laws regarding the bride-price, whereby the price given by the groom to the bride's family was slowly transformed into a settlement on

the bride herself, is traced by Louis-Maurice-André Cornuey, *Le régime de la dos aux époques mérovingienne et carolingienne* (Thèse, Univ. d'Alger, 1929).

45. *Lex salica*, Text D, 15, 1, in *MGH, Legum Sectio* 1, 4, pt. 2: 54–55 compensated an injured husband with two hundred solidi. But if a bridegroom changed his mind and broke the engagement, he had to pay only sixty-two and a half solidi, *Lex salica*, 17 in *MGH, Legum Sectio* 1, 4, pt. 2: 168–69. A further law, *Lex alamannorum*, 51, in *MGH, Legum Sectio* 1, 2 pt. 1: 85 provided that a woman who broke her engagement and married another must pay three hundred solidi and her husband was required to prove that he was unaware of her prior engagement. If he could not prove it, he was subject to the death penalty.

46. W. Rullkoetter, "The Legal Protection of Woman Among the Ancient Germans" (Ph.D. Dissertation, University of Chicago, 1900), argues that these laws aimed at safeguarding the honor of free maidens, but the texts are more concerned with the honor of the family. On the punishment of rape, see Ganshof, "Le statut de la femme," p. 44, and n. 117 for further studies.

47. *Lex saxonum*, 40, in *MGH, Legum Sectio* 1, 5: 69–70. Frisian law, likewise, required that the abductor give the bride price to the family if he had not obtained their consent: *Lex frisionum*, 9, 1, in *MGH, Legum Sectio* 1, 3: 664.

48. *Lex anglorum*, 47, in *MGH, Legum Sectio* 1, 5: 135–36. A similar penalty was prescribed by Roman Law according to Merêa, "Le mariage 'sine consensu parentum' dans le droit romain vulgaire occidental," *Revue internationale des droits de l'antiquité* 5 (1950): 203–17. *Lex visigothorum*, 3, 1, 2, 7 in *MGH, Legum Sectio* 1, 1: 99–100. If the girl was betrothed and took another man against the will of her parents, she was to be given with her husband into the power of the man whom she had jilted. If her parents were implicated, they had to pay a pound of gold to the king.

49. *Leges burgundionum liber constitutionum*, 12, 1–4; 44, 1, in *MGH, Legum Sectio* 1, 2, pt. 1: 51, 74, tripled the *wittemon* if the union took place without parental consent. If the girl did not consent, the abductor had to pay the *wittemon* nine-fold but only six-fold if he returned her uncorrupted. Ripuarian law was slightly more lenient, requiring the raptor only to pay the equivalent of the bride gift, *Lex ribuaria*, 35, 2 in *MGH, Legum Sectio* 1, 5: 228.

50. *Formulae Turonenses*, 16, in *MGH, Formulae*, p. 143; *Formulae Marculfi* 2, 16, in *MGH, Formulae*, p. 8. The view that marriage was also invalid among Visigoths without a *dos*, which was upheld by A. Lemaire, "Origine de la règle 'Nullum sine dote fiat conjugium,'" *Mélanges Paul Fournier* (Paris, 1929), p. 421, is disputed by P. D. King, *Law and Society in the Visigothic Kingdom* (Cambridge, 1972), p. 225, n. 4.

51. Boniface's letters, *MGH, Epistolae merowingici et karolini aevi*, 1: 215 ff. give ample evidence of the sorry state of the Frankish kingdom. Evidence for some limited conciliar activity during the latter part of the seventh century has been found and collected by C. de Clercq, the editor of the *Concilia Galliae, A. 511–A. 695*, *CCSL*, 148A.

52. *Epistolae* 26, 50, 51, *MGH, Epistolae merowingici et karolini aevi*, 1: 276, 299–304.

53. Canons 4, 5, 6, 7, 8, 9, in Mansi, 12: 263. Fleury, *Recherches historiques*, p. 136, has suggested that the Roman legislation aimed at conformity with that of the Byzantine church and therefore *cognatus* meant any relative of the wife. Esmein, *Le mariage*, p. 421, preferred the strict interpretation, brother-in-law.

54. Canon 5 in *MGH, Concilium II: Concilium aevi Karolini*, 1: 13–14. *Capitulare Pippini Regis*, anno 754–55, *MGH, Capitularia regum francorum*, 1: 31. Fleury, *Recherches historique*, 180, n. 23, discusses the problems involved in dating this capitulary, connecting it to the council of Compiègne held in 757.

55. Fleury, *Recherches historiques*, 183f. discussed the incest legislation of these councils in detail.

56. Compiègne (757), canon 13 provided that if a man violated his son's betrothed, neither he nor the girl could ever marry, although the son, if he were not party to the crime, could contract another union. Canon 17 required the dissolution of the marriage of a man who had sexual relations with a mother and a daughter and then subsequently married. His wife could remarry but he had to remain celibate; the mother and daughter could marry if they had been unaware of the incest, but once they knew of it, they had to leave their husbands and do penance, while their husbands could remarry. See also canon 18, referring to sexual unions with two sisters. *MGH, Capitularia regum francorum*, 1: 38–39.

57. Rome's unyielding attitude in cases of affinity is seen in Pope Zachary's letter to Pepin in 747, prohibiting the union of a woman to two brothers, a man to his god-daughter, and her mother, etc. based on canon 2 of Neocaesarea, in Mansi, 12: 326 and *PL*, 89: 930; no. 2277 in P. Jaffé and P. Ewald, *Regesta pontificum romanorum* (Leipzig, 1888), vol. 2; henceforth cited as "J. E." followed by number of document.

58. Verberie (756), *MGH, Capitularia regum francorum*, 1: 40.

59. This date is supported by H. Wurm, *Studien und Texte zur Dekretalensammlung des Dionysius Exiguus* (Amsterdam, 1964), p. 33. F. Maasen, *Geschichte der Quellen und Litteratur des kanonischen Rechts im Abendland bis zum Ausgang des Mittelalters* (Graz, 1870), 1:469, thought that the collection was received at the Synod of Aachen in 802.

60. *Capitulare missorum generale* (802), 33, *MGH, Capitularia regum francorum*, 1:97; on Charlemagne's incest regulation see Fleury, *Recherches*, pp. 202–13.

61. *Capitulare Haristallense* (779), *Forma communis*, 5, *MGH, Capitularia regum francorum*, 1: 48. *Capitulatio de partibus Saxoniae*, 20, *MGH, Capitularia regum francorum*, 1: 69. *Capitulare missorum generale* (802), 33, *MGH, Capitularia regum francorum*, 1: 97.

62. *Concilium Cabillonense* (813), 31, in *MGH, Concilium*, 2: 279.

63. *MGH, Epistolae merowingici et karolini aevi*, 1: 278; J. E., 2174 (1667). Fahrner, *Geschichte der Ehescheidung*, p. 83 showed that Pope Alexander III interpreted this to refer to a union which was never consummated and added that even if the marriage were consummated, Pope Gregory was merely giving a dispensation to a specific individual. Fahrner, therefore, believed that it was not intended to change the general position of the church.

64. *Concilium Suessionense* (744), canon 9, in *MGH, Concilium*, 2: 35.

65. *MGH, Epistolae merowingici et karolini aevi*, 1: 348 and 1: 482; J. E. 2278 and 2277.

66. A capitulary of Carloman at this period gave bishops jurisdiction over incest and adultery cases: *Karlmanni principis capitulare Liptinense, an.* 743, 3, in *MGH, Capitularia regum francorum*, 1: 28. Daudet, *Jurisdiction matrimoniale*, p. 37, n. 3, dates this capitulary in 743 or 745. Pepin, however, did not emulate his brother and treated these offenses as subject to secular authority. The property of the offenders was to be confiscated or, if they had no property, they were either to be imprisoned or flogged according to their status. *Capitulare Pippini regis, 754–55*, 1, in *MGH, Capitularia regum francorum*, 1: 31. See note 41 *supra* for references to formulae for divorce by mutual consent.

67. Pope Stephen III, *MGH, Epistolae merowingici et karolini aevi*, 1: 560 reminded Charlemagne and Carloman that Pope Stephen II had persuaded their father not to divorce their mother Bertrada.

68. Cap. 5, 9, 16, 19, 20, 21, in *MGH, Capitularia regum francorum*, 1: 37–39.

69. On penitential literature in general see P. Fournier and G. Le Bras, *Histoire des collections canoniques en occident depuis les Fausses Décretales* (Paris, 1931), 1: 107 and H. J. Schmitz, *Die Bussbücher und die Bussdisziplin der Kirche* (1883; reprint ed., Graz, 1958). For rules concerning divorce and remarriage in the penitentials, Daudet, *Jurisdiction matrimoniale*, pp. 61–64.

70. *Penitentiale Egberti*, 1, 19, 26 in Mansi, 12: 438; and *Exceptiones* 122–23 in Mansi 12: 424. Also edited by F. W. H. Wasserschleben, *Die Bussordungen der abendländischen Kirche* (1851), pp. 231–47, who believed it was composed in the Frankish kingdom. See also Fournier and Le Bras, *Histoire des collections*, 1: 316–20. *Concilium Romanum* (826) 36 in *MGH, Concilium*, 2: 582.

71. G. H. Pertz, *MGH, Legum* 2, pt. 2: 17 has it among spurious documents, but the council is not regarded as spurious by A. Dumas in his article on Pope Eugenius II in *Dictionnaire d'histoire et de géographie écclésiastique* 15 (1963): 1347–49. Cap. 36 was incorporated in *Hlotharii imperatoris capitula langobardica: exerpta canonum* 1, in *MGH, Legum*, 1: 372.

72. *Admonitio generalis* (789), 43 in *MGH, Capitularia regum francorum*, 1: 56; included in *Dionysio-Hadriana* and also in the extracts for the *Dionysians* sent to Pepin by Pope Zachary.

73. *Concilium Forojuliense*, c. 10, in *MGH, Concilium*, 2: 192 and in Mansi 13: 849. H. Barion, *Das fränkisch-deutsche Synodalrecht des Frühmittelalters*, Kanonische Studien und texte, ed. A. M. Königen, 5–6 (Bonn and Köln, 1931): 222, n. 24, said that this council was convoked by Charles to reform the Italian church.

74. *Capitulare missorum* (802) 22, in *MGH, Capitularia regum francorum*, 1: 103. The same principle was reiterated by a member of Charlemagne's court, Theodulf of Orléans (790–818), in his *Capitulare* in *PL*, 105: 213.

75. Einhard, *Life of Charlemagne*, trans. L. Thorpe (London, 1970), p. 58. Pepin is mentioned in another context as being the son of a concubine, *ibid.*, p. 60.

76. *Codex Carolinus*, 45 in *MGH, Epistolae merowingici et karolini aevi*, 1: 560–63; J. E. 2381.

77. *MGH, Epistolae merowingici et karolini aevi*, 1: 561.

78. Einhard, *Life of Charlemagne*, p. 58.

79. Notkar the Stammerer, *Charlemagne*, trans. L. Thorpe (Penguin, 1971), p. 162.

80. Paschasius Radbertus, *Life of Saint Adelard*, trans. A. Cabaniss (Syracuse, 1967), 7: 29.

81. On the significance of the reforms of these four synods of Toulouse, Mayence, Lyon, and Paris, see Barion, *Das fränkisch-deutsche Synodalrecht*, pp. 257–58.

82. *Concilium Parisiense* (829) 3, 2, in *MGH, Concilium*, 2: 671 and in Mansi, 14: 596. See also *Addimenta ad Hludowici Pii capitularia*, 54, 20 in *MGH, Capitularia regum francorum*, 2: 46.

83. *Episcoporum ad Hludovicum imperatorem relatio*, 55 in *MGH, Capitularia regum francorum*, 2: 46. *Capitularia pro lege habendum Wormatiense*, 3 in *MGH, Capitularia regum francorum*, 2: 18.

84. In 818-19, *Capitulare ecclesiasticum* 24, in *MGH, Capitularia regum francorum*, 1: 279, addressed itself to the problem of the rape of a betrothed girl, citing the council of Ancyra that the rapist must restore the girl to her fiancé and must undergo public penance even if the girl had consented. The rapist and the girl could not marry under pain of anathema, though she could marry her former fiancé if he was willing to accept her or another man if she had not consented to the rape. *Capitula legibus addenda* 9, of the same year in *MGH, Capitularia regum francorum*,

1: 282, stipulated that the raptor must pay the groom *(sponsus)* a composition according to his law and sixty additional solidi to the king. If he refused he would be exiled and could not have the woman.

85. *MGH, Epistolae Karolini aevi*, 3: 446-47.

86. *MGH, Capitularia regum francorum*, 2: 18.

87. *Concilium Cabillonense* (813), c. 18 in *MGH, Concilium*, 2: 277, on the interpretation of this article, see Daudet, *Recherches historiques*, p. 44, n. 2.

The Council of Tours (813), 41, called for secular coercion of those incestuous parties who were not willing to listen to the admonitions of piety, in *MGH, Concilium*, 2: 292. The same plea for secular coercion was reiterated in 826. *Concilium Ingelheimense*, 13, in *MGH, Concilium*, 2: 552.

88. *Concilium Turonense*, 41, in *MGH, Concilium*, 2: 292.

89. Hincmar of Reims, *De divortio*, in *PL*, 125: 655 A-B.

90. Sources on Judith are generally hostile but the story is outlined in *The Anonymous Life of Louis the Pious*, in *Son of Charlemagne*, ed. A. Cabaniss (Syracuse, 1965).

91. See K. F. Morrison, *The Two Kingdoms* (Princeton, 1964) and W. Ullmann, *The Growth of Papal Government in the Middle Ages*, 2nd ed. (London, 1962), pp. 219ff.

92. *Capitula in synodo acta . . . apud Meldensem urbem* (845), 71, in *MGH, Capitularia regum francorum* 2: 415.

93. *Epistola Synodi Carisiacensis ad Hludovicum regem Germaniae directa* (858), 7 in *MGH Capitularia regum francorum*, 2: 432. *Conventus Suessionensis* (853), 11 in *MGH Capitularia regum francorum*, 2: 266.

94. The Council of Mainz, convened in 852, added penance and perpetual celibacy to the sentence of exile which was delivered by the king against a certain Albgis who publicly abducted the wife of Patricius; *Concilium Moguntium*, 11, in *MGH, Capitularia regum francorum*, 2: 189.

95. In cases of abduction, the council did not insist on the dissolution of the resulting marriage even though the woman had previously been engaged, so long as penance was performed and the injured *sponsus* suitably compensated. Moreover, a man accused of rape could clear himself by furnishing proofs of his innocence or be defending himself according to canonical rules: *Concilium Meldense Parisiense*, 68, in *MGH, Capitularia regum francorum*, 2: 414. Canon 69, in *MGH, Capitularia regum francorum*, 2: 414, imposed a purely canonical requirement on the secular courts in cases of adultery to encompass the possibility that an adulterous woman might marry her lover after her husband's death. If, in consequence, the second husband were accused of adultery, he must do public penance after which he might reunite with the woman provided that neither "are suspected of having murdered the deceased of their marriage." But if murder were proved, then both must submit to perpetual penance without hope of being reunited. If the man denied that he committed adultery with the woman while her husband was alive and that either was party to the homicide, and if neither could be convicted with suitably tested witnesses, they would be allowed to purge themselves legally of the aspersion of rumor and be reunited if, as we have said, no other impediment stood in the way of their marriage.

96. Rudolf von Scherer, *Über das Eherecht bei Benedict Levita und Pseudo-Isidor* (Graz, 1879), discussed the broader problems of marriage law in both sources. For indissolubility: *Benedicti capitularia* 2, 87, 191, 209, 235; 3, 73, 179, in *MGH, Legum*, 2 (pars altera): 77, 83, 84, 85, 107, 113. Pseudo-Evaristus, *Epistola 4*, in *Decretales Pseudo-Isidorianae*, ed. Hinschius, p. 90. On this collection, see Schafer Williams, *Codices pseudo-Isidorianae*, Monumenta iuris canonici, ser. C, vol. 3 (New

York, 1971). See also *Ansegisi capitularium*, 42, in *MGH, capitularia regum francorum*, 1: 400.

97. Hincmar's position in the case was described by Flodoard, *Historia Remensis ecclesiae* 3, 10, 21, 28, in *MGH, Scriptores*, 13: 483, 518.

98. *Concilium Moguntinum* 12, *MGH, Capitularia regum francorum*, 2: 189.

99. *Epistola* 22, *Collectio Brittaniae*, ed. P. Ewald, *Neues Archiv* 5 (1880): 385-86. For Hincmar's relations with Leo IV, see *Hincmari regesta*, 15, 28, 44, 50-54, 61, 62, ed. H. Schors in *Hinkmar, Erzbischof von Rheims* (Freiburg i. B., 1884), which is still the best published account of Hincmar's life.

100. Esmein, *Le mariage*, 2: 125-39 showed that the church sometimes regarded concubinage as a legal union and therefore indissoluble but at other points maintained that the relationship must either be legitimated by marriage or abandoned.

101. *De divortio Lotharii et Tetbergae*, in *PL*, 125: 649 A-B. Hincmar was drawing his definition almost verbatim from Pseudo-Evaristus, *Epistola* 2, in *Decretales Pseudo-Isidorianae*, p. 87.

102. Daudet, *Jurisdiction matrimoniale*, p. 95, gives date 855, while C. E. Smith, *Papal Enforcement of Some Medieval Marriage Laws* (Ph.D. Dissertation, Louisiana State University, 1940) gives 857 as the date of the marriage following Regino Prumiensis, *Chronicon*, in *MGH, Scriptores*, 1: 571, which is not as reliable as Hincmar's own *De divortio*, in *PL*, 125: 619-772. Smith failed to consult the two basic studies on the affair, Max Sdralek, *Hinkmar von Rheims kanonistisches Gutachten über die Ehescheidung des Königs Lothar II* (Freiburg i. B., 1881) and R. Parisot, *Le royaume de Lorraine sous les Carolingiens, 843-923* (Paris, 1889), pp. 83-88, 143-324, and some other accounts listed by Daudet, *Jurisdiction matrimoniale*, p. 94, n. 2. See also C. Brühl, "Hincmariana, II. Hinkmar im Widerstreit von kanonischen Recht und Politik in Ehefragen," *Deutsches Archiv* 20 (1964): 55-77.

103. *De divortio*, in *PL*, 125: 629C-D.

104. *Annales Bertiniani* (858) in *MGH, Scriptores*, 1: 450.

105. *De divortio*, in *PL*, 125: 630C-632B; 636A-637B. On the threat of torture, *De divortio*, in *PL*, 125: 641B; at least, that was what she told Pope Nicholas. See his letter in *PL*, 119: 1179-80.

106. *De divortio*, in *PL*, 125: 639D. On the king's request for remarriage, see *De divortio* in *PL*, 125: 641B. See also *MGH, Capitularia regum francorum*, 2: 463-69, for records of the two synods and for an additional document of 865 concerning the affair. In addition to Hincmar's treatise, there are two other treatises extant in Mansi, 15: 626-39, attributed by Sdralek to Adventius, bishop of Metz. According to E. Dümmler, *Geschichte des ostfränkischen Reiches* (Berlin, 1862), 1: 476 n. 6, Arnulf bishop of Toul and Hougue bishop of Utrecht, also wrote against the dissolution of the marriage.

107. *De divortio*, in *PL*, 125: 680C.

108. Hincmar's letter to Adventius explaining his absence is included in *De divortio*, in *PL*, 125: 646-647D.

109. *Ibid.*, 646A.

110. Hincmar discussed the juridical problems presented by the situation extensively in *De divortio*, in *PL*, 125: 634B, 639D-640A, 644C, 658D, 672D-673A, 680D, 682B, 687A.

111. Sdralek, *Hinkmar*, pp. 16-17. Brühl, "Hincmariana," pp. 56-57, argues that Waldrada was not a mere concubine but was bound to Lothar in "germanischer Friedelehe." The fact that she was of noble birth and bore the king several children may explain why Lothar's own bishops were sympathetic to the king's desire to marry her. But notwithstanding Waldrada's birth and her "Friedelehe," she was not

legally married to Lothar (although when all arguments for an annulment failed, Lothar tried to use this one). The dispute was over the annulment of his marriage to Tetberga, a fact that Brühl acknowledges in a footnote, 13a, p. 59. Since Hincmar was willing to concede that the marriage may be annulled, he could hardly be called a political opportunist. See also *De divortio, PL*, 125: 736D.

112. *De divortio*, in *PL*, 125: 695C.
113. Daudet, *Jurisdiction matrimoniale*, p. 143.
114. *De divortio*, in *PL*, 125: 658B.
115. *De divortio*, in *PL*, 125: 645A.
116. *De divortio*, in *PL*, 125: 736D.
117. *De divortio*, in *PL*, 125: 652C. For further discussion of the "sacerdotalis or episcopalis conscientia," see Daudet, *Jurisdiction matrimoniale*, pp. 119 ff. *Epistola* 1, 17; 1, 31 in *MGH, Epistolarum 6: Karolini aevi*, 4: 321, 330.
118. The following letters by Nicholas are listed on the subject of Lothar's divorce: J. E., 2725, 2752, 2755, 2758, 2764, 2766, 2768, 2788, 2870, 2871, 2872, 2873, 2874, 2878.
119. The Synod of Metz was condemned for violation of the orders of the Apostolic See and their acts were annulled "just like the robber synod of Ephesus." The pope reported these acts in a long series of letters to Charles the Bald, Louis the German and the Frankish, German, and Lotharingian bishops: Hincmar, *Annales*, in *MGH, Scriptores*, 1: 460–61. Lothar's main supporters, Gunther and Thietgadus, were summoned to Rome where they were placed under anathema. To Lothar himself the pope wrote denouncing his lust and the indignity he had inflicted on Tetberga. Convinced that the charges against her were fraudulent and that she had confessed under duress, Nicholas ordered Lothar to dismiss Waldrada and restore Tetberga under threat of excommunication and deposition, *Epistolae* 58, 59, in *PL*, 119: 869–70; J. E., 2755.
120. In 865, under pressure from his uncles, Lothar compiled. See *Relatio de Theutbergae receptione scripta*, in *MGH, Capitularia regum francorum*, 2: 468–69. But in 869 he again attempted to seek dissolution and coerced Tetberga to request separation from the pope on the ground that she was childless and wished to enter a monastery, *Epistola* 146 in *PL*, 119: 1136–38; J. E., 2870. Nicholas answered that childlessness was not a cause for separation and that Lothar could not remarry if Tetberga took the veil but must remain celibate, *PL*, 119: 1146; J. E., 2871.
121. Hincmar, *Annales* in *MGH, Scriptores*, 1: 462; Regino Prumiensis, *Chronicon, MGH, Scriptores*, 1: 580; and *MGH, Epistolarum 5: Epistolae karolini aevi*, 3: 269.
122. In his *Responsio ad consulta bulgarorum*, 26, 28, in *MGH, Epistolarum 6: Epistolae karolini aevi*, 4: 580. Nicholas acknowledged lay competence to judge adultery. A bishop could interfere only if the accused sought asylum in a church. Some rule applied to incest, although it is preferable to give preference to ecclesiastical jurisdiction in this instance.
123. *De divortio*, in *PL*, 125: 654D. In the case of Northilda, *PL*, 125: 655. Our point is supported by Esmein's observation, *Le mariage*, 1: 23, n. 2.
124. See bibliography on this affair in K. Hefele and H. Leclercq, *Histoire des conciles* (Paris, 1911), 4: 248ff. Nicholas wrote to Hincmar and Charles the Bald in 860; to Ado of Vienne in 863; to Louis the German and to the German clergy in 867. See nos. 1, 2, 18, 49, in *MGH, Epistolarum*, 6: 267–68, 286, 333.
125. *Epistola* 24, in *PL*, 126: 154–61. The father-in-law may have been Raymond, Count of Toulouse, see Daudet, *Jurisdiction matrimoniale*, p. 123, n. 2.
126. *De nuptiis* in *PL*, 126: 132C–153C.
127. See Esmein, *Le mariage*, 1: 160, on this point.

128. *De nuptiis*, in *PL*, 126: 134D and 143A.

129. Judith was already the source of some embarrassment to her father and was in confinement as a result. Having gone to England as the wife of King Aethelwulf of Wessex after a marriage celebrated in France by Hincmar himself, she remained after her husband's death and married his son Aethelbald. The biographer of her stepson Alfred the Great, Asser, was shocked by the marriage and apparently the Franks were even more deeply upset; see Duckett, *Carolingian Portraits*, pp. 219–20. Judith's life has been treated by H. Sprömberg, "Judith, Königin von England, Gräfin von Flandern" *Revue belge de philologie et d'histoire* 15 (1936): 397ff, 915ff. Chaney, *Cult of Kingship*, discusses the implications of this marriage in terms of the requirements of pagan cults. The incest which she had presumably committed was completely ignored by Hincmar in discussing her marriage to Baldwin, possibly because her father did not wish to diminish her chances to marry someone else.

130. Hincmar, *Annales* (862–63), in *MGH, Scriptores*, 1: 456, 462.

131. Under secular law her father claimed that as a widow she was under his paternal *mundium* and the *tuitio* of the church. *Hludowici, Karoli et Hlotharii II, Conventus apud Saponarias* 5, in *MGH, Capitularia regum francorum*, 2: 160.

132. *MGH, Epistolarum*, 6: 272; no. 7, to Charles the Bald, 23 November 862; p. 274, no. 8, to Judith's mother dated 24 November 862; p. 360-61, no. 57, to the synod of Soissons dated 3 April 863; and p. 369, no. 60 to Charles the Bald dated 3 April 863. See also p. 275, no. 9, where he interceded on behalf of Charles' son who married likewise without paternal consent.

133. *Epistola* 2, in *PL*, 126: 26A; J. E., 2741. Also E. Duckett, *Carolingian Portraits*, p. 222.

134. Jean Devisse, in his "Hincmar Archevêque de Paris, 842–882" (Thèse, Sorbonne, 1972), p. 523, reached the conclusion that the Archbishop's attitude was enigmatic. Brühl, *Hincmariana*, assembled with great care all the evidence relating to this case. K. F. Werner, "Die Nachkommen Karls der Grossen bis um Jahr 1000," *Karl der Grosse* (Düsseldorf, 1967), 4: 439ff., disputed Brühl's dating of the Stammerer's second marriage but supported his conclusion that Hincmar was a politician who simply waived canon law when expedient. This interpretation can be disputed by the statement of Regino Prumiensis (864), in *MGH, Scriptores*, 1: 590: "Sed quia sine genitoris conscientia et voluntatis consensu suis amplexibus sociaverat, ab ipso patre ei postmodum est interdicta, et ab eius consortio in perpetuum separata." As both Devisse and Brühl have pointed out, Louis probably decided entirely on his own to divorce Ansgar, but this does not vitiate Regino's statement, for Louis probably blamed the whole affair on his father. Hincmar implied that the marriage was concluded without paternal consent for in 862 Louis was in rebellion against his father. But the same year, father and son reconciled and Charles instructed Louis "cum uxore de Neustria ad se venire . . .," *Annales Bertiniani* (862), in *MGH, Scriptores*, 1: 458. This is the last reference Hincmar made to Ansgar. Much later, he noted that Louis could not persuade the pope to crown his second wife, *Annales Bertiniani* (882), in *MGH, Scriptores*, 1: 508. We know from Flodoard that Hincmar felt obliged to explain to Ansgar's sons, Carlomann and Louis, why he did not object to their mother's repudiation, *Historia Remensis ecclesiae*, 3, 19, in *MGH, Scriptores*, 13: 510. Unfortunately this letter is not extant.

135. The differences between papal interpretation of ecclesiastical competence and that of Hincmar was accentuated under John VIII. Both K. T. Morrison, *The Two Kingdoms*, pp. 264ff. and W. Ullmann, *The Growth of Papal Government*, pp. 219ff. have discussed the pope's tendency to uphold papal supremacy in ecclesiastical and temporal affairs. His letters to the Frankish and German bishops show his desire to attribute exclusive jurisdiction over matrimony to the Roman church: nos. 154, 156,

159, 195, 294 in *MGH, Epistolae,* 7: 129, 130–31, 156, 256. On John's sources, see P. Ewald, *Neues Archiv* 5 (1879): 505–96. Though he left it to bishops to verify facts and judge whether the laws of the church had been transgressed on adultery, repudiation, or incest, he did not always sustain their verdict in handling appeals (though he did in *Epistola* 154). Some cases were returned for further investigation and deliberation (nos. 156–59) and at least one case was reversed.

    136. P. Daudet, *L'éstablissement de la compétance de l'église en matière de divorce et de consanguinité* (Paris, 1941). In *Jurisdiction matrimoniale,* the same author has shown that the Rhenish councils of the late ninth century, especially Mayence (888) and Tribur (895), upheld ecclesiastical precedence in matrimonial cases. So did Regino of Prüm in his *De synodalibus causa.* The weakening of princely power in the course of the tenth century contributed to the disappearance of dual jurisdiction, and both in France and Italy synods of bishops became solely competent to judge such cases. On this see Esmein, *Le mariage,* 1: 27–29.

Barbara A. Hanawalt

⇢✣ The Female Felon in Fourteenth-Century England

Lies, tears and spinning are the things God gives
By nature to a woman, while she lives.
> Geoffrey Chaucer, *The Canterbury Tales,*
> tr. Neville Coghill (London, 1951), p. 287.

Although a murderess occasionally finds her place in fourteenth-century crime, she is less common than the thief, the burglar, or the receiver of stolen goods. Furthermore, female felons appear considerably less frequently than males both in medieval court records and also in modern British and American criminal statistics. Because the crime pattern of women differs somewhat from that of men in amount, methods, motivation, and types of crimes, a special study of their criminality is warranted. Such a study gives valuable information on at least one aspect of women's activity in medieval society and is also helpful in giving an historical perspective to modern criminal statistics.

Medieval records are rich in information on the foibles, transgressions and crimes of the medieval populace. Court rolls from all jurisdictional levels have been preserved: for this study, three types are employed. The chief source will be the gaol delivery rolls for 1300–48 from the counties of Norfolk, Yorkshire, and Northamptonshire.[1] These rolls yield a total of about 10,500 felony cases. Gaol delivery was a royal circuit court with jurisdiction over felony cases: larceny, robbery, burglary, arson, receiving,

Originally published in *Viator: Medieval & Renaissance Studies,* vol. 5, pp. 253–68, edited by Lynn White. Copyright © 1974 by the Regents of the University of California; reprinted by permission of the University of California Press. I would like to thank the American Philosophical Society for the financial aid they have given me through the Penrose Fund and also the American Association of University Women for their aid in 1968–69 with the Irma E. Voight Fellowship.

rape, homicide, and some minor treason cases such as counterfeiting. In addition to these rolls, I have used the coroners' rolls for the counties of Bedfordshire and Northamptonshire.[2] The county coroners were crown officials whose duty was to investigate all violent or suspicious deaths and to hold an inquest to determine the cause of death, murderer (if any), and motive. These records, while not as complete as gaol delivery, are very valuable for their full descriptions of the circumstances surrounding homicides. Finally, I have used the court records of two manorial courts to provide some information on misdemeanors and more minor offenses.[3] In all of these records, the women who appear are most often peasants and villagers.[4]

The court rolls provide information on the ratio of men to women accused of crimes, acquittal-conviction ratios, types of crimes committed and goods stolen, and even on cooperation in crime. Generally, however, they stop short of telling why a person did the deed or anything about the accused's background. Putting all the bits of evidence together, one can reach tentative conclusions about the motivations for female crime, describe the types of crimes women committed, their methods and their treatment by the law.

A consideration of the medieval feloness must begin with the problem of her relative infrequency in criminal statistics. In Norfolk, Yorkshire and Northamptonshire between 1300–48 there was only one woman to every nine men accused of felony. It is surprising how little this ratio has changed over the centuries. In modern Britain the ratio is 1:7.4, and in America in 1955 the ratio was 1:8.[5] The apparently low criminality among women has led to much speculation among criminologists not only about the nature of the female offender but also about the reliability of the criminal statistics. Are women, indeed, the gentle creatures that chivalric literature of all centuries assumed them to be, or do they commit just as many crimes as men but get caught less frequently?

Those who claim that women are less criminal than men base their arguments either on the assumption that women's psychological drives make them gentle and motherly or that, culturally, women are taught to take a less aggressive and more subordinate role in society.[6] In terms of their crime pattern, the first argument suggests that women are, by their instinctual makeup, not prone to violence and antisocial behavior. Coupled with this mild-mannered psychological portrait is that of comparative physical weakness which, before the days of the gun, limited the crimes women could commit. On the other side are those who claim that in crime, as in all other aspects of life, women have been forced into a submissive, nonaggressive role. Women, therefore, commit fewer crimes than men because it is less culturally acceptable for them to do so. As the criminologist W. A. Bonger concludes: "[Women's] smaller criminality is like the health of a hothouse plant; it is due not to innate qualities, but to the hothouse which protects it from harmful influences."[7]

The effects of either psychological or cultural factors on female criminality in the middle ages is impossible even to speculate on at this time. No systematic or exhaustive study has been done on the role of women in medieval society.[8] The literary, chronicle, and letter sources provide conflicting images of women. On the one hand there are the helpless damsels in courtly romances who are prone to victimization by dragons, while on the other hand there are women like Margaret Paston, who commanded the defense of a manor house against siege, or like the wife of Edward II, who led a successful coup d'etat. Ecclesiastical texts. biased the case against women by starting all arguments with Eve. In manorial records, however, women appear in a variety of capacities as property owners, brewers, bakers, cultivators, weavers and plaintiffs or defendants in business matters. Certainly, the illuminations of peasant women hard at work in the fields should eliminate the argument that physical weakness was a major deterrent to women in crime. But the lack of information on the role and social attitudes of medieval women need not deter the present study. Even modern criminal researchers, who have the advantage of being able to interview prisoners and consult voluminous studies on the position of women in society, are reluctant to argue conclusively for either the nature or the nurture explanation.

Another common explanation for the paucity of female offenders is that women are more able to conceal their crimes than men. For instance, very few cases of women killing newborn children appear in either the coroners' rolls or in gaol delivery, and yet one assumes that unwanted babies were sometimes killed. We cannot know how many mothers, like the peasant woman in Pearl Buck's *The Good Earth*, suffocated their children at birth and then claimed that the child was stillborn. The manorial records indicate that many of the lesser antisocial acts were concealed. Petty thefts were called trespass, assaults on children regarded as disciplinary, and even the prostitute could claim to be a housekeeper, as is shown in a Waksfield case:

> The Earl's villeins of Stanley complain, as they have frequently done before, that Richard del Ker has lived an incestuous life among them, and has allowed a harlot, forbidden by the Steward, to return again, the penalty assigned being 40s. He was, therefore, attached and came, saying it was true that the harlot lived in the house with him, to bring up his children but he had no relations with her. An inquisition is taken of the whole graveship, who find otherwise.[9]

But whether felonies were as easily concealed as misdemeanors or more women than men hid illegal acts is certainly not clear in the records.

The one explanation for the lower incidence of women than men in criminal records, which can be documented in both medieval and modern statistics, is that the courts treated women more leniently. Fewer women than men are arrested and, even when they are brought into courts, they are more likely to be acquitted. Medieval English juries and judges were no exception to this rule: of the women tried in gaol delivery 83.7 percent were acquitted compared to 70.3 percent of the men.[10] If trial juries showed a reluctance to convict women, then indicting juries and local officials responsible for making the arrests may have been less anxious to indict women. Indeed, since there was often an overlap of personnel on the two juries, we may regard this as a safe assumption. Thus, fewer women would appear in the courts. One cannot, therefore, trust the criminal statistics on the number of female offenders. This does not mean that we must dismiss the possibility that instinctual and cultural factors played a role in limiting female criminality, but the effects of these factors cannot be tested with the type of information available. An analysis of the types of crimes women committed and their methods and motivations will, however, give some idea of the nature of the medieval feloness.

One of the first works on female antisocial behavior, *Malleus Maleficarum*, written in 1487, had a ready explanation for both the methods and the types of offenses women committed against society. Women, according to the authors, were prone to deceit, lies, and concealment because:

> . . . there was a defect in the formation of the first woman since she was formed from a bent rib, that is, a rib from the breast, which is bent as it were in a contrary direction to a man. And since through this defect she is an imperfect animal, she always deceives.[11]

In terms of appropriate felonies, this theory implies that women would be found most frequently in crimes involving concealment such as larceny, counterfeiting, and receiving and that their methods would involve ruses to hide the deeds.[12] Luke Owen Pike, writing in the nineteenth century, also claimed that medieval women were more likely to be concentrated in nonviolent property crimes because medieval weapons such as swords, battle axes and staffs required more brute strength than the gun.[13] The authors all based their conclusions on personal biases about women, with little regard to evidence in the courts. An analysis of the gaol delivery and coroners' rolls for the types of crimes women committed and, where possible, for their methods and motives will give a more accurate picture of female offenders.

Whether the reasons were the crudity of medieval weaponry, the gentleness of the sex, or the preference for more devious methods than physical assaults, women do appear somewhat less frequently than men in cases of crimes against the person. The figures in the Appendix indicate that 26.3 percent of the men tried in gaol delivery were accused of homicide whereas only 16 percent of the women were suspected. These percentages represent the relative frequency with which men and women were accused of homicide compared to other types of crimes. The discrepancy between male and female participation in homicide is more dramatically shown by looking at the category of homicide by itself. Of the 2,696 cases of homicide tried in the three counties, women were accused of only 7.3 percent. (See Appendix.) In the coroners' rolls only 5.4 percent of the suspects were female.[14] One might argue, following the lead of L. O. Pike, that women were more likely to be involved in assaults rather than homicides because of the physical strength required to wound a victim fatally. But, of the 632 assault cases in Wakefield manor court, women committed only 11 percent—just slightly higher than their homicide record.[15] Women are also less conspicuous than men in other crimes against the person. In rape cases there were, as one might expect, no women, and only .4 percent of the men appearing in gaol delivery were accused of rape. In robbery cases, 10.3 percent of the men were tried for this felony compared to 6.2 percent of the women. Of the 1,049 arrests for robbery, 6.5 percent were women.[16]

Looking at the percentage of women involved in crimes against the person tells only part of the story of their anti-social violence. Although women did commit fewer homicides and robberies than men, they were nevertheless the third most common felonies among women. Obviously, physical weakness did not hinder the female suspects who committed murder or assaulted in connection with robbery. In order to understand the nature of female participation in violent crimes, one must investigate the weapons women used, their victims, and the extent to which they acted with accomplices.

For the most part, women did not act alone in violence. In 64.4 percent of the homicides another person aided them, and in 84.2 percent of the robbery cases they had companions. Usually, the women acted with male associates (52.9 percent in homicides and 84.2 percent in robberies). Indeed, about half of the fellow participants were members of the woman's own family—usually her husband or perhaps her children or parents. Alice le Frenshe, her husband William, and an associate robbed and murdered a foreign Hospitaller on the king's highway and stole ten silver marks from him.[17] One of the classic criminal combinations—a woman and her lover murdering her husband—accounted for the deaths of Robert son of John Presson of Cullingworth and Thomas Darel.[18]

The court rolls give little and, indeed, conflicting information on the part women played in criminal associations. They may have actively participated in, planned, and incited the crime or simply aided and abetted the real felons. In a burglary case in Bedfordshire, which ended in brutal maiming and murder, the neighbors testified that two women, Agnes and Maud Pikhorn, had concealed and incited the deed.[19] On the other hand, when Isabel daughter of Stacie of Rudham was brought to trial for aiding a band of robbers to hold Hertford Bridge and rob all who crossed, the jurors excused her on the grounds that her husband had forced her to do it.[20]

Although women often had aid in violent crimes, they showed complete capability of handling weapons on their own. Coroners' roll evidence indicates that knives and hatchets were the most popular weapons among women: 53.8 percent of the murderesses used knives, and 30.8 percent used hatchets or axes. It is hardly surprising that these instruments were most commonly employed, for women had considerable practice with them in the kitchen and cutting wood. Women virtually never used the staff, sword, bow and arrow, and battle axe which were favored among men. In later ages, poison gained the reputation of being the woman's weapon, but medieval peasant women seemed to have ignored the possibilities of deadly nightshade and poisonous mushrooms—possibly because their effects were too recognizable.[21] One woman in Northamptonshire whipped her ten-year-old son to death in a fit of anger, and perhaps more children died of beatings than the jury of neighbors admitted.[22] Drowning also might have been more popular as a method of murder than the jurors confessed. Certainly, the number of children who drowned was very high; some of these may have been well-concealed murders. Alice Grut and Alice Grym drowned a three-day-old child in a river. They did it with the consent of Isabelle of Badenham, her daughter Alice, and her son John.[23] We have no record, however, of whose child it was and why it was drowned.

One might assume that the victims of women's wrath were often children or other women, who could be more easily overpowered than men, but, in fact, in 68.4 percent of the cases in the coroners' rolls and in 81.6 percent of the gaol delivery cases, the slain person was male. Of course, since women often had male assistance in homicide, they were not limited to attacking only the weaker sort of victim. About a quarter of women's prey were members of their own family—31 percent in the coroners' rolls and 21.1 percent in gaol delivery. Of these intrafamilial homicides, husbands were the most common victims (59.3 percent), children were second (26.5 percent—13 percent of mothers killing sons and 13.5 percent killing daughters), and siblings third (13.6 percent). There was only one case of infanticide in 2,933 homicides reported in gaol delivery and coroners' rolls.[24] Aside from the child killed by Alice Grut and Alice Grym, most of the young victims were already a year or more old and they were usually killed by their mentally deranged mothers. Perhaps the church prohibition against taking life inhibited women from killing unwanted babies. One tends to be somewhat sceptical that such a moral injunction could be so successful and looks instead at the possibility that women concealed the murders. Perhaps illegitimacy was readily accepted by the community or mothers suffocated the babies and claimed that they were stillborn.[25] In a devastating famine similar to the one Pearl Buck described, Johannes de Trokelowe, a chronicler, claimed that during the crop failures of 1315–17 some parents killed their offspring and ate them.[26] Whatever the truth is about the low incidence of infanticide, the court rolls give no hint.

What motivated women to turn to acts of violence against other people, especially against their own families? We have already seen that some women were forced into their felonies by their husbands and that others, if Trokelowe's account of canibalism is true, killed from sheer desperation. But from what can be concluded from the scanty evidence in the records, it seems as if the motives for violence were similar to those of men: personal grudges, material gain, sadism, self-defense, fits of anger, and familial arguments.[27] Generally speaking, the rolls are silent on the question of motives. For instance, one assumes that domestic anger arising from jealousies must have motivated the murder of spouses, but I have found no explicit case of a wife killing her husband for this reason. Perhaps the two Yorkshire women teamed up with their lovers to murder their husbands because divorce was difficult and murder seemed a convenient way to be rid of the third member of a triangle. One woman who killed her husband as he was lying in bed claimed that he had a fit of insanity, and that she thought he was "siezed by death." This hardly seems an adequate reason for helping death along by cutting his throat with a small scythe and breaking his skull with a billhook. To add to our suspicions, instead of pleading that she had acted in self-defense, she fled to a church and abjured the realm.[28]

Cases arising from insanity were among the few in which motivations were fully discussed.[29] Insanity was a fairly uncommon plea in gaol delivery, but of these cases, that of a mother killing her children was the most usual.[30] These unfortunate women all had a history of derangement, or were suicidal, or had been sick with a high fever. Agnes wife of Roger Moyses, an example of the first type of case, killed her young son Adam during one of her frequent bouts of insanity (amentia).[31] Emma wife of Henry Wolfrom of Cantele also suffered a period of "demented and vexed" behavior before killing her child.[32] Other women, like Matilda widow of Mark le Waleys of Buthamwell, tried to commit suicide before returning and murdering the children.[33] Juliana Matte of Killingbury, on the other hand, was ill and became crazed from fever; in this state she drowned her one-year-old son in a well.[34] Sadistic violence might also accompany murders by the insane as it did in the case of Margery wife of William Calbot who killed her two-year-old daughter with a knife and forced her four-year-old to sit in the flames of the hearth.[35] The court cases contain insufficient information about the murderesses to label their particular type of mental derangement.

Although a quarter of the female offenders were involved in violent attacks on the person, the bulk were concentrated in property crimes. The preference for property crimes can hardly be said to stem from a specifically female quality, for, among male offenders as well, property crimes were quite common. Larceny was slightly more common among men than women (34.3 percent to 31.8 percent), but in other property crimes women had a slight edge: 27.8 percent of the females were accused of burglary compared to 23.4 percent of males, 14 percent of the females were charged with receiving while only 3.7 percent of the men were, and in arson and counterfeiting the percentage was about the same (see Appendix). Of all of the property crimes, then, only receiving seems to have been specifically female. The reasons for the predominance of women as receivers, the relatively large percentage of women committing burglary, the types of goods stolen, the methods employed, and the motives for the commission of property crimes must now come under consideration.

Women are, then and now, in a particularly vulnerable position to become receivers, for they must often welcome into their homes felonious husbands, lovers, and children along with their stolen goods. They are, therefore, less often professional "fences" than simply family receivers.[36] The gaol delivery rolls are full of cases of women tried for receiving family members who have committed crimes. To give but one example, the sister of John Benne of Ormesby received her brother after he had broken into a house and stolen goods worth one hundred shillings.[37] Generally speaking, these cases ended in acquittal. There were, of course, those women who seemed to have more sinister motives for receiving, as was the case of the woman who took into her home a gang of robbers and murderers fresh from their latest murder.[38] In another case the woman had a reputation for being a regular receiver of malefactors.[39]

Perhaps the most surprising of the property crimes in which to find a heavy concentration of women is in burglary. As the Appendix shows, women committed 12 percent of all burglaries—a considerably higher percentage than in modern burglary, where women figure only 3.3 percent of all cases.[40] In this felony, as in homicide and robbery, physical strength was a prerequisite for breaking and entering walls and doors. Were medieval women stronger than modern women, medieval walls weaker, or has the woman's role changed? The court rolls can hardly provide answers to all of these questions. One of the common ways of illegally entering a house was breaking down a door or walls.[41] The walls of the poorer houses were, often enough, insubstantially constructed of plaster and wattles and would yield to the assault of a woman. But, not surprisingly, in 46.6 percent of the burglary cases women acted with an accomplice, usually a male. Matilda, sister of Richard ad Fres had the help of Robert of Pinkney of Westmorland and William of Strikland, clerk, in the burglary of a house in Baggeby, Yorkshire.[42]

Despite their relatively large participation in burglary, larceny was the most common crime among female offenders. Of all the larcenies recorded in gaol delivery rolls, women were arrested for 9.6 percent of them.[43] The types of goods women stole varied somewhat from the pattern of thefts by men and reflect the economic interests of women. Foodstuffs (grain, bread, cheese, meat, and fish) comprised 30 percent of the goods women stole, whereas they accounted for only 12 percent of men's thefts. The value of these stolen items was often very low. For instance, one woman was indicted at Wakefield for making a practice of stealing from her neighbors' vegetable gardens at night.[44] Even more common were cases of women stealing sheaves of wheat from the fields at harvest time, as did Agnes of Weldon and her three children who stole eight sheaves of grain worth four pence.[45] Another category of small items usually stolen by women rather than men was clothing and household goods—17 percent of female thefts compared to 8 percent of male thefts. These thefts could be rather valuable as in the case of the thirty-two clothes worth forty shillings stolen by Matilda Waraunt and her sister.[46] Aside from thefts of foodstuffs, clothing, and household goods, however, women tended to steal less in the other categories than men. Industrial products such as cloth, tools, timber, and metals accounted for only 10 percent of the thefts among women compared to 16 percent among men. Women also stole less money, plate and jewels—7 percent to 11 percent. The largest category of thefts among both men and women was livestock—women 30 percent and men 44 percent. Livestock thefts included small animals like poultry, but even larger animals presented no obstacle to women who could easily lead away an animal and find a cooperative butcher to buy it. Agnes Pegere of Thornes stole two sheep and sold them to Peter de Acom and John le Leche, butchers.[47]

Although two-thirds of the women stole small items without the help of accomplices, there were women who made something more of a profession of larceny and who joined gangs of thieves. Alice Garlic of Great Houghton stole one horse worth ten shillings and robbed three different men of clothing in Creton.[48] Other women joined up with roaming bands of vagrants and thieves.[49] Sometimes, as in the case below, they married one of the members; other times they were cited in the rolls as concubines.[50]

On 28 April 1272 Adam of Deddington of Oxfordshire, Isabel of Moreton of Bukinghamshire, Walter Scot of Berwick-upon-Tweed and his wife Joan of Stratford, outside London, came to Dunton and Walter offered a pelt for sale through the whole town. They then sought hospitality through the whole town, but did not find any and later withdrew from the town to 'Godeshull', where a quarrel arose between Adam and Walter. Adam struck Walter under the left ear to the throat with a knife called 'swytel'. . . . Joan immediately raised the hue and the townships came, found Walter dead and arrested Adam and Joan. Isabel heard the hue from the other side of the town, took a *(sic)* child in her arms and immediately fled to Dunton church, where she stayed until 5 May and then confessed before the coroner that she had stolen a coat of brightly coloured material, a rochet, a veil, a sheet and many other things. . . .[51]

The gang that Isabel and Joan belonged to seems to have been a small group of vagrants involved in petty thefts. Of Joan and Walter it might be said that the vagabond life brought them together—he from Berwick-upon-Tweed and she from London—until she was left a widow in Bedfordshire.

Arson and counterfeiting seem to have been very much a family affair for women in fourteenth-century England. In 60 percent of the arson cases women were part of a family group, and the same for a third of the counterfeiting cases.[52] One counterfeiting gang contained three generations of women—Richard of Causby and his wife, Albreda, their son John, their daughter Anicia, and her child, Matilda.[53]

The motivation of women in committing property crimes varied from desperation to acquisitiveness to vindictive reprisals. The individual circumstances leading to thefts are given in court records even less frequently than those surrounding homicides, so that much must be left to speculation. Certainly, both men and women were reduced to desperate straits for survival during the early fourteenth century and especially during the famine of 1315-17.[54] Women, in particular, might have felt pressed to steal rather than see their children die of starvation. The gaol delivery rolls, however, show only a slight tendency toward a higher proportion of women in crime before the third decade of the fourteenth century and no marked increase during the famine years. From 1300-25, roughly the period of greatest pressure on the agricultural resources of the countryside, women committed 11.6 percent of the crimes.[55] After 1325, when grain prices dropped, women account for only 7 percent of the total crimes. The woman who stole vegetables from her neighbors' gardens did so in the height of the famine and may have been driven by hunger. For other women we may assume that the motivation was acquisitiveness, as it is for most thefts. After all, crime did pay very well in the early fourteenth century when the average value of pilfer from a single theft was three pounds six shillings. A woman who drove off a cow or several sheep to the butcher could do quite well without moving into the realm of armed robbery which paid somewhat better. Finally, there were the women who stole to spite their victims, perhaps a neighbor or more likely a family member. An example of an indictment for this type of theft appeared in a Wakefield tourn in 1307.

Alice wife of John Kyde of Wakefeud was abducted by night by the servant of Nicholas, the parish chaplain of Wakefeud, on the chaplain's horse and by his command, and with the woman's consent; she was taken to Aylisbiry, with goods belonging to her husband, to wit, 11d. taken from her husband's purse; 3 gold rings worth 18d.; a cup of mazer, 12d.; a napkin, 12d; a towel, 6d.; a gown, 6s. 8d.; a new hood taken from her husband's pack, 12d. with many other things unknown. Afterwards Alice returned to her husband.[56]

Women, then, committed crimes for a variety of motives. If they predominated in one motive over another or if their reasons for committing crimes differed radically from those of men, our records give no hint. If not in motive, then certainly in other respects the pattern of crime among women differs from that of men, as we have shown in this section. But the question remains of society's attitude toward the female offender.

In the absence of reliable literary sources, our evidence for the attitudes of medieval society toward the feloness must rest primarily upon laws and legal records. A study of medieval English laws applicable to women is a separate and very interesting study in itself, but I will concentrate in this brief section on provisions for processing the female suspect in the administration of criminal law.

The treatment of suspected and convicted female offenders was virtually the same as for males. From the moment of confinement in the king's gaol, women and men were treated to equally miserable conditions. Indeed, in the early fourteenth century women and men were usually put into the same cell, since prisons with separate quarters for women were rare.[57] Both sexes received the same type of trial and, if found guilty, were punished by hanging. Only if they had committed a treasonable offense, such as counterfeiting, were the punishments differentiated: the treasonous man being drawn and quartered and the woman being burned at the stake. If a man killed his lord, he was guilty of treason. If a woman killed her husband, hence her lord, she would be burned. The law made the woman's position clear in relationship to her husband and therefore Lucia widow of Thomas Tasseburgh, who killed Thomas in Norwich, was duly burned for her crime in 1326.[58]

If women were singled out for special brutal treatment for killing their spouses, the law also gave especially generous consideration to the convicted mother-to-be. Since canon law prohibited killing the unborn child in the womb of the convicted feloness, a woman could plead that she was pregnant and prolong her life at least until the baby was born. The court, of course, did not take the woman's word about her condition, but appointed a jury of matrons to examine her. If her pregnancy were confirmed, she was returned to prison until the child was born. Such was the case with Margery wife of Simon of Berewik, who was found guilty of breaking into the house of Hugh son of Hugh of Berwik.[59] As these women do not normally reappear in the records, they were either hanged after the birth of the baby or perhaps were able to break out of gaol. One woman, Matilda Hereward of Branndeston in Northamptonshire, was able to prolong her life at least one year and three months by being pregnant every time the justices came to deliver the gaol. She and her husband were found guilty of larceny in the Northamptonshire delivery of 21 June 1301. They were sentenced to be hanged but she was returned to gaol because of pregnancy. Again on 25 September 1301 she was returned to prison because she was pregnant. Likewise, the justices found her pregnant on 15 January 1302, 5 June 1302, 26 October 1302 and 22 January 1303.[60] After that date there is, unfortunately, a gap in the records, so that we do not know the ultimate fate of Matilda. Since her husband had been hanged in 1301, one assumes that the mixed prison conditions must have made repeated pregnancy possible—indeed, almost impossible to avoid.[61]

With the exception of special treatment for pregnant women and a distinctive punishment for women who killed their husbands, the law in theory offered equal treatment to the suspected and convicted person regardless of sex. However, our data have shown that only one woman was indicted to every nine men and that only 16 percent of the women were convicted compared to 30 percent of the men. Furthermore, when indictments were made, the names of the suspected women in a case generally followed those of the men, even if the women were guilty of planning the crimes. The male jurors and judge obviously held some beliefs about the essentially gentle nature of women which inhibited them in indicting women and especially in sending them to the gallows.

The question of whether or not women were the uncriminous creatures of the jurors' imagination must remain unanswered, as it is in modern studies of the female offender. Although we cannot know conclusively why fewer women than men were accused of felonies, I have outlined in this study the recorded pattern of female crime in the early fourteenth century. Women certainly did not limit themselves to crimes like larceny, receiving, and counterfeiting, which require more cunning than physical strength. Although larceny was the single most common crime among women, over half of the felonies women committed involved violence to persons and property. In these acts, women had accomplices in about half of the cases, but they were equally capable of committing even murder alone. Their weapons in homicide were knives and hatchets, instruments which were in daily use, and their victims were, for the most part, men. Children were more often victims of their mother's violence than their father's, but in most of the cases in the gaol delivery rolls the mother was insane. Receiving was the only crime which seemed to be decidely a female offense, partly because a

APPENDIX

Males and Females Tried for Particular Felonies

Felonies	Males		Females		Total Number of Males & Females	Total Percentage Tried	
	N	%age	N	%age		Females	Males
Larceny	3262	34.3	348	31.8	3610	9.6	90.4 = 100%
Burglary	2228	23.4	305	27.8	2533	12.0	88.0 = 100%
Robbery	981	10.3	68	6.2	1049	6.5	93.5 = 100%
Homicide	2498	26.3	198	18.1	2696	7.3	92.7 = 100%
Receiving	349	3.7	153	14.0	502	30.5	69.5 = 100%
Arson	111	1.1	14	1.3	125	11.2	88.8 = 100%
Rape	38	0.4	—	—	38	100.0	— = 100%
Counterfeiting	45	0.5	9	0.8	54	16.7	83.3 = 100%
Total	9512	100.0%	1095	100.0%	10,607		

woman was often placed in the difficult position of receiving her felonious family. If familial duty was the special motivation for women in receiving, their motivation for other crimes covers the same range as it did for men.

NOTES

1. Public Record Office class Justice Itinerant III 1300–48; hereafter referred to as JI 3.

2. R. F. Hunnisett, ed., *Bedfordshire Coroners' Rolls*, vol. 16 (Bedfordshire Historical Society, 1960). Public Record Office class Justice Itinerant II 1300–48; hereafter referred to as JI 2. Total number of homicides in this study from coroners' roll data is 237.

3. *The Court Rolls of the Manor of Wakefield*, ed. W. P. Baildon and others (Yorkshire Archaeological Society Record Series, 1901–45), vols. 27, 29, 57, 68, 109. Hereafter referred to as *Wakefield* with the volume number. *Court Rolls of the Manor of Ingoldmells in the County of Lincoln*, ed. W. O. Massingberd (London, 1902). Hereafter referred to as *Ingoldmells*.

4. For the most part, the people who appear as the accused in the gaol delivery rolls are villagers and peasants. This is because the wealthier elements of the society used their influence to remove their cases to other courts or to have the indictment rejected. Towns very often had their own courts so that most of the gaol delivery rolls represent rural conditions.

5. H. Mannheim, *Comparative Criminology*, 2nd ed. (Boston, 1967), p. 697.

6. I have relied on O. Pollak, *The Criminality of Women* (Philadelphia, 1950), p. 3, for a summary of the two positions in criminological literature.

7. W. Bonger, *Criminality and Economic Conditions*, abridged by A. T. Turk (London, 1969), p. 64.

8. D. M. Stenton, *The English Woman in History* (London, 1957), chapt. 1. E. Power, "The Position of Women," *Legacy of the Middle Ages*, ed. C. Crump and E. Jacob (Oxford, 1926), pp. 401–33.

9. *Wakefield*, 57: 94–95.

10. In New York in 1940, jurors convicted 14 percent fewer women than men. In the late nineteenth century in France the male jurors acquitted as many as 20 percent more women than men. Pollak, *Criminality of Women*, p. 5.

11. H. Kramer and J. Sprenger, *Malleus Maleficarum*, trans. Montague Summers (London, 1928), p. 44.

12. Pollak, *Criminality of Women*, pp. 8–14.

13. L. O. Pike, *History of Crime in England* (London, 1873), 2: 527. This view differs from his description of medieval women in volume one where he places greater emphasis on their brutality. Perhaps he held strong personal views about the helplessness of women which caused him to forget his earlier material.

14. W. A. Lunden, *Crimes and Criminals* (Ames, Iowa, 1967), p. 102. In the United States in 1963, 82 percent of arrests for murder were male and 18 percent were female. Comparisons with modern criminal statistics are, of course, always somewhat suspect because social conditions, legal definitions of crimes, and methods of crime detection have changed so much. It would be helpful to have other medieval data or even sixteenth-and seventeenth-century figures, but these are not available.

15. *Ibid.* Modern figures show women arrested for 14 percent of assaults.

16. *Ibid.* This is close to the modern figures in which 95.1 percent were men and 4.9 percent were women.

17. JI 3/51 m. 2.

18. JI 3/77/2 m. 3 and JI 3/75 m. 13–16.

19. Hunnisett, *Bedfordshire Coroners' Rolls*, p. 14. At twilight on 23 April 1271, felons and thieves came to the house of John Reyd of Ravensden while John, his wife Maud, and his servants, Walter of Astwood and Richard Pikhorn, were sitting at supper. They entered by the door towards the courtyard on the west side and immediately assaulted John, striking him on the head near the crown to the brain, apparently with an axe, and to the heart with a knife, of which he immediately died. They wounded Maud on the right side of the head, almost cut off her left hand, and heated a trivet and placed her upon it so that they left her almost dead. Walter and Richard were tied up, and all the goods of the house were robbed and carried away.

20. JI 3/125 m. 9d.

21. JI 3/78 m. 5. There was only one case of poisoning in 10,500 cases, and it ended in acquittal.

22. JI 2/106.

23. JI 3/48 m. 4d.

24. The seemingly low incidence of infanticide is particularly noteworthy because it was a serious problem in the eighteenth and nineteenth centuries. Mannheim, *Comparative Criminology*, p. 696.

25. Richard M. Smith, *The Sir Nicholas Bacon Collection, Sources on English Society, 1250–1700: A Catalogue of an Exhibition at the Joseph Regenstein Library of the University of Chicago* (Chicago, 1972), pp. 10–11. Illegitimacy was between 8 percent and 11 percent in the early fourteenth century on these East Anglian estates. It is unclear how he arrived at these percentages, and they may not be very meaningful.

26. Johannes de Trokelowe, *Annales (Chronica Monasterii s. Albani)*, ed. H. T. Riley, Rolls Series (London, 1866), 28: 95.

27. JI 3/48 m. 3. A woman in Norwich was attacked by a madman and dragged around by the hair until she managed to kill him in self-defense. Another woman committed homicide defending her husband against the assault of a burglar. JI 3/48 m. 12.

28. Hunnisett, *Bedfordshire Coroners' Rolls*, p. 102.

29. In cases of both insanity and self-defense, the defendant asked for pardons from the king. Therefore, the rolls contain a fairly full description of the motivation of the act and the circumstances.

30. There are only about twenty cases in the combined data of the gaol delivery and coroners' rolls.

31. KB (King's Bench) 27/273 m. 29.

32. KB 27/327 m. 36d.

33. JI 3/119 m. 14d. Also see Hunnisett, *Bedfordshire Coroners' Rolls*, p. 114 for a case of a woman who killed her three children and then hanged herself from a beam.

34. JI 3/52/3 m. 13. Another woman killed her husband while she had a high fever and had no recollection of doing so until she recovered two weeks later. KB 27/327 m. 36d.

35. JI 3/48 m. 6.

36. Pollak, *Criminality of Women*, p. 87.

37. JI 3/76 m. 3–3d.

38. Hunnisett, *Bedfordshire Coroners' Rolls*, p. 66.

39. *Wakefield*, 29: 57.

40. Lunden, *Crimes and Criminals*, p. 102.

41. B. A. Hanawalt Westman, *A Study of Crime in Norfolk, Yorkshire, and*

Northamptonshire, 1300–1348 (Ph.D. Dissertation, University of Michigan, 1970), p. 178.

42. JI 3/74/2 m. 11.

43. Lunden, *Crimes and Criminals*, p. 102. In modern criminal statistics women were arrested in 19 percent of all larceny cases.

44. *Wakefield*, 58: 179.

45. JI 3/74/3 m. 12.

46. JI 3/117 m. 10.

47. *Wakefield*, 29: 128–29.

48. JI 3/51/4 m. 3d.

49. JI 3/106 m. 3 for an example.

50. JI 3/79/1 m. 2d. for an example.

51. Hunnisett, *Bedfordshire Coroners' Rolls*, p. 48.

52. JI 3/74/3. A husband and wife burned the home of Richard le Provost of Hundesley.

53. JI 3/75 m. 34.

54. There was a very close correlation between the fluctuations in the number of cases coming into gaol delivery and the price of grain for the first quarter of the century, particularly in the famine years. B. A. Hanawalt, "Economic Influences on the Pattern of Crime in England, 1300–1348," *The American Journal of Legal History* 18 (1974): 281–97.

55. M. M. Postan, "Medieval Agrarian Society at its Prime, England," *Cambridge Economic History of Europe*, ed. M. M. Postan (Cambridge, 1966), 1: 565.

56. *Wakefield*, 29: 93. For another case of a woman delivering her husband's goods to her lover, *Wakefield*, 57: 45.

57. R. B. Pugh, *Imprisonment in Medieval England* (Cambridge, 1968), pp. 257–58.

58. KB 27/263 m. 32.

59. JI 3/48 m. 22.

60. For the respective sentencings and examinations, JI 3/100 m. 17, JI 3/101 m. 1, JI 3/101 m. 10, JI 3/101 m. 13, JI 3/102 m. 9, and *ibid.*

61. In some cases the gaoler or another peace officer raped the female prisoners. KB 27/322 m. 32.

Brenda M. Bolton

⁕ Mulieres Sanctae

The early thirteenth century was an extraordinary period in the history of piety. Throughout Europe, and especially in urban communities, lay men and women were seized by a new religious fervor which could be satisfied neither by the new orders nor by the secular clergy. Lay groups proliferated, proclaiming the absolute and literal value of the gospels and practicing a new life-style, the *vita apostolica*.[1] This religious feeling led to the formation, on the eve of the fourth lateran council, of numerous orders of "poor men" and, shortly afterwards, to the foundation of the mendicant orders. From this novel interpretation of evangelical life women by no means wished to be excluded and many female groups sprang simultaneously into being in areas as far distant as Flanders and Italy. Yet how were such groups to be regarded because current attitudes to women were based on inconsistent and contradictory doctrines?[2] It was difficult to provide the conditions under which they could achieve their desire for sanctity as they were not allowed to enter the various orders available to men. How then were men to reply to the demands of these women for participation in religious life? That there should be a reply was evident from the widespread heresy in just those areas in which the ferment of urban life encouraged the association of pious women. And heretics were dangerously successful with them! For the church, the existence of religious and semi-religious communities of women raised, in turn, many problems, not least the practicalities involved in both pastoral care and economic maintenance. Only after 1215, when it attempted to regulate and discipline them, did it realize the widespread enthusiasm on which their movement was based.

Originally published in *Studies in Church History*, vol. 10, pp. 77–85, edited by Derek Baker. Published for the Ecclesiastical History Society by Basil Blackwell, London, and Barnes and Noble, New York. Copyright © 1973 by the Ecclesiastical History Society; reprinted by permission of the Ecclesiastical History Society.

For men the problem was less difficult, for an astonishing variety of new religious orders had begun to appear at the beginning of the twelfth century.[3] Premonstratensians, Augustinians, Grammontines and Cistercians alike enjoyed an immediate and overwhelming success. In spite of this stimulus, there was no comparable, parallel attempt to enrich the religious life of women, with the possible local exception of the Gilbertines in England.[4] Nunneries remained exclusive and few in number. Instead, many women attached themselves to itinerant religious leaders whose teaching had a wide appeal. The first such charismatic preacher was Robert of Arbrissel, who settled his large and heterogeneous female following in a new convent at Fontevrault in the Loire valley, but within a generation it had become entirely aristocratic, looking no further than the northern French nobility for its recruits.[5] Another such preacher, Norbert of Xanten, received a most enthusiastic reception from women in the neighbourhood of Valenciennes in the early 1120s.[6] The Premonstratensian order, which he founded, immediately assumed the protection of pious women and established a number of double monasteries. In 1137 the general chapter decreed the separation of monks and nuns for reasons of convenience, although successive popes repeated that adequate maintenance should be provided for women. Yet, by 1150, apparently undeterred by powerful influences at work against them, the women were said to number over ten thousand.[7] Finally, in 1198, Innocent III's bull *de non recipiendis sororibus* confirmed and commended the decision of the general chapter no longer to accept them into the order.[8]

The community at Fontevrault and the early Premonstratensian nunneries had flourished initially because of the help which they had received from their male protectors. But other protectors of female communities appeared in different and unexpected guises. Large numbers of women began to form convents which followed the customs of Cîteaux and yet which held no formal place in the structure of the order.[9] In Spain many great families, who were responsible for the settlement of Cistercian monks, also created large, aristocratic houses of Cistercian nuns. Possibly because of this noble patronage and because of the grandeur of aristocratic Spanish women, individual Cistercian abbots appear to have supported and supervised these nunneries. The abbesses enjoyed a remarkable degree of independence.[10] By the 1190s the Cistercian order, which had at first ignored the existence of female intruders, became increasingly aware of the large number of women who claimed its protection without being subject to its organization or control. The contrast between the discipline of the male order and the freedom of the large and rapidly growing female branch was becoming very apparent.

In Flanders, too, there is evidence that the Cistercians supported the foundation of nunneries and that abbots, such as Walter of Villers, in the diocese of Liège were responsible for their supervision and welfare.[11] Of the popularity of these houses we are left in no doubt. The contemporary view of the situation in this diocese alone was that there were three times as many pious women as there were Cistercian houses able to receive them.[12]

From 1213 the general chapter began an attempt to discipline them. The number of nuns was limited; they were strictly enclosed; they were forbidden to receive visitors, and their opportunities for confession were limited.[13] In 1228 the general chapter issued a peremptory statute forbidding all further attachment of nunneries to the order and refusing the benefit of visitation and pastoral care to existing communities.[14] But the severity of this decree was more apparent than real for, if they could support themselves economically, Cistercian convents could continue to exist and new foundations to be made.[15] Yet despite this, the Cistercian general chapter had made the point most forcibly that there was no place for these women in its order and that they were accepted only with extreme reluctance.

There was thus a strong reaction in both the Premonstratensian and Cistercian orders against the large numbers of women who wished to join them. What is so difficult to explain is why this reaction should have occurred. The general ecclesiastical attitude to women was at best negative if not actively hostile. Nor, indeed, was a woman's vocation necessarily regarded in a serious light.[16] It was thought that women inevitably contributed to indiscipline.[17] As the church became increasingly institutionalized so it was less able to tolerate any disruptive force in its midst.[18]

Women were also considered to be receptive to all forms of religious prophecy and to be completely unrestrained in relationships with their leaders or patrons. Just as, in the first half of the twelfth century, orthodox and heretical preachers had become the founders of orders and sects, so later the Cathars confronted the Cistercians and the mendicants. Sects were generally only too glad to accept women, and women accompanied preachers through the land, sometimes preaching themselves. Here was the dilemma. The church in turn had to provide some measure of approval for their aspirations or heresy would materialize amongst these women.

Women could not, however, under any circumstances be allowed to regulate their own forms of religious life. In the view of the church, the only possible role for them was one of attachment to existing male orders. But these orders did not want them and were reluctant to provide pastoral care and administrative oversight. So the importance of a male protector to advance and secure their interests and, possibly, to ward off accusations of heresy was increased for these communities of pious women.

Women who had thus been catered for erratically in the twelfth century moved by 1200 into a different situation. They began to demand recognition of their real and separate identity. The question of their status in religion could no longer be answered solely by placing them in houses attached to the male orders, often as unwanted appendages. As enthusiastic women began to share the aspirations of the Friars and like-minded religious groups, the logical outcome ought to have been the creation of a separate female order. Instead, in 1215, the Fourth Lateran Council issued a decree which epitomized the contest between those who would have allowed new forms of religious life within the church and those who supported the forces of tradition and reaction. As a result of this, there were to be no more new orders and henceforward anyone who wished to establish a religious community had to do so within the framework and rule of an approved order. [19]

Although it may not have been possible to measure an increase in piety, yet contemporaries undoubtedly believed that female piety was increasing at the beginning of the thirteenth century. In 1216 Jacques de Vitry, protector of a group of pious women in the diocese of Liège, travelled to Perugia where the curia then was and, in a letter to his Flemish friends, described those groups of religious women which he had seen in Lombardy and Umbria. [20] In Milan, among the *humiliati*, he found pious women, some who lived separate and ascetic lives in religious communities and others who lived at home and practiced strict evangelical precepts by stressing the importance of family life, prayer, exhortation, and manual work. Although they were called heretical by their enemies, he was convinced of their orthodoxy and reported that they alone were resisting and actively working against heretics in Milan. [21] In Umbria he encountered the Poor Clares and early Franciscan tertiaries who were following the example of the primitive church in various hospices near the towns. They would accept nothing and lived entirely by the work of their hands. He reported that they were greatly distressed because, by clergy and laity alike, they were honored more than they would have wished to be. [22]

Why was Jacques de Vitry so interested in female communities? Like many devout men of his day he eagerly gathered information about the variety and extent of such pious groups and individual female mystics. He wrote about them in his *Historia Occidentalis*, in his *Exempla*, and in his *Sermon to the Beguines*. [23] Above all, he wrote about them in his life of the "new" saint, Mary of Oignies, around whom centred female piety in the diocese of Liège. [24] Irresistibly attracted to voluntary personal poverty from an early age, she had eventually renounced her marriage, distributed her wealth to the poor, and together with her husband, served the leper colony at Williambroux, outside Nivelles. After several years, she had moved into a cell at the Augustinian priory of St. Nicholas of Oignies, there living in complete poverty save for what she earned at her spindle. In 1209 she prophesied the Albigensian crusade after a vision in which she saw a great number of crosses descending from heaven. [25] Jacques de Vitry, who himself preached this crusade in Flanders in 1211, was drawn to Oignies by Mary's renown and by his desire to identify himself with her work.

At her instigation, he was ordained in 1210 and remained in the community as her confessor. After her death in 1213, he continued to be the enthusiastic protector of her followers. To enhance her memory and expressly to counter heresy in the south of France, he wrote her *Life* and seems to have taken it with him on his journey to Perugia, but there is no evidence that he showed it to Honorius III.[26] Mary exercised a considerable influence over him and he, personally, was very close to her, even carrying around with him her finger in a reliquary.[27]

The pious women whom Jacques de Vitry was protecting in Liège were known as Beguines and were to be found also in France and Germany.[28] Their movement was essentially urban in character. They followed no definite rule of life; they had no real founder; at their inception they sought no authority from the hierarchy and imposed no irreversible vows upon their adherents. Their objectives were twofold: chastity or continence and the renunciation of worldly goods. They did not protest at the wealth of others but voluntarily renounced property and possessions to fulfill their evangelical ideal. They lived by the labor of their hands, for the injunction to work was essential to such semireligious associations in their pursuit of a penitential life and it also enabled them to meet in some measure the religious needs of the new urban populations.

What other contemporary evidence may we use to match Jacques de Vitry's experience of the Beguines? His manuscripts belong to the period of his cardinalate, 1229 to 1240.[29] At about the same time, between 1229 and 1235, Robert Grosseteste, bishop of Lincoln, declared privately to the Franciscans at Oxford that the Beguines, who, unlike the Mendicants did not live on alms but only by manual work, had achieved through their way of life the highest degree of Christian perfection through this poverty.[30] Shortly afterwards, Robert de Sorbon declared that at the last judgment the Beguines would give a better account of themselves than many a learned *magister,* jurist, or theologian.[31] And later still, in 1243, the English chronicler, Matthew Paris, wrote of those women "who have adopted a religious profession, though it is a light one. They call themselves 'religious' and they take a private vow of continence and simplicity of life, though they do not follow the rule of any saint, nor are they, as yet, confined within a cloister. They have so multiplied within a short time that two thousand have been reported in Cologne and neighbouring cities."[32]

The Beguine movement differed from the heretical poverty movement in that it made no polemical demands on clerics and did not stress to the same extent the merit of the priesthood.[33] Yet Beguines were often confused with heretics and it was probably from their supposed Albigensian affiliations that their name derived.[34] Jacques de Vitry discounted the accusations of heterodoxy against them and, in his role as protector, worked to save them from this charge. The Beguines fascinated him by the fervor and spontaneity of their personal religion and he saw that, in common with the *humiliati* of Lombardy, they could provide an effective barrier against heresy if contained within the church. We know that he was not alone in this view from the wholehearted admiration shown to the Beguine communities by Bishop Fulk of Toulouse, who arrived in the diocese of Liège in 1215 or early 1216.[35]

Jacques de Vitry was interested in pious women's communities because he saw them as being significant and potentially useful to the church. His enthusiasm for the Beguines was, however, tempered by the possible dangers of their extraregular status. He seems to have wished them to be completely incorporated into the ecclesiastical structure so that their obedience could be ensured. In spite of his representations to the curia on their behalf, no independent female order came into being. Perhaps he had hoped for assistance from Innocent III, but his arrival in Perugia coincided with the death of the pope, and he saw instead Honorius III, whom he described as a kind and simple man, ready to aid the poor in any possible way.[36] But he only obtained from him oral permission for the Beguines in Flanders, France and the Empire to live together in religious communities and to assist one another by mutual exhortations.[37] Shortly before Jacques de Vitry's mission to the curia in 1216, John de Liro, a friend and preacher in the Liège area, had set out for Rome with much the same purpose, only to perish in the Alps.[38]

Jacques de Vitry obviously considered the Poor Clares of Umbria and the religious women's communities which he knew in Flanders as a united, cohesive phenomenon, for he said nothing about the generic and organizational differences between them. But were there, perhaps, differences which Jacques de Vitry did not see? Superficially, the two groups might have been similar, yet from one emerged the order of Poor Clares, while the Beguines were never officially organized. Why, if there was an order of Poor Clares, was there no order of Beguines or, for that matter, of Cistercian nuns? Perhaps we could approach the problem from two directions by first looking at the social composition of these groups and then at the institutional problems which the attempts to found one order raised.

Who were these women who, in the early thirteenth century, wished to live in poverty and humility in areas as widely separated as Flanders and Lombardy or Umbria? In the initial stages they appear to be almost exclusively aristocratic. In 1218 Cardinal Hugolino commented that the Italian women, whose cause he had adopted, were of noble birth, assured of a comfortable existence and yet still wished to renounce the world to live instead in communities alongside their chapels.[39] Jacques de Vitry also describes the patrician status of Beguines and Cistercians alike.[40] Surely neither Hugolino nor Jacques de Vitry should have been surprised that these were aristocratic women. Such women were far more likely to question their way of life than those from lower classes, and their natural self-assurance must have helped them to win acceptance.

Here the religious factor seems to have been of prime importance. The religious poverty movement appeared to represent a reaction to landed wealth or newly acquired urban prosperity among those circles best placed to participate. Perhaps they felt that competition to achieve status was irreconcilable with their interpretation of the gospel. These women, whether Beguines or Poor Clares, wished not only to be poor but to live with the poor. Against the natural order of society they deliberately chose to deny their noble or rich background and turned instead to a way of life scorned by those they had known. It seems likely that poverty and chastity represented for these women a personal and social *renovatio*—a spiritual renewal through the adoption of a new life-style—the *vita apostolica.*[41]

Jacques de Vitry described two groups of women in these religious communities. There were those married noblewomen who, with the consent of their husbands, had renounced their earthly marriage, together with lands and possessions, in favor of a spiritual marriage and a life of voluntary poverty. Mary of Oignies, the child of rich and respected parents, was married at the age of fourteen but later separated voluntarily from her husband. Many other women like her, in the first half of the thirteenth century, parted from their husbands and became Beguines or nuns, attached to a Franciscan or Dominican house.[42]

Jacques de Vitry also talked of young girls from the nobility who, scorning not only their parents' wealth but also advantageous marriage, preferred to live humbly, sparsely clothed, and poorly fed, and to follow religious precepts outside their accustomed social circle.[43] Clare herself, at her conversion by Francis in 1212, gave away her property in order to serve God in voluntary poverty.[44] There were many examples of noble and unwilling brides-to-be who attempted to escape marriage in order to join a religious community. Christine of Stomeln, aged twelve, ran away to join a Beguine group in Cologne. The Beguines, however, received her coolly and sent her home. She endured several years of hardship and suffering, living as a beggar, before she eventually managed to convince them of her vocation.[45]

Was the number of pious women really increasing or was it that there were simply more women? Could the *Frauenfrage* be explained in demographic terms alone? Did these new religious groupings stem from women's social and economic needs at this time?[46] Such questions have received lengthy discussion elsewhere but it is perhaps worth making some points again. By 1200 the population of certain areas of western Europe was beginning to reflect an imbalance between men and women. Factors bringing this about were female longevity, a masculine proclivity to death in battle or permanent absence on crusade, and the large numbers of men entering the priesthood.[47] There may thus have been a high proportion of nubile women for whom there was no prospect of marriage and who therefore sought release in a mystical, contemplative life. We may even wonder tentatively if the intense interest in virginity, expressed through devotional literature, did not create a strong aversion in the minds of many girls towards marriage.[48] Practical considerations may here have played some part, for early marriage brought attendant risks in childbirth.

Possibly this women's movement towards religion was stimulated by the disadvantageous position which they appear to have held in feudal society. Primogeniture became more usual and depressed the independent status of some aristocratic women in landowning families.[49] Nobles could no longer necessarily afford large dowries for their daughters. Such insecurity may often have provided an incentive to enter a religious house or join a Beguine community. As a disadvantaged group in society, women looked for anything which might improve their personal status. They turned to religion, as nothing else was available for them. It is possible to argue that they might indeed achieve status through austerity in this world or, if not that, "what they cannot claim to *be,* they replace by the worth of that which they will someday *become.*"[50]

The argument is thus circular and returns constantly to religious factors. Poor Clares, Beguines, Cistercian nuns; all seemed to spring initially from the same social environment. Their motivation was basically religious but was, perhaps, complicated by other factors.

It is now worth examining the institutional differences between the Poor Clares and the Beguines which led to the development of an order in one case but not in the other. One man alone grasped the significance of the feminine piety movement. In his treatment of Francis, Innocent III had taken a long step towards creating the possibility of an order for women. He had already enabled new religious movements such as the *humiliati* to develop within the church and, by his farsighted actions, had saved many groups from heresy. It was logical that Innocent III should have been in favor of adding a women's order to the church to strengthen it in its struggle with heresy and its current political difficulties.

Francis had come to him in 1210 seeking approval for his way of life, yet unwilling to accept a traditional rule.[51] In the face of considerable hostility from the hierarchy, Innocent had to determine how this movement might be incorporated into the church and thus allowed Francis to continue on two conditions. He and his companions were to be tonsured and, as clerks, could then be given the *licentia praedicandi ubique.* The question of leadership was solved when Francis promised obedience to Innocent III and received oral approval from the pope.

The recognition of Francis by Innocent III had very wide implications for Clare. The oral permission given to him by the pope in 1210 contained no justification for the formation of a female order, nor was such permission subsequently issued. In 1212, after her conversion by Francis, Clare established her community in the church of St. Damian of Assisi. The community did not follow any usual, recognized rule, but a simple *formula vitae* which Francis had given them and which was essentially similar to his in its profession of evangelical poverty.[52]

When, in 1215, the Lateran Council imposed on all new movements the obligation to accept an approved rule, the community at St. Damian had to apply for a privilege to enable it to maintain its renunciation of property and its profession of strict proverty. At the same time, Clare was appointed as abbess of St. Damian and strict claustration was introduced.[53] She received from Innocent III the *privilegium paupertatis,* a privilege which allowed the sisters of St. Damian to live without an assured income.[54] All previously approved rules had been based on the presupposition that, although individuals were without property, houses would have to maintain themselves by a sufficient income from corporate possessions. So this privilege represented for Clare a guarantee that her community could not be obliged to adopt an existing rule. It seemed that Innocent had, therefore, helped her to create an entirely new form of convent community, which maintained itself on alms and the profits of manual labor in the same way as the Franciscans.

Innocent may have issued this document in May 1216 at Perugia or possibly earlier, in 1215, when Clare was made abbess of St. Damian.[55] Could he have been concerned, as indeed he was with Francis in 1210, that the question of leadership in the community should be regulated? What we do know is that Innocent actually wrote the privilege with his own hand *cum hilaritate magna* and that he therefore knew very well how unique it was.[56] At whatever time this privilege was issued, whether before, during, or after the council, it was unquestionably opposed to the decree since it made possible a new form of religious community not based on an existing order.

The Beguines, however, did not have the same advantages. Jacques de Vitry might have received a similar reception from Innocent III if he had been able to tell this pope about the Beguines. But there were other considerable difficulties. Mary of Oignies's death in 1213 had deprived the Beguines of Flanders of a leader, and they were soon to lose their protector, as Jacques de Vitry, now bishop-elect of Acre, was about to depart for the Holy Land.[57]

Is it possible that Innocent III's intervention on behalf of the Poor Clares might have led to the creation of a separate male order? A separate order for women would have horrified most medieval ecclesiastics. For this reason, Clare represented a potential revolution within the church. Why, therefore, with Innocent's help did not her community develop into an independent order? Perhaps Francis had hoped that this might happen, for he certainly did not wish to be too greatly involved with the convent of St. Damian. Nor indeed could he be. The Poor Clares lived in convents; the Friars were mendicant preachers and as such were unable to live a stable, cloistered life.[58] Jacques de Vitry, in 1216, described how, after their annual gatherings, they would disperse throughout the year in Lombardy, Tuscany, Apulia, and Sicily.[59] As they became more popular and spent more time in preaching over a wide area, so Francis, beset by other problems, could devote less time to the community of St. Damian.[60]

Yet there was certainly no lack of interest in a community such as Clare's. All over Italy there was a tremendous demand from women to join similar religious groups, and in 1218 Cardinal Hugolino applied to Honorius III on their behalf, asking that they should be placed under papal protection. He wished to institutionalize them but was not satisfied with simply congregating them under a nominal Benedictine rule to fulfill the provision of the lateran decree.[61] They still lacked connection with a male order, so Hugolino wanted all of them, including St. Damian's, to adopt one uniform rule and also make the Franciscans responsible for overall pastoral care of such communities. Francis appeared to agree that Clare's community should adopt Hugolino's rule, as it made no statement about the possession of property and thus contained no essential contradiction to her original *formula vitae*.[62] On the issue of pastoral care, however, he was adamant.

St. Damian was the only convent community which he would tolerate. He ordered that no others were to be founded or supported by his followers or attached to his order in any way at all. He rejected the use of the word "sister" to describe the women saying, "God has taken away our wives, and now the devil gives us sisters."[63] His violent reaction to Hugolino's attempt to involve the Friars in the service of the women's convents during his absence has been reported by one of the brothers. Francis had said, "Up to now the disease was in our flesh and there was hope of healing but now it has penetrated our bones and is incurable."[64] He managed to have this decision declared void and remained convinced that he had narrowly avoided the ruin of the order. Francis, like Innocent III, might have aimed originally at creating a separate female order under Clare. In the light of his hostility to women it would have given more coherence to his actions. Or did the possibility of a separate order for women come about almost by default—an attempt to prevent the friars from getting too involved with female communities? Whether this is so or not can only be a matter for conjecture.

What of Dominic's attitude to women? He had set out to create a new form of religious life for them long before he had created his own preaching order. The foundation of the nunnery at Prouille in 1206 was closely associated with the struggle against heresy in the south of France.[65] At first, Dominic attracted to Prouille the daughters of the impoverished lesser nobility whose education and upbringing were likely to be entrusted to the cathars.[66] Then older, aristocratic women, often former heretics, came to satisfy their demands for an austere life which, previously, catharism alone had offered in that area.[67] In 1215 Prouille was taken into papal protection by Innocent III and, when the Order of Preachers was established, the convent

became its property.[68] Other convents were also linked with Dominic. In
1218 he founded a house for nuns in Madrid which was supervised by his
brother.[69] In 1219 he was given the task of reforming the convent of St. Sisto
in Rome.[70] While in Bologna in the same year, Dominic approved the
suggestion of another house, on the lines of Prouille, which later became the
convent of St. Agnes.[71] All this activity in relation to foundations for women,
and especially the community at Prouille, raises a particular question. Was it
possible that Dominic was really trying to found a female order? This might
have been so in the years immediately after 1206, but he certainly felt
differently by the early 1220s. On his deathbed he warned his followers most
urgently about communion with women, especially young women.[72] It
seems likely that he was considering the future of his order and how far it
should put itself at the disposal of women's communities, which might then
draw it away from its greater task of preaching.[73]

   Both Francis and Dominic had thus, by the end of their lives, refused in
highly emotive terms to allow the general attachment of women to their
orders. Yet this represented a denial of their *raison d'être* as preachers.
Everywhere they went they were met by a huge wave of female piety.
Heinrich, first Dominican prior of Cologne, specialized in preaching to
women and enjoyed such success among "virgins, widows, and female
penitents" that his early death was bewailed by women throughout the
city.[74] There was considerable and constant pressure on the curia to
recognize these women and incorporate them somehow within the church.
But before such communities could exist they had to be institutionalized and
firmly regulated. So in 1227 the curia returned to the policy of creating
female branches of male orders and turned its attention to the mendicants to
examine how far it was possible to link the women to these orders. Thus
ensued a struggle between the women supported by the curia and the
orders. This struggle centered on two particular problems: the extent to
which pastoral care could be provided without detracting from their original
mendicant character, and the nature and extent of the economic support
required by female communities.

   In 1227 Gregory IX placed more than twenty central Italian convents of
pauperes moniales reclusae in the care of the general of the Franciscan order
and henceforth grouped them under the title of the Order of St. Damian.[75]
In the same year the curia mediated with the Dominicans to achieve the
incorporation of the nunnery of St. Agnes in Bologna, and this process was
repeated on many subsequent occasions.[76] Thus, within a short time of their
deaths the curia had succeeded in doing just what Francis and Dominic had
striven so hard to prevent during their lives. But the orders resisted vigo-
rously. In 1228, the year in which the Cistercians, too, refused to accept
nunneries, the general chapter of the Dominican order forbade not only the
incorporation of women's convents but also threatened with censure any

brother who accepted their vows, tended to their pastoral needs, or allowed them to wear religious habits.[77] This prohibition of pastoral care was completely ineffective against vigorous feminine demands. We know this from a bull of 1238, directed to the general of the order by Gregory IX, which reversed a previous chapter decision to release the brothers from the *cura mulierum* and thus to dissolve all connection between the order and its convents.[78]

At the request of the nuns of Prouille and Madrid, Gregory instructed that Dominican friars should be reappointed to undertake care of souls but in 1239 the order managed to secure an assurance that it would not in future be obliged to take on pastoral duties in convents or of other female groups unless this was expressly permitted by an abrogation clause.[79] In 1242 an attempt was made to forbid any Dominican activity within convents not legally in the care of the order, which further diminished its responsibilities towards women.[80] Against this, Innocent IV and the Dominican nuns launched a massive counteroffensive, and, from 1245 to 1250, thirty-two convents in Germany alone were incorporated into the order.[81]

The equally vain attempts of the Franciscans to deny responsibility for women were likewise frustrated by Innocent IV, who in 1246 authorized the incorporation of fourteen convents in France, Spain, and Italy and also groups of *sorores minores* who were wandering, undisciplined, and unregulated, save for their desire to join the order of St. Damian.[82]

The problem of economic provision of these convent communities faced both the curia and the mendicant orders. How far could religious women be allowed to live in absolute poverty without a guaranteed income? This was almost impossible to achieve. Dominican and Franciscan nuns and Beguines alike attracted gifts and benefactions from patrons and admirers.[83] Clare alone managed to resist. In 1247 the question of convent property came to a head when Innocent IV attempted to impose uniform regulations in the convents of the Order of St. Damian by ordering them all, irrespective of any earlier and contradictory regulations, to accept property and income.[84] Clare reacted strongly to this threat to her privilege. Not only did she succeed in rejecting this decree but used the opportunity to create a specific rule approximating as closely as possible to that of the Friars. In 1252 she received confirmation of the *privilegium paupertatis* and also of the essential characteristic of her rule—the profession of the strict principle of poverty in accordance with the directions of Francis.[85] In a sense, therefore, she took her own community out of the Order of St. Damian to avoid the property regulations which the curia was attempting to impose.

The situation was complicated by the fact that by no means all female communities succeeded in gaining incorporation by the mendicant orders. Many women, therefore, remained in Beguine communities with no uniform rule or defined leadership. Again there was the problem of their supervision and pastoral care. The parish clergy on the one hand claimed them as part of their regular flock; the mendicants, on the other, resisted them by general legislation or by the appointment of special confessors from outside their orders.[86] But these Beguine-type groups arose independently of the mendicant orders as a result of the movement towards the *vita apostolica*. In the Rhineland especially we find numbers of women who wished to lead a religious life, singly or in small groups, in inherited family houses, or in those bought by pooling resources.[87] In Flanders similar groups had close relations with the Cistercians.

Despite the statutes of the general chapter of the order, many Cistercian abbeys were spontaneously interested in the fate of religious women.[88] They defended them against the Cathar adepts whose danger lay in their austere guise and pious way of life, and to whom women were easy prey. Two abbeys in particular, Villers and Aulne, both in the diocese of Liège, were noted for their patronage of pious women under a succession of abbots.[89] Why was there never an order of female Cistercians? The answer, perhaps, is that there was no need for one, at least not in Flanders. There, both the Cistercians and the Beguines seemed content with the situation as it was. The Cistercians not only defended them against their detractors but supported them in difficulties as Jacques de Vitry had done previously. Abbot Walter of Villers wanted "nothing more than to attract men to the religious life and to found convents for women." But he saw the danger of an excessive multiplication of Cistercian nunneries, for "he reflected that he was sufficiently occupied by the government of his own monastery." Besides, "he knew that if he sent the older, more enthusiastic monks to these convents to hear confessions, then the younger ones, missing their example, would become less humble and the discipline of the house would be weakened."[90]

The Cistercian general chapter remained firm in its attempt to keep women out of its order, yet certainly in Flanders it showed itself to be tolerant towards those abbots who themselves encouraged some degree of affiliation of convents and Beguine groups. To the Beguines of the diocese of Liège, protection from the monks of Villers and Aulne was a valuable safeguard, not only against the penetration of heresy but as a defense against their detractors. Nor was this a one-way process. The Beguines' lives embodied an idea of sanctity which was most attractive to contemporaries and especially to the Cistercians in Flanders.[91]

The Cistercians in Liège entered into spiritual relationships with nuns and Beguines through which both sides benefited. St. Bernard appeared to Mary of Oignies in a vision, and she had a great admiration for his order.[92] But feminine emotion often went beyond the limit recommended by the abbot of Clairvaux. Diedala, a Beguine, experienced a vision in which, one Christmas night, the Infant Jesus appeared and lay in her arms. She explained that she could not sufficiently wonder at this marvel unless her friend, a monk at Villers, could enjoy it also. So, miraculously, she was transported to the abbey and there presented the child to the monk who was saying mass.[93]

The appearance of such large numbers of women in such diverse forms, demanding that they should be allowed to participate in the large-scale religious changes which were in progress in the early thirteenth century perplexed the church and all those associated with it. A small number of like-minded men, whose activities covered a very wide area and who had influence with these women, attempted to deal with the problem. Jacques de Vitry in Flanders; Bishop Fulk in Languedoc; some Cistercian abbots in Spain and Flanders; Francis and Dominic in a wider European context; all had the interests of the church at heart. These interests were reflected, above all, by Pope Innocent III, who led these men in their common aim to fight current heresies and to keep within the church any movements which might be of value. Alone, his farsightedness, his breadth of vision, and his skill in seeking out such movements, regulating and incorporating them into the church, might have made possible the creation of an independent female order worthy of Clare or Mary of Oignies. But to recognize women in this way proved impossible in the face of antagonism from the traditional forces in the hierarchy. The Lateran Council of 1215 and Innocent's death in the following year combined to hinder still more any progress towards meeting the demands of religious and semi-religious women alike.

Subsequent popes indicated a willingness to support them, but by this time the church was too rigid, the mendicants too widely dispersed and too preoccupied with their internal strife to care what became of them. Left to themselves, the women reverted, becoming branches of the male orders, some vigorous shoots such as the community of St. Damian and the Cistercian nuns and Beguines in Flanders, and others, such as the incorporated Dominican and Franciscan convents, proliferating like suckers and risking always severance from the main life-giving trunk of the church.

NOTES

1. An account of the way in which these groups practiced the *vita apostolica* is given by M. D. Chenu, *Nature, Man and Society in the Twelfth Century* (Chicago, 1968). See also C. Violante, "Hérésies urbaines et rurales en Italie du 11e au 13e siècle," in J. Le Goff, *Hérésies et sociétés dans l'Europe pré-industrielle 11–18 siècles*, Ecole pratique des hautes études. *Civilisation et Sociétés*, 10 (Paris, 1968) who offers an analysis of the movement towards the *vita apostolica*.

2. These doctrines placed woman either on a pedestal or in a bottomless pit; exalted her as the virgin mother of Christ or denigrated her as "the supreme temptress, the most dangerous of all obstacles in the way of salvation." See E. Power, "The Position of Women," in *The Legacy of the Middle Ages*, ed. C. G. Crump and E. F. Jacob (Oxford, 1962), pp. 401–3.

3. R. W. Southern, *Western Society and the Church in the Middle Ages* (Harmondsworth, 1970), pp. 240-72.

4. R. Graham, *St. Gilbert of Sempringham and the Gilbertines* (London, 1901).

5. J. -P. Migne, ed., *Patrologiae cursus completus* (Latin series) vols 1-222 (Paris, 1844-1864), 162: 1053 (henceforth cited as *PL*).

6. *PL* 170: 1273. See also S. Roisin, "L' efflorescence cistercienne et le courant féminin de piété au xiiie siècle," *RHE* 39 (1943): 349-50.

7. *PL* 156: 997; Southern, *Western Society*, p. 313.

8. *PL*, 214: 174; Potthast, *Bibliotheca historica medii aevi*, 2 vols. (1896; reprint ed. [*Repertorium fontiom historiae medii aevi*] Rome, 1962), 1: no. 168 (henceforth cited as Potthast).

9. Southern, *Western Society*, pp. 314-18.

10. They held their own chapters, undertook the benediction of their own nuns, preached and had their own dependent houses. *PL* 216 (1855): col. 356; Potthast, 1: no. 4143.

11. Roisin, "L'efflorescence cistercienne," pp. 354-55.

12. Jacques de Vitry, *Jacobi de Vitriaco libri due quorum prior orientalis sive Hierosolimitanae, alter occidentalis historiae nomine inscribitur*, ed. Franciscus Moschus (Duaci, 1597), p. 306.

13. E. Marténe and U. Durand, *Thesaurus novus anecdotorum* (Paris, 1717), c 2, p. 1312; c 10, p. 1324; c 4, 1327; c 6, p. 1340.

14. *Ibid.*, c 7, p. 1348.

15. Between 1220 and 1240, almost fifty houses for women were incorporated into the order in places as far apart as Castile and Hungary, Ghent and Marseilles. For a comprehensive list of these foundations see Roisin, "L'efflorescence cistercienne," pp. 351-61.

16. The cluniac nunnery of Marcigny, founded specifically for women whose husbands had already become monks, provided a refuge in which "mature women, tired of matrimonial licence, might purge themselves of past errors," Southern, *Western Society,* pp. 310-11.

17. St. Bernard, who was horrified at the dangers implicit in the association of men and women, was only expressing a common contemporary belief in feminine wantonness when he warned that "to be always with a woman and not to have intercourse with her is more difficult than to raise the dead," *PL* 183: 1091.

18. And women could be disruptive as we are reminded in the parody of the chapter of nuns at Remiremont by C. S. Lewis, *The Allegory of Love*, 8th ed. (Oxford, 1965), pp. 18-19.

19. Cap. XIII, Lateran IV in *Conciliorun Oecumenicorum Decreta*, ed. J. Alberigo et al., 2nd ed. (Freiburg, 1962), p. 218. For a discussion of this decree see M. Maccarrone, "Riforma e sviluppa della vita religiosa con Innocenzo III," *Rivista di storia della Chiesa in Italia* (Rome, 1962), 16: 60-69.

20. Jacques de Vitry, born c. 1160-70, probably in Rheims, was a regular canon of St. Nicholas of Oignies in the diocese of Liége from 1211-16, Bishop of Acre from 1216-27, auxilliary Bishop of Liége from 1227-29 and cardinal from 1229-40. See McDonnell, *The Beguines*, pp. 17-21 (n. 28 below). The text of his letters is from *Lettres de Jacques de Vitry*, ed. R. B. C. Huygens (Leiden, 1960), pp. 71-8. But see also "Les passages des lettres de Jacques de Vitry rélatifs à Saint François d' Assise et à ses premiers disciples," ed. R. B. C. Huygens in *Homages à Léon Herrman*, *Collection Latonius* (Brussels, 1960), 44: 446-53.

21. On the *humiliati*, see L. Zanoni, *Gli Umiliati nei loro rapporto con l'eresia l'industria della lana ed i communi nei secolo xii e xiii, Biblioteca historica itialia*,

Serie II, 2 (Milan, 1911); Maccarrone, "Riforma e sviluppo," pp. 46-51: H. Grundmann, *Religiöse Bewegungen [im Mittelalter]* 2nd ed. (Darmstadt, 1970), pp. 70-97, 487-538, and my article "Innocent III's treatment of the *Humiliati*," in *SCH* 8 (1971): 73-82.

22. J. Moorman, A· *History of the Franciscan Order from its origins to the year 1517* (Oxford, 1968), pp. 32-39, 205-25.

23. Jacques de Vitry, *Historia Occidentalis*, pp. 304-7, pp. 334-37; *The Exempla of Jacques de Vitry*, ed. T. F. Crane, *Folk Lore Society Publications*, 26 (1890); *Die Exempla aus den Sermones feriales et communes*, ed. J. Greven (Heidelburg, 1914); *Die Exempla des Jacob von Vitry*, ed. G. Frenken, *Quellen and Untersuchungen zur lateinischen Philologie des Mittelalters* (Munich, 1914), 5:1-153.

24. *Vita Maria Oigniacensis, ASB* 5 (1867): 542-72.

25. *Ibid.*, p. 556.

26. Grundmann, *Religiöse Bewegungen*, p. 173.

27. It was the possession of this to which he attributed his safe arrival in Milan in 1216, despite the hazards of crossing rivers in flood in Lombardy. *Lettres*, p. 72, lines 34-46.

28. For a guide to the huge bibliography on the Beguines see E. W. McDonnell, *The Beguines and Beghards in Medieval Culture* (Rutgers University, 1954). Also a review by J. Van Mierlo in *RHE* 28 (1932): 377-83 of H. Grundmann, *Zur Geschichte der Beginen im XIII Jahrhundert, Archiv für Kulturgeschichte* (1931), 16:292-320. Of special value have been Grundmann, *Religiöse Bewegungen*, pp. 170-98, 319-54 and A. Mens, "Les béguines et béghards dans le cadre de la culture mediévale," *Le Moyen Age* 64 (1958): 305-15.

29. McDonnell, *The Beguines*, p. 21.

30. Southern, *Western Society*, p. 320.

31. Grundmann, *Religiöse Bewegungen*, pp. 322-23.

32. Translated by Southern, *Western Society*, p. 319.

33. Grundmann, *Religiöse Bewegungen*, p. 197.

34. For the origin of the word "beguine," see R. P. Callaey, "Lambert li Beges et les Bèguines," *RHE* 23 (1927): 254-59, and Mens, "Les bèguines et beghards," p. 309.

35. Fulk of Toulouse, poet, *jongleur*, monk, and then Cistercian abbot of Florège, was created Bishop of Toulouse in 1206. In 1212 he was driven from his diocese by heretics and went to preach the crusade in Flanders. His interest in religious women's communities as a bulwark against heresy led him to support Dominic's foundation at Prouille and it was at his request that Jacques de Vitry wrote the life of Mary of Oignies. C. Thouzellier, *Catharisme et Valdéisme en Languedoc à la fin du xii siècle*, 2nd ed. (Louvain, 1969), p. 192.

36. *Lettres*, p. 73, lines 61-70.

37. *Ibid.*, p. 74, lines 76-81.

38. *ASB* 4 (1867): 197.

39. Potthast, 1: no. 5896.

40. Jacques de Vitry, *Historia Occidentalis*, pp. 305-6; J. Greven, "Der Ursprung des Beginenwesens," *HJch* 35 (1914): 26-58, 291-318.

41. For discussion of this question see J. L. Nelson, "Society, Theodicy and the Origins of Heresy: Towards a Reassessment of the Medieval Evidence," *SCH* 9 (1972): 65-77; Chenu, *Nature, Man and Society*, pp. 202-69.

42. *ASB* 5 (1867): 547-50.

43. Jacques de Vitry, *Historia Occidentalis*, pp. 305-6.

44. Grundmann, *Religiöse Bewegungen*, p. 235.

45. *ASB* 5 (1867): 236-37. Two of many other examples are Ida of Nivelles, aged nine, who fled from home to avoid marriage, becoming a Cistercian nun six years

later, and Yolande of Vianden, whose noble family, which included the archbishop of Cologne, tried for years to persuade her to accept an advantageous marriage. They were unsuccessful, and she eventually entered a Dominican convent. See Grundmann, *Religiöse Bewegungen*, pp. 192–93.

46. G. Koch, *Frauenfrage und Ketzertum im Mittelalter* (Be. in, 1962).

47. Power, "The Position of Women," p. 411.

48. Southern, *Western Society*, p. 311.

49. Nelson, "Society, Theodicy and the Origins of Heresy," pp. 71–72.

50. M. Weber, *The Sociology of Religion* (London 1965), p. 106.

51. For a detailed account of Innocent's treatment of Francis see Grundmann, *Religiöse Bewegungen*, pp. 127-35.

52. *Ibid.*, pp. 253–54.

53. It seems that Clare may not have wanted strict claustration at all. See Moorman, *The Franciscan Order*, p. 36.

54. Grundmann, *Religiöse Bewegungen*, pp. 149–51.

55. For a discussion of dates, *ibid.*, p. 150 n. 147.

56. *ASB* 2 (1867): 757. "Et ut insolitae petitioni favor insolitus arrideret, pontifex ipse cum hilaritate magna petiti privilegii primam notulam sua manu conscripsit."

57. *Lettres*, pp. 77–78.

58. Moorman, *The Franciscan Order*, p. 206.

59. *Lettres*, p. 76, lines 124–32.

60. The friars could not help the Poor Clares by collecting alms for them, and the community of St. Damian experienced great hardship, eking out a living from spinning and making altar linen. See Moorman, *The Franciscan Order*, p. 36.

61. J. H. Sbaralea, *Bullarum Franciscanum* (Rome, 1759), 1:264; Grundmann, *Religiöse Bewegungen*, pp. 258-59.

62. *Ibid.*, p. 260. Grundmann thinks that Francis agreed to the adoption of Hugolino's rule by the community of St. Damian before he left for Egypt in 1218 or 1219.

63. Moorman, *The Franciscan Order*, p. 35.

64. Grundmann, *Religiöse Bewegungen*, p. 62.

65. Thouzellier, *Catharisme et Valdéisme*, p. 253.

66. *Ibid.*, p. 200.

67. These women confessed to Dominic that they had admired those who originally converted them to heresy for their ascetic form of life. See Grundmann, *Religiöse Bewegungen*, p. 209.

68. *Ibid.*, p. 211.

69. Jordanis de Saxonia, *De initiis ordinis; opera ad res ordinis Praedicatorum spectantia*, ed. J. J. Berthier (Freiburg, 1891), p. 19.

70. Grundmann, *Religiöse Bewegungen*, p. 213.

71. *Ibid.*, pp. 213–19 for a full discussion of the foundation of this convent.

72. Jordanis de Saxonia, *De initiis ordinis*, p. 28.

73. Grundmann, *Religiöse Bewegungen*, p. 215.

74. Jordanis de Saxonia, *De initiis ordinis*, p. 25.

75. Sbaralea, *Bullarum Franciscanum*, 1:36.

76. T. Ripoll, *Bullarum ordinis fratrum Praedicatorum*, ed. A. Bremond (Rome, 1729) 7:7.

77. Grundmann, *Religiöse Bewegungen*, pp. 218–19.

78. *Ibid.*, p. 241.

79. Ripoll, *Bullarum ordinis fratrum Praedicatorum*, 1:107.

80. Grundmann, *Religiöse Bewegungen*, p. 245.

81. *Ibid.*, pp. 246–52.

82. Sbaralea, *Bullarum Franciscanum*, 1:413; Grundmann, *Religiöse Bewegunge*, pp. 270-1.
83. *Ibid.*, pp. 224-26.
84. Sbaralea, *Bullarum Franciscanum*, 1:476.
85. *Ibid.*, 1:671.
86. Grundmann, *Religiöse Bewegungen*, pp. 274-75.
87. Southern, *Western Society*, pp. 323-24.
88. Roisin, "L'efflorescence cistercienne," p. 346.
89. *Ibid.*, pp. 358-60, 362-64.
90. *Ibid.*, p. 355.
91. *Ibid.*, p. 372.
92. *ASB* 5 (1867), p. 567.
93. Roisin, "L'efflorescence cistercienne," p. 373.

Sue Sheridan Walker

⟶❖ Widow and Ward: The Feudal Law of Child Custody in Medieval England

The feudal family was dominated by the demands of its social and tenurial position. Land in Anglo-Norman England had been parcelled out on the basis of a society organized (at least theoretically) for war. By the late twelfth century, feudal land was clearly heritable though subject to the well-defined and heavy burdens of nonfiduciary guardianship, in which until the heir came of age and was able to do homage and fealty for the lands of his late father, both the land and the heir's person were at the disposal of the feudal guardian.[1] The estate or estates of the deceased tenant were considered to be in wardship as was also the heir himself as a person; wardship of the land was separable from wardship of the body. In nonfiduciary guardianship, the feudal lord, or his assignee, as guardian of the land enjoyed the whole profits of the estate, subject to the mere maintenance of the heir; wardship of the body carried with it the lucrative right to arrange the heir's marriage.[2] Because of the distinction between wardship of the land and wardship of the body, different lords could receive the custody of lands held of them by the late tenant—the child's father and their vassal—but the custody of the body was considered indivisible. A ward might have many nonfiduciary guardians— several as custodians of the land and one as custodian of the body—yet none of these would, of right, be his mother.

Early death of military fathers and children, combined with early and frequent marriage, made the feudal family a complex structure. This complexity makes difficult the interpretation of the large body of extant

This paper was read at the Second Berkshire Conference on the History of Women at Radcliffe, October 1974, and will appear among the Berkshire Papers in *Feminist Studies* 3, no. 3/4 (1975); reprinted by permission of the publisher. Copyright © Feminist Studies Inc. My appreciation is due to the staff of the Public Record Office (London, England) and the Newberry Library (Chicago) for facilitating my research.

legal and administrative records. Was the widow the mother of the heir or a subsequent wife? Was she perhaps also the mother of a family of children debarred from succession by the existence of the present heir? I have examined more than fifteen hundred royal administrative records and the rolls of the royal courts for the period from the twelfth to the mid-fourteenth century—many of them court rolls of hundreds of membranes—and if there is much that is still obscure, one may see something of the significance of the female feudatory in regard to her children, even if her rights related more to her position as a property holder and member of a great family than to her role as a mother.[3]

Inheritance to feudal lands in this period was determined by rules of primogeniture; the eldest male child succeeded to the fief or, failing a male heir, any surviving females were joint heirs.[4] When there was a male heir who was the ward, in all probability the other siblings stayed in the custody of the mother, to be reared upon her dower and family lands. The death of the ward would draw into feudal wardship the survivors who had been in maternal custody. Records are rarely informative about the fate of the heir's siblings but a writ of Henry III illustrates this point by ordering the delivery of the daughter, now the heiress, to take the place of her dead brother:

> To Mabel late the wife of Roger Torpell. She must well remember that the king gave the custody of the land and heirs of the said Roger de Tropell, with the marriage of the heirs, to R. bishop of Chichester, the chancellor, during the minority of the heirs, whereof because William the eldest son and heir, has died, the king commands her, as she loves herself and her goods, not to eloign Acelota, sister and next heir of the said William, whom the chancellor committed to her ward to nurse, but to deliver her to the messenger of the said bishop bearing these letters with letters of the bishop testifying that he is his messenger.[5]

The sheriff of Northampton was ordered to enforce the writ. If the widow did not deliver the child to the bishop or his messenger, the sheriff was "to distrain her to do so by her lands and goods in that county."[6] The guardian had, of course, the right to arrange the heir's marriage, so that the daughter who had lived with her mother then had to take the place of her dead brother in the guardian's hands.

Because the child and the feudal lands returned to the overlord on the death of the tenant and father, the mother had no right to the guardianship of her child. Not sentiment as to who would most suitably nurture the infant shaped minority in medieval England, but rules which governed land tenure. Although debarred by right from the custody of feudal heirs in their role as mothers, they were, however, not weak creatures without a recognized place in feudal society nor the capacity to assert their influence over the lives of their children. Claims on the basis of motherhood were largely ignored by laws dominated by concepts relating to the holding of land, but women of the feudal class could themselves hold feudal lands both in virtue of their dower rights and family lands in *maritagium*.[7] The term "dower" refers to the widow's share of her husband's estate, not to a gift made by her parents to the young couple on marriage. Such gifts were frequently made but were termed lands in *maritagium;* designed to help the new family, they also provided support for future generations. Dower was usually a cumulative life interest in roughly a third of the husband's feudal estate; the more times a woman was widowed and remarried, the more her substance. When the widow died, her "third" returned to the estate from whence the dower came, while the lands in *maritagium* would pass to her heirs in whatever way had been stipulated by her family when the grant was made; the stipulation could have set lands aside as patrimonies for her daughters. Women feudatories were habitual suitors in the courts for their dower rights and jealously protected their feudal interests, including the rights of guardianship over their tenants' wards, both by law and by "self-help," that is, by seizing property with an armed force.

There is no reason to assume that widows would wish to keep their sons at home, since their raising involved primarily military training, but there were two ways that mothers could indeed secure the custody of their children: by retaining the *de facto* control of the child at the guardian's discretion, or to buy or receive the guardianship of the heir from the feudal overlord who had the right of custody. After the death of the father and before the custody was sold, the child normally resided with the mother, though in royal custodies the child and the lands were said to be under the jurisdiction of the escheator, a crown official in charge of collecting royal feudal revenues.[8] If, when the guardian came into possession of the lands, the child continued to reside with the mother, the guardian was obligated to pay a maintenance for the child's support.[9] Royal records contain copious examples of the payment of such maintenance allowances.[10] A writ of 30, Edward I appropriated funds for the maintenance of several wards while carefully asserting that the arrangement was to be only temporary until permanent grants were made.[11] This period of "nurture" with the mother varied according to the guardian's wishes, but the usual termination was the arrangement of the child's marriage, or betrothal, probably at the age of six or seven.[12] It must have been a convenience to the purchaser of a wardship, if he were without an ample household, to have the infant feudatory stay with the mother as an alternative to leaving it in a convent or to paying someone else to care for it.[13]

Once the marriage was arranged, it was customary for the heir or heiress to reside with the future in-laws.[14] Administrative records contain many orders to take the child from its mother and deliver it to the ultimate purchaser of its marriage. The *Register of the Black Prince,* for instance, records that messengers coming to him on business were "to cause the body of the daughter and heir of Sir John Dauney to be brought to him at London as quickly as possible, doing what courtesy they can to the damsel's mother without damage to the ["Black"] prince."[15] One may presume sadness in such parting; certainly there is a melancholic note in the following mandate of Henry III:

> (1238) Mandate to A. late the wife of Ralph son of Bernard, in accordance with the bond she made by letters patent to surrender at the king's demand the heirs of the said Ralph, her lord, the custody of whom the king granted to her at the time because of their tender years, to deliver them to Blaise de la Mare and William Moissun, messengers of the king's special clerk, Master Simon de Esteilland, to whom the king has granted their custody and marriage.[16]

The infant bride or groom must have passed from the nursery of the mother to that of the mother-in-law, to be raised with its future spouse. The new family had, of course, an investment in preserving the heir's wellbeing until majority when its own child would share in the enjoyment of the estates.[17] A child bride did not necessarily go to live with the grooms's family; the groom might be as likely to join her nursery. The family who purchased the marriage of either the male or female ward would be the most likely host, but the young couple could have been entrusted to a third party, kin to neither bride nor groom.

Not satisfied with merely the prospect of the temporary nurture of the heir and the loss of the right to arrange its marriage, some widows entered the feudal wardship market to purchase the heir's custody. In the reign of John, Isabella de Clinton was successful in outbidding a wardship buyer by one hundred marks, thereby securing both the custody of the lands and the heir.[18] The pipe, fine and memoranda rolls show mothers who purchased at least the wardship of the body.[19] The market on occasion was even manipulated to favor the mother as when Edward I enjoined the escheator:

> Whereas the king wills, that Margaret, late the wife of John Giffard, tenant in chief, shall be preferred to others in buying the wardship during the heir's minority of the land and of the marrying of his son and heir and of the castle of Brunnesfeld. If she cannot find security for the whole sell her at least the castle and the marriage.[20]

There is no reason to believe such preference was based on sentiments favoring mothers as guardians, for this same close roll entry continues that Margaret was to have "the custody of the prisoners in the castle"—obviously in this case the tender mother was also an experienced jailor.[21] A mother could be given the custody of the heir by favor, as when the daughter of

Edward III gave such custody to Philippa, the widow of Roger Mortimer, along with one hundred marks a year to sustain the heir.[22] The escheators regularly sold minor wardships in the counties.[23] Usually the names of the purchasers were not recorded but it is probable that many such wardships were returned to familial if not to maternal hands.

So little is known of medieval childhood, either within the paternal home or elsewhere, that the scraps of evidence provided by economic documents such as wardrobe accounts are worth mentioning. Some idea of the lives of the wards can be gathered from the provision of new clothes (fur-trimmed or not according to the child's station in society), of endless pairs of shoes (perhaps a testimony to rough use in children's play), of a psalter for a bishop's ward which records his pet name in the ecclesiastical household, the provision of syrups and medicine to "drive away death."[24] The children of Henry III's nursery had occasional visits from a royal minstrel to entertain them and apples were provided by royal stewards to feed the pet porcupine—a dubious choice for a child's plaything.[25] Older male wards on the way to becoming knights received "allowances," but the lot of the little wards of both sexes must have been shaped by the nurses and tutors provided for them, of whom little is known save for names in account books.[26] The lives of children in their mother's household would probably have been little different.

No provision for feudal heirs was final. Because of the tangle of tenurial relations that was a part of subinfeudation and plural lordships, persons with some species of right over the child might at any time enter the scene to challenge the existing arrangements by the initiation of litigation or sometimes by "self-help" in seizing the wardship or the heir. Time and again mothers were forced to answer pleas of the so-called writ of right of ward (*quod reddat custodia*) by guardians who claimed they had been "deforced" of the ward.[27] Fortunately for the historian, simple denial was not enough to explain the defendant's species of right to the wardship and thereby refute the claims of the plaintiff that she was a deforcer. Especially in cases concerning wardship of the body alone, mothers would often reply that they claimed nothing in the wardship or only by nurture.[28] What was implied in the claim "by nurture"? *Nutriciam* was not used with precision in medieval English legal records; one has the impression it meant only that the mother kept her *de facto* custody of the child until a proper guardian was forthcoming.[29]

As a part of their defence, mothers usually offered to yield the child to the rightful guardian.[30] There is an entry in the King's Bench rolls of Edward III recording a case on error where a widow had yielded her child, an heir, to a wrongful guardian, presumably at the mistaken direction of the Court of Common Pleas.[31] Occasionally, compromises such as that in a case of *quod reddat*, where a widow agreed to give up claim to the lands in wardship in order to receive the custody of the child until its majority, indicate the possibility of the heir remaining with the mother.[32] Some plaintiffs do not win the right to the custody, so that the child's fate was not yet settled.[33] All cases were, of course, decided on the basis of feudal right, not maternity.

How intricate were many of these cases can be seen in the disputes concerning Juliana, the widow of Robert Underburgh. Summoned in 1329 to the Court of Common Pleas to answer three separate writs which demanded that she render to the complainant the land and heir of the late Robert, she responded that she was no deforcer but the guardian of the heir by right of nurture and was in possession of a portion of the land in question as her dower. The singularity of the case is not in the number of guardians who claimed they had the same ward but in the expeditious way in which the court handled the matter: the order was given to but one jury to determine which of the three complainants had the right to the wardship. The jury decided that the prior of Walsingham should recover the custody from Benedict, the second plaintiff, damages were fixed at one hundred shillings, and Benedict was also fined for false claim. John, the third plaintiff, took nothing by his writ and he and his pledges were fined for false claim. The ward was declared now to be in the care of the prior and Juliana went free, correct in her contention that she should not have been the defendant.[34] In a less tangled 1279 Essex *quod reddat* case, the court did hold the lady at fault. Constance, widow of the ward's father, lost the land in custody to the plaintiff and on the court roll is shown to owe a fine. No damages were listed, however, possibly in recognition of extenuating circumstances.[35]

Maternal custody was more common in socage lands, a free tenure closer to the peasant level in which the land and the heir were placed in the familial custody of a relative who could not inherit in the event of the child's death—a grim reminder that improper care of the child might hasten the inheritance. Socage guardianship was custodial and designed to protect the property and benefit the heir.[36] Mothers who acted as guardians ("next friends") of socage lands were especially liable to be involved in litigation if their late husbands held any land by feudal tenure.[37] It was common to hold land by a variety of tenures; if any land were held by military tenure, the rules of nonfiduciary guardianship described above would apply here. Under no circumstances would socage lands be placed in feudal guardianship, although the heir himself and his feudal lands would be subject to those feudal rules of minority which were discussed above.[38]

Writs of wardship normally would assert mothers were guilty of "deforcing" wardships through their passive continuance of nurturing the heir, but there were instances when mothers were accused of "ravishing" their own children—that is kidnapping them and arranging a marriage contrary to the guardian's interest.[39] The mother might well have seized her own child not for the sake of its companionship but rather to gain the right to sell the child's marriage, a matter of material consequence dependent upon the size of the estate and the social importance of the family. Or perhaps she was attempting to fulfill a family arrangement of the marriage, as in a Kent ravishment case which runs through a dozen years of the plea rolls. This was a family quarrel within a feudal dispute where the litigants were sisters-in-law. The defendant, Goditha, was accused of having ravished Agatha's son by marrying him to her daughter. Goditha tried to justify her action by claiming that the marriage was planned in the lifetime of the fathers.[40] The ultimate disposition of the case is not known, but at least during the same stage of the proceedings Goditha was put into jail—one of the few persons ever imprisoned for ravishment as provided by statute.[41] When mothers such as this vindictive Agatha did secure the feudal guardianship of their own child, they were liable to lose the enjoyment of the estate to "ejectors" or "ravishers." But in common with any guardian in possession of a wardship which suffered such deprivation, they could sue writs of ejectment from custody (ejectio custodia) or ravishment and abduction (rapuit et abduxit) if the heir were kidnapped and married contrary to their wishes.[42]

Much research still remains to be done to estimate how many mothers in each reign did become guardians of the heir. Who had the right to the custos corporis and the right to sell the marriage can be determined, but often it is not easy to say who had actual possession of the child for the purposes of nurture. Sometimes the facts come to us accidentally through the garrulousness of a scribe who had included in the record that the heir was in the custody of the mother.[43] Diverse legal actions must be studied, not only litigation in which the custody itself is called into question but also cases of dower in which the heir would be vouched to warrant—that is, to give substantiating evidence that the widow was indeed the wife of the heir's late father. Cases in which the heir was called to warrant are valuable to the historian because the record always stated in whose actual care the ward was found; the guardian was expected to give such warranty for a child who was too young to do so. Court cases of this kind balance the comparative absence of private administrative records against the wealth of royal administrative records.

As has been seen, the documents do not always make clear the precise relationship of a widow to the ward whose guardianship is in dispute. Widows frequently remarried, but this is not always evident in the entry.[44] An exhaustive search of the court rolls would have to be combined with improved geneological material in the form of a Dictionary of National Biography for the minor feudality if the historian were to be able to distinguish with greater clarity social and economic as well as regional differences in the patterns of maternal custody.

On the basis of my reading of the plea rolls and other legal and administrative records for this period, I would conclude that many, probably most heirs were not raised by their widowed mothers and therefore must have spent part of their brief childhood apart from their siblings. However this might have been true had their father lived; because of early marriage and the English emphasis on education and social formation outside the home, it was not expected that the heir was to remain under his mother's care.[45] Mothers sometimes obtained custody of the heir, but most of the evidence points to the infrequency of widows being guardians of the body of the heir with the concomitant right to sell the child's marriage.[46] Even when mothers were among the guardians or portions of the land in wardship, the control of the heir was not in their hands.[47]

Among the major feudatories, it was rare for the child heir to be left in the care of the mother. How could her nurture have been an introduction to the skills of a military society? It is not surprising, then, to find the heir of a great magnate like Mortimer in the wardship of the king, or like Bello Campo in the guardianship of the queen.[48] Nor can one doubt the social suitability of the household of prominent ecclesiastics like Roger the bishop of Coventry and Lichfield, or the abbot of Tewkesbury, or noblewomen such as the Countess of Gloucester and Hereford or the Countess of Wynton; all of these were certainly desirable places in which to raise a young heir.[49]

The great feudatories themselves offered in turn obvious advantages to the minor heirs of their tenants "in chivalry." The court rolls show the same Mortimer family as guardians of their feudal wards, as they do of other baronial families such as the Wakes and the de Ros.[50] The homes of minor feudatories would have had much of the same advantages for lesser feudal tenants.[51] Within the feudal pyramid, with the royal household at the apex down to the lesser lords, the feudal lords—if they chose to exercise their rights of guardianship personally—offered the heirs of their tenants social and educational advantages as important as any school.

Feudal guardianship was nonfiduciary as well as custodial. Wardships were vendible feudal rights and were often sold and resold. When examples are found of mothers who bought the custody of their child, there is no reason to doubt that she would in turn sell the marriage and the child would pass from her custody.[52] There is a Berkshire case in 1288 where Alice, the widow of William de la Penne, sued a man for having ravished John her son and the heir of her late husband. The defendant replied that Alice had indeed obtained the right to the custody of her child, but she had in turn sold the custody and the marriage to someone who had sold it to him, the defendant. The jury agreed and Alice lost the case.[53]

That feudal women did not make greater attempts to secure control over their children does not suggest weakness or indifference, but rather their acceptance of prevailing societal attitudes as to the raising of future feudatories, male and female. Long ago Eileen Power wrote that "books of deportment are singularly silent as a whole, on the subject of maternal duties."[54] Motherhood for the upper classes in medieval Europe, she pointed out, was not demanding because of wet nurses and short childhoods determined by early marriage and the custom of "sending both boys and girls away to the households of great persons to learn breeding."[55]

Legal records reveal that while much ingenuity was applied to withdraw parts of or to avoid altogether the burdens of the wardship of lands, little was done to avoid wardship of the body and the operation of the feudal marriage law. If feudal society in general did not protest these arrangements, it is hardly surprising that the widow, herself a feudatory, voiced no complaint.

NOTES

1. *Tractatus de legibus et consuetudinibus regni Anglie qui Glanvilla vocatur,* ed. with intro., notes and trans. by G. D. H. Hall (London, 1965) 7: 9, 10, 11; 9: 4 (henceforth cited Glanvill). S. E. Thorne, "English Feudalism and Estates in Land," *The Cambridge Law Journal* 17 (1959): 193-209, argues heritability of feudal lands was not fixed until 1200. But the practice of feudal wardship was well established by the reign of Henry II, as can be seen in the material in *Rotuti de dominabus et pueris et puellis de xii comitatibus (1185),* Pipe Roll Society 35, (London, 1913). The complex story of wardship practice from Henry II to the early years of Henry III can be pieced together from the pipe and eyre rolls, as I have shown in "Royal Wardship in Medieval England," (Ph.D. dissertation, University of Chicago, 1966), Chapter 3, pp. 50-76.

2. Bracton, *De Legibus et Consuetudinibus Angliae,* ed. G. E. Woodbine, trans. with revisions and notes by S. E. Thorne, (Cambridge, Mass., 1968), 2: fol. 86, re "marriage" fols. 88 and 89, (henceforth cited Bracton).

3. For an earlier review of the kinds of evidence examined see my "Proof of Age of Feudal Heirs in Medieval England," *Mediaeval Studies* 35 (1973): 306, no. 2.

4. Glanvill, 7:3.

5. *Calendar of Patent Rolls,* Henry III, 6 vols., (London, 1901-1913), 3:301 (henceforth cited *CPR, Henry III*).

6. *Ibid.*

7. Glanvill 6, and editor's note, pp. 183-84 re "dower" and 7:1 and note pp. 186-87, re "maritagium." See also T. F. T. Plucknett, *The Legislation of Edward I* (Oxford, 1962), pp. 120-135.

8. Allowance to the widowed mother of William de Cortelingstok, a ward of a ward of Edward I by virtue of the estate of Patrick de Cadurcis being in the king's hand, Public Record Office (henceforth cited as PRO)MSS E 136/3/7 m 3. The Countess of Ulster, a kinswoman of the king, in 1334 received an enlargement of her grant of one hundred marks for the sustenance of Elizabeth, daughter and heir of the late Earl of Ulster and ward of the king. The countess was to receive a total of one hundred and fifty marks yearly at the exchequer "for such time as the heir shall stay in her custody." *Calendar of Patent Rolls,* Edw. III, 25 vols. (London, 1891-1916), 2:31 (henceforth cited as *CPR, Edward*).

9. For example, in 1295 Edward I ordered that Joan, widow of Owen de la Pole, tenant-in-chief, was to have twenty marks yearly from the estate of her husband for the "sustenance of his son and heir, a minor in her ward." *Calendar of Fine Rolls,* (London, 1911-49) 1:351 (henceforth cited as *CFR*). The liberate rolls of 38, Henry

III (1254) allow one mark to Margery of Womford, "the king having granted her the wardship of her son, John, and that sum for his maintenance." *Calendar of Liberate Rolls,* Henry III, 4 vols. (London, 1916 in progress), 4:177. Edward III adjusted a grant which had been made five years previously to Agnes, the widow of Laurence of Hastynges, Earl of Pembroke, and a subsequent husband (also deceased) of certain castles during the minority of the earl's heir. She was now to pay only 160 pounds yearly into the royal wardrobe, instead of 240 pounds as had been first stipulated, as long as the sustenance of the heir remained at her cost. But if the marriage of the heir were sold by the king so that she would no longer keep the heir, she would have to pay 240 pounds. If in the past she had paid more for the wardship or for the heir than 80 pounds yearly allowed for his maintenance she was to be reimbursed, *CFR,* 7:33.

10. W. O. Ault, "Manors and Temporalities," in *English Government at Work* eds. Willard, Morris, and Dunham, 3 vols. (Med. Acad., 1940-50), 3: 16, contains several examples from the fine rolls; notes 7 and 8 also contain a good deal of information.

11. *PRO* MSS E 153/1/5 m 8.

12. The fact of early marriage is well recognized; see for example F. Jouon des Longrais, "Le statut de la femme en Angleterre dans le droit commun médiéval," *La Femme,* Societè Jean Bodin, 12 (Brussels, 1960), esp. p. 203 ("au moyen âge, les mariages sont en Angleterre singulierement precoces)," and D. M. Stenton, *The English Woman in History* (London, 1957), pp. 44-45. Because of the church law that required free consent for marriage, there is a difficulty in determining the passage from betrothal to binding marriage. Charles Donahue, in an important paper for the 1972 international canon law congress in Toronto, "The Policy of Alexander III's Consent Theory of Marriage," addresses himself to this and to other problems concerned with medieval marriage. The church unsuccessfully opposed child marriage: the papal petitions contain several examples of the dissolution of marriage between minors, even though issue was born of the marriage; see my paper "The Marrying of Feudal Wards in Medieval England," *Studies in Medieval Culture* 4/2 (1974): 209-224.

13. Mary Green, *Lives of the Princesses of England,* 6 vols. (London, 1849-1955), 2: 433-35, concerning girls under the special tutelage of Mary, the sixth daughter of Edward I and a nun at Amesbury. Later, in the reign of Henry VII, Catherine de la Pole, abbess of Barking, received 50 pounds for expenses incurred during her custody of Edmund and Jasper "ap Meredity ap Tydier" by command of the king. F. Devon, *Issues of the Exchequer, Henry III to Henry VI* (London, 1837), pp. 437-438.

There is a receipt dated 22 Edward III for Roger de Creting for his expenses in maintaining the three children of Thomas de Cornerde. PRO MSS C 47, Chancery Mis. Bundle 3, No. 32, Part IV (formerly Dep. 891). Two more examples of such accounts exist for the reign of Henry VI; a much defaced "particulars of the account for the maintenance of the heirs and possessions of Richard Hankeford," PRO MSS E 101/514/25, 10-17 Henry VI m 4, and a long membrane of the account of Margaret Frampton for the expenses of Hugh Camays and Elizabeth Drayton, minors in the king's ward, *ibid.,* File 10. Sometimes it is not clear if the child is in the family hands, the care of a royal custodian, or if arrangements had been made such as described above. For example, monies appropriated for the maintenance of John, son and heir of Henry Reyhill "senior," where are listed also some stipulated repairs to the estate, PRO MSS E 136/3/8 m 18, and several sums listed for the son and heir of John de Bello Campo, *ibid.,* m 18, m 22.

14. See Philippe Ariès, *Centuries of Childhood,* trans. Robert Baldick (London, 1962), pp. 329, 332.

15. *Register of the Black Prince*, 4 vols. (London, 1930), 1: 15.

16. *CPR, Henry III*, 3: 229.

17. For a guardian who has custody of the body of John, heir of Galfridi Russel and Isabella his wife, PRO MSS Court of Common Pleas CP 40/141 m 189 (North), (henceforth cited CP 40/).

18. *Rotuli de Oblatis ... Johannis*, (London, 1835), p. 61; a similar example, *CPR*, Henry III, 3:107.

19. See Pipe Roll 16, Henry II, Pipe Roll Society, 15 (London, 1892); p. 63; and Pipe Roll 2, Richard I, PRS, 39 (London, 1925), p. 21 for two of many examples of this common practice.

For fine rolls see, for example, *Excerpta e Rotulis Finium ... Henrici III*, Records Comm. 1835-1836), 1: 75 (re widow of Robt. de Ver fined with Henry III for the custody of the lands and heirs of her late husband), and p. 420 (re widow of John le Viere); *CFR* 2: 333 (re custody of John de Mares).

PRO MSS Exchequer Memoranda Rolls E 159/14 m 19d (Devon) (1235-36), widow of William de Meysy fines with the king fifty-three pounds, two marks for the custody of the land and heir of her late husband (henceforth cited E 159); E 159/16 m 6 (1237-38) Margary, the wife of Henry la Pringe, fines for the custody of the land and heir of her late husband Henry de la Pomeye; E 159/72 m 56r (26-27 Edward I), Gena the widow of Roger de Caleston pays forty pounds to the king to have the license to marry herself as she wishes and the right to marry the heir without disparagement; m 69d, Isabella, the widow of Fulcon de Penebrugg, gives one hundred pounds to have the marriage without disparagement, of Fulcon, son and heir of her late husband; m 70r, Joanna, the widow of Bertin de Cughtrescate, ten marks for the right to marry John, son and heir of Bertin, without disparagement. Joanna's entry notes that if the heir died, for the same fine the king granted her the marriage of the next heir.

20. *Calendar of Close Rolls*, Edward I, 5 vols, (London, 1900-1908), 4: 254-55.

21. *Ibid.*

22. *CPR*, Edward III, 13: 37-38.

23. For example, *Calendar Patent Rolls*, Edward I, 4 vols. (London, 1893-1901), 1: 77, (henceforth cited *CPR*, Edward I); *CFR*, 1: 46; *CFR*, 2: 213; *CPR* Edward I, 2: 151 (in this case addressed to the sheriff of Glamorgan and keeper of the Clare estates).

24. PRO MSS Escheators' Files E 153/1/ File 5 m B 8 (20, Edw I) expenses for wardship of Henry de Erdington, ten marks for robes and food for the period prior to the sale of his marriage to Thomas de Walneye of county Warwick. More details are given of the clothing for the ward of the Bishop Swinfield in *A Roll of Household Expenses of Bishop Swinfield*, Camden Society, Old Series, vol. 63 (London, 1855), pp. 184-85. Clothes and "harness" are mentioned in the pipe roll for 25 Henry II, *Pipe Roll 25 Henry II*, Pipe Roll Society, 37 (London, 1907), p. xxii, concerning the heir, "Baldwin de Reviers." In Madox, *Baronia Anglica* (London, 1741), p. 74, the entry appears "and for clothes for the use of William de Elinton's daughter who is in the king's wardship for the present year and two years past"; Hilda Johnstone, *Edward of Carnarvon* (Manchester, 1946), p. 11; *Household Expenses of Bishop Swinfield*, pp. 131-32; Johnstone, *Edward of Carnarvon*, pp. 12-13, describes medication purchased for the king's son and other wards in the household.

25. Green, *Lives of the Princesses*, 2: 226-27, and T. F. Tout, *Chapters in Medieval Administrative History*, 6 vols. (Manchester, 1923-35), 5: 243. Green, *Lives of the Princesses*, 2: 2, discusses the purchase of a dove for the royal children.

26. "Household Ordinances of York, 1318" in T. F. Tout, *The Place of the Reign of Edward II in English History* (Manchester, 1936), p. 277; younger wards with their exhibitions, *ibid.*, p. 252. Hilda Johnstone, "The Wardrobe and Household of Henry,

Son of Edward I," *Bulletin of the John Rylands Library* 7 (1922-23): 387-90; for rewards to nurses of the royal children in the reign of Edward III, *Calendar of Close Rolls*, Edward III, 14 vols. (London, 1896-1913), 8:26.

27. For example, CP 40/14 m 37 Leyt), m 56 (Norf) (1276); CP 40/21 m 87d (Wylt) (1277); CP 40/32 m 35 (Linc) (1280), where the widow in her defence refers to previous litigation on the same subject; CP 40/103 (Wylt) (1294) where a mother and a clergyman are defendants concerning John, the son and heir of her late husband; similarly PRO MSS Court of Common Pleas Bench Writ Files CP 52/1 (Hilary 20 Edward I [1301]), where the child is claimed as the ward of a ward; CP 40/132 m 199 (Ebor) (1300): CP 52/1 Easter 6 Edward I (Suff) (1278) and CP 52/1 (Mich. 27-28 Edward I [1299]) (Staff) (henceforth cited CP 52/1).

28. PRO MSS Court of Curia Regis KB 26/169 m 27 (Oxon) (1259-61) (henceforth cited as KB 26/); PRO MSS Court of the Justices Itinerant 1/178 m 2 (1269-70 (henceforth cited Just 1/); CP 40/102 m 49 (North) (1293) and CP 40/194 m 33 (1312); CP 40/277 m 18d (1327).

29. CP 40/22 m 5 (1278), widow suing for dower is accused by the defendant of maliciously eloigning the custody of the heir so that if she gives him up she will get her dower; Just 1/89 m 19d (1285-6), where "nutriciam" is used in regard to a socage ward in care of relatives.

30. A widow brings her child into court for this purpose, CP 40/27 m 160d (Essex) (1327); *Year Book* 6, Edw II, Seldon Society, vol 34 (London, 1918), pp. 171, 178, and YB 40-50, Edw, III fol. 32R #28; a widow actually does turn over her child, CP 40/8 m 41 (Horff). See further, Plucknett, *Legislation of Edward I*, p. 117.

31. KB 27/395 m 38 (Warr) (1359).

32. Just 1/1055 m 72d (1278-9): Just 1/487 m 19 (1280-81) indicating the carrying out of the concord, including transfer of "seisin"—interesting terminology referring to the custody of the heir himself.

33. CO 40/42 m 6 (Horht) and CP 40/69 m 41d (Ebor), both mothers go "*sine die*" and the plaintiffs were fined for false claim.

34. CO 40/277 m 152 (1329), a mother and other defendants in two suits relating to the same heir; CP 40/132 m 33 (Ebor) and another m 66d (1300).

35. KB 27/26 m 36d (1276); a similar case in Warwickshire, CP 40/31 m 126 (1279).

36. Bracton, fol. 86, 87b and 88; Glanville, 7: Pt. 2.

37. Socage guardians as defendants: KB 26/136 m 7d (1249), KB 26/138 m 18 (1250) (Northumb); relatives and socage heirs but no mother, CP 52/1 17, Edward I (Hertf). Widows and other relatives of men who held by socage tenure were routinely put to suit to secure the guardianship as "next friend" as in KB 26/137 m 16 (Oxon); KB 26/136/1/2 Trinity 56, Henry III (Sussex), for three instances where the mother was the plaintiff in cases of ravishment and abduction: CP 40/23 m 28 (Berk), CP 40/148 m 163 (Hoting) and KB 27/255 m 77 (Sussex).

38. 25, Edward I Magna carta C 27 (1297) *Statutes of the Realm*, 11 vols. in 12 (Rec. Comm., 1810-28), 1: 117 (henceforth cited as *Statutes*); a case indirectly illustrating the guardianship rule when a mother of a son and heir in socage was sued for disseisin and the court upheld her right to the custody and she went *sine die*, KB 27/159 m 35d (1299).

KB 26/165 m 14 (Devon) (1260). The Countess of Devon was sued by a mother who was the "next friend" of a ward in socage, but went *sine die;* a mother who was the next friend in socage suing one Agnes Berton, who was identified as the custodian of the feudal lands and the body of the heir of the plaintiff's late husband, to recover the guardianship of the socage land, KB 26/136 m 7d (1249), and continued on KB 26/137 m 17d (1250), still with no result recorded.

39. Just 1/1055 m 61 (York) (1278-79); KB 27/212 m 27d (Lanc) (1313), widow and three others defendants; E 13/17 m 31 (Ebor) (1290-92), mother accused of "subtracting" the heir and marrying him against the king's will; CP 40/138 m 148 (Hereford) (1303) Johanna, widow of Adam de Lorymer, went *sine die* in a plea of ravishing Walter, the son and heir. Johanna disputed the tenural claims of the plaintiff and the jury supported her. Probably she had taken her son from the plaintiff but he had had no right to the custody, and hence there was no case against her.

40. KB 27/184 m 10 (1306), cancelled but gives a good summary of previous litigation; there is more on m 30.

41. KB 27/191 m 5 (1308): KB 27/205 m 90 (1311). For a sister-in-law who received the custody of her nephew, E 159/72 m 57d (26-27 Edward I). There is another quarrel over a feudal custody in CP 40/19 m 19d (Cant) (1277). Statute of Merton, 20 Henry III (1236); *Statutes*, 1:3, 5-6; Westminster II (1285)c 35 went further and provided terms of imprisonment alone as punishment for ravishers, *Statutes*, 1: 88. See Plucknett, *Legislation of Edward I*, p. 114.

42. CP 40/26 m 142d (Horht) (1278); CP 52/1 Trinity 10, Edward I (Soms) (1282).

In KB 27/110 m 16d (Berk) (1288), Gilbert, the defendant, declared and the jury agreed that the mother was seized of the body of the heir but had sold the marriage to Gilbert. The mother was put in mercy for false claim. In CP 40/148 m 163 (Hoting) (1278), the plaintiff claimed ravishment of a socage heir but the defendant said the land was feudal—no result was recorded. In KB 27/255 m 67 (Sussex), again the plaintiff is a socage guardian but also alleged the asportation of chattels—there is no result listed.

43. Just 1/643 m 5 (1268-69), or CP 40/24 m 52 (Essex) (1278), where the queen is the plaintiff and her attorney alleges that the abductor took the child from the home of Walter le Fletcher and Anna his wife, in whose custody the child was, or as in n. 32 above, where the ward was declared to be now in "the *curia* of the prior," or CP 40/138 m 135 (Leyt/Linc) (1301) where the land is in the king's custody but the child is said to be in the mother's custody.

44. A female plaintiff or defendant listed as the wife of one man suing for or sued about the custody of the heir of another man might be the widow remarried or a stranger. CP 52/1 Mich. 27, Edw I (Noting) gives information showing the plaintiff was formerly married to the father of the heir. Financial records are often more satisfactory in identifying persons both as to present and former husbands; for example, E 159/16 m 6 re "Margia ux' Henr la Pringe," fining to secure the custody of land and heir of former husband Henr de la Pomeye.

45. And the fifteenth-century author Sir John Fortescue, *De Laudibus Legum Anglie*, ed. S. B. Chrimes (Cambridge, 1942), pp. 110-11, waxed eloquent about the moral advantages to young orphans of the princes of the realm or other lords who held immediately of the king being raised in the royal household. Few feudal heirs were actually raised in what Fortescue called "the supreme Academy." Urban T. Holmes, "Medieval Children," in the Book Review section of *The Journal of Social History* 2 (1968-69): 168-69, disagreeing in part with Ariès *Centuries of Childhood*, concedes that "there was undoubtedly a persistent practice of entrusing a boy or girl to one's overlord; or to a prosperous friend or relative. . . . There is no need to labor this point. It is granted that in the majority of instances children were sent away—but in numerous cases the child remained home under direct parental control."

46. For maternal custody: KB 26/166 m 20d (horf) (1262); CP 40/8 m 23 (Essex) (1275); CP 40/27 m 20 (Linc) (1278); CP 40/122 m 23d (Surr/Lond) (1. . . . 98); CP 40/132d m 13 (pencil number) (1300); CP 40/148 m 15d (Ebor) (1303); CP 40/154 m 107 (1305). For nonmaternal custody: KB 26/180 m 5 (Berk/Midd) (1267), two cases;

CP 40/8 m 18 (Leyt) (1275); CP 40/141 m 100 (Ebor) m 108 (Warr) m 207 (Ebor) m 189d (Suff/Essex) (1302); CP 40/152 m 74 (Cant/Sussex) m 128 (Ebor) (1304); CP 40/330 m 303 (Staff) (1342). Such examples are legion; there is more evidence of nonmaternal custody in n. 47–51 below.

47. CO 40/122 m 132d (Wygorn) m 177d (Noht/Leyt) (1298); CP 40/138 m 161 (Surr) (1301); CP 40/141 m 211 (Lanc/Surr) (1302); CP 40/154 m 139 (Staff/Salop) (1305); KB 27/167 m 38 (Hibn/Kent/Essex) (1302), where the mother had custody of some of the land but the king had custody of the daughter.

48. For Mortimer's wardship: CP 40/71 m 53d (1288) and m 43, another lesser feudatory Loveday also in royal custody, and KB 27/167 m 38, an Irish ward with lands also in Kent and Essex. For Bello Campo's guardianship: CP 40/57 m 52d (1285). The queen is a constant recipient of royal wardships.

49. Just 1/47 m 9 (1283–84), where Roger the bishop of Coventry and Lichfield is *custos terre et heredis* of Roger, son of William de Englefeld; Just 1/1005, Pt. 1 m 20d (1280–81), the abbot of Tewkesbury as guardian of the son and heir of Hugh Poltone; CP 40/16 m 62d (1276), guardian is master of the Hospital of St. Lazarus; CP 40/16 m 67d (1276); CP 40/4 m 4 (1273), the Countess of Wynton is custodian of the land and heir of Baldwin de Bassingburn.

50. CP 40/2B m 4 (1273), Roger de Mortuo Mari is *custos* of the heir of John, son of Alan; CP 40/71 m 7d (1288), William de Mortuo Mari is *custos* of the heir of Robert de Musgrose. For other baronial families see, for example, CP 40/3 m 2 (1273), *custos* Robert, son and heir of Baldwin de Veer, and KB 27/177 m 34 (1304), *custos of* Johanna, daughter and heir of Hugh de Barton.

51. CP 40/3 m 28 (1273) (Horf); CP 40/4 m 26 (Cornub) m 24d (Horht) m 9d (Dors/Herf) (1273); CP 40/16 m 61d (Midd/Herf/Horf) (1276); CP 40/57 m 47d (Ebor) (1285); Just 1/63 m 9 (1285–86); CP 40/71 m 62d (Dors) (1288); CP 40/77 m 74d (Ebor) (1288–89).

52. CP 40/5 m 96 (Horf) (1274); CP 40/71 m 2 (Essex), lands in royal custody, child in mother's by fine; m 76 (Lanc) (1288), widow and new husband are guardians, or in the instances cited above n. 46.

53. KB 27/110 m 16d (Berk) (1288). In one of the few articles to focus directly on the widow, Constance Fraser indicates that widows spent most of their energies in trying to get control of the land, restoring castles, or getting a son recognized as heir. "Four Cumberland Widows in the 14th Century," *Transactions of the Cumberland and Westmorland Antiquarian & Archaeological Society* 64 n.s. (1964): 130–37.

54. Eileen Power, "The Position of Women," Chapter 7 of *The Legacy of the Middle Ages,* ed. C. G. Crump and E. F. Jacob (Oxford), 1926), p. 420.

55. *Ibid.*

Stanley Chojnacki

⸺❧ Dowries and Kinsmen in Early Renaissance Venice

In the fifteenth canto of the *Paradiso* (ll. 103–105) Dante wistfully observed that in contrast to his own time, the epoch of his great-great-grandfather, Cacciaguida, did not see fathers taking fright at the birth of daughters. In those good old days, dowries had not yet "fled all limitation." Dante may have been indulging in a familiar kind of romanticizing; certainly twelfth-century Florentine fathers also had to face responsibility for their daughters' dowries. But his laments about the rise in dowries had plenty of echoes. In fact, the problems that the dowry institution itself, and especially dowry inflation, posed in the early Renaissance (fourteenth-fifteenth centuries) are a familiar theme in the historical literature on the period.[1]

The fact of dowry inflation is fairly well documented. An example from Venice can give a sense of the trend. In a sample of fifty mid-*trecento* patrician dowries, the average was about 650 ducats and the largest, about 1540 ducats.[2] By the fifteenth century, however, it was a rare patrician dowry that fell below 1,000 ducats, and there was a strong tendency to go much higher.[3] This tendency was alarming enough to induce the Venetian Senate in 1420 to place a limit of 1,600 ducats on patrician dowries, a good indication that many dowries were larger. But such measures did no good. There are many instances of larger dowries in the years after 1420; and at the beginning of the sixteenth century the Senate passed another law reaffirming the principle of dowry restraint—but resignedly raising the ceiling to 3,000 ducats.[4]

It would be valuable to know whether the rise in dowries was greater, smaller, or about the same as price movements generally in the period. Were Dante and the Venetian senators alarmed because dowries were soaring out

Originally published in *The Journal of Interdisciplinary History* 5, no. 4 (Spring, 1975): 571–600. Copyright © The M.I.T. Press; reprinted by permission of the publisher.

of all proportion to other expenses—and to incomes? Or were their laments over dowries just symptomatic of a general concern over a rising cost of living? Sketchy data, great variations year-to-year in the availability of articles of consumption, and a complex monetary system that fluctuated dizzily during the period make it impossible to plot with any precision general movements in prices or, on a broader level, in the overall cost of living—even without getting into the delicate and complex question of different levels of wealth in the consuming, and dowry-raising, population.[5]

In general, there seems to have been a rise both in prices, particularly in manufactured goods, and in the standard of living.[6] However, there has not been much research on this question in the Italian context. As a center of exchange Venice certainly escaped the worst of the "price scissors" that afflicted the agrarian sector. Yet wheat prices appear to have risen during the period. In 1342–43, a *staio* (2.3 bushels) of wheat cost a Venetian house-holder 22 silver *grossi*, equal at the time to just under one ducat. By 1390 importers were selling wheat to the Venetian government's grain office at about 1.7 ducats per *staio*—a wholesale price that still prevailed, however, in 1432.[7] But wheat prices are a notoriously unrepresentative index of prices generally. Although other isolated bits of evidence testify to a rise in the cost of living, they do not add up to a clear enough picture against which we can gauge the relative impact of the dowry rise. Yet the leading authority on medieval Italian dowries speculated that the increase in dowry levels could be attributed in large part to prospective bridegrooms' growing dowry pretensions in the face of the rise in the cost of living.[8]

But if we cannot be sure whether the increase in dowries was greater than general increases in the cost of living, there is good documentation of a development that helps to explain the concern of fathers in the fourteenth and fifteenth centuries. It is the great squeeze that governmental exactions, especially in the form of forced loans (*prestiti*), put on private wealth. This important question cannot be dealt with in detail here (studies by Luzzatto and others have treated it thoroughly), but its bearing on the rise in dowries can be stated briefly.[9]

Military expenses throughout the third quarter of the fourteenth century put a mammoth burden on the nobles and citizens of Venice—the assessable part of the population. At their worst, during the years of the desperate War of Chioggia with the Genoese, the fisc's levies in two years, 1379–81, drained away about one quarter of the private wealth in Venice.[10] It is true that the impost-paying public gained interest-bearing shares of the state debt (*Monte*) for most of these exactions. It is also true that *Monte* shares could be negotiated for various purposes, including dowry transactions. But by this time the government had given up its former practice of making amortization payments in addition to interest payments; moreover, after 1382 interest payments effectively dropped from 5 to 4 (and for some even

3) percent—considerably lower than the return on commerical or real estate investments; and the market price of *Monte* shares, at its low point of 18 percent of face value in 1382, had risen only to 63 percent of face value by 1400, despite governmental efforts to shore up the *Monte* by buying shares through a sinking fund.[11] So dowry payments in *Monte* shares, whether computed at the market price or at face value were not a one-for-one solution to the squeeze on private wealth that endless *prestiti* levies had effected.

Considering the effect of these fiscal burdens on private wealth, the growth of dowry standards must have been particularly painful for Venetian patricians—"insupportable" in the words of the Senate act of 1420.[12] It is probable that dowries came to demand a much larger chunk of the family patrimony than had been the case earlier. For these reasons, the rise in dowries had important ramifications for Venetian economic life. However, we are primarily concerned here with effects rather than with causes. Specifically, we shall deal with the way in which these ever-larger dowries were assembled. It happens that, at least in Venice, at the same time that dowry inflation was straining the resources of Dante's frightened fathers, the fathers were in fact getting a good deal of help to meet the challenge. This nonpaternal involvement in the raising of dowries is a little-known fact of Venetian social history during the early Renaissance. Yet it has importance not just for the dowry as an institution, but for the family and kinship system of Venice's ruling class. Stated briefly, a widening circle of dowry contributors encouraged a patrician social orientation in which the traditional emphasis on lineage was increasingly complemented by nonlineage ties of affection and interest.

According to Roman dowry practice, the main pupose of the dowry was to help the groom bear the burden of matrimony (*sustinere onera matrimonii*).[13] In its medieval Italian version, however, the Roman *dos* had a special twist. Unlike original Roman practice, the medieval Italian dowry came to be regarded as the girl's share of the patrimony. From this principle flowed several important effects. One was that girls were excluded from a share in the patrimony (the *exclusio propter dotem*). The *fraterna*, or enduring joint inheritance, was for brothers alone: sisters, provided with dowries, had no further legal part to play in their paternal family's economic life. Another effect was that dowries were supposed to be "congruent"—to equal a full share in the patrimony. It was, Pertile observes, to guarantee that dowries would not *exceed* an equal share under the pressure of dowry inflation, that Venice and other cities legislated against excessive dowries.[14] Finally, and most fundamentally, the view that a girl's dowry represented her rightful share of the patrimony meant that she had an indisputable right to a dowry. This was the source of the fathers' fright.[15]

Of course not all girls received marriage portions, no matter what the legal principles demanded. Closeting them in convents was a regular practice, and at its worst led to the scandalous situation in which convents, it was said, were little better than brothels. The 1342 will of the patrician Leone Morosini illustrates why the practice was widespread.[16] He bequeathed to his daughter Lucia a dowry of 576 ducats, along with a *corredum* (in effect, a trousseau of movable goods: personal effects, household items, etc.)of 346 ducats. But his wife was then pregnant and might give birth to another daughter. Rather than divide Lucia's portion between two girls—which would have led to two undistinguished marriages—Leone simply instructed that the second daughter be placed in a convent and given an annuity of ten ducats—quite a saving over Lucia's marriage portion.

Leone proposed the convent for his unborn daughter—in fact, the child turned out to be a son—because it was cheaper than an adequate dowry. But his motive was not simply to rid himself of the burdens of daughters. If two girls were too much to deal with, Leone, like other fathers, still viewed a well-dowered daughter as a social asset. In the same will he provided that if the unborn child was a boy, then Lucia was still to have a dowry "of the right amount for a patrician girl." It was the fathers' interest in effecting favorable matrimonial alliances that kept the marriage market booming and contributed to the rise in dowries—and operated to give concrete application to the legal principles governing families' responsibilities for their daughters' dowries.

But if, according to law, fathers bore primary responsibility for their girls' marriage portions, the responsibility did not stop with them. Contemporary commentators on Roman law and the Venetian statutes asserted that when a man died or became feeble-minded (*mentecaptus*) without providing for his daughters' dowries, his sons, the girls' brothers, took on the charge. This was consistent with the principle of the *fraterna*: the sons who assumed joint proprietorship of their deceased father's estate also assumed his obligations. The same principle further dictated that when male descendants were lacking, dowry responsiblity went to the deceased father's male ascendants.[17]

Even more interesting, and usually unremarked in discussions of the early Renaissance dowry, is the principle that mothers were sometimes obliged to provide dowries, specifically when the father was too poor to do the girl justice. Since mothers were not part of the lineage (they had no membership in their husbands' and sons' patrimonial group), this responsibility signifies that dowries were not exclusively the concern of the patriline. But this slight hint of economic matriliny in a society usually regarded as stoutly patrilineal may have gone even further. If an unmarried and undowered girl lacked parents, brothers, and paternal ascendants, then according to one authority responsibility passed to her maternal grandfather and other maternal ascendants.[18]

What this indicates is that the jurists considered dowry provision important enough to commit a fairly wide kinship web to participation in it. And even though in medieval practice the dowry took on the appearance of a share in the patrimony, which was the classic patrilineal institution, the maternal line also figured in this central fact of the family's social and economic life. But though the confluence of paternal and maternal kin around dowry-raising seems by itself to caution against overemphasizing the patriarchal character of Venetian upper-class society, what we have seen so far is only legal prescription. Did it correspond to actual practice? More specifically, did hard-pressed Venetian fathers receive the help in dowering their daughters that these legal prescriptions promised?

The evidence indicates that they did, and more. In the fourteenth and fifteenth centuries, patricians showed a strong and increasing disposition to contribute to the dowries of their young kinswomen. These conclusions are based on the testimony of 305 patrician wills, all but seven from the period 1300–1450. The wills were written by members of the sprawling Morosini clan or by wives of Morosini. Although one clan cannot be regarded as representative of the entire patriciate, the Morosini wills do offer something of a cross-section. This clan was a large one, spread over the city; there were at least fifty property-owning Morosini males in 1379, at all levels of wealth; and nearly half of the wills, 140, were written by women from other families who married into the Morosini clan.[19] It should be acknowledged at the outset that testamentary bequests for dowries are not the same as actual contributions; Venetians frequently rewrote their wills, thus cancelling their original bequests. However, each bequest indicates an intention valid at the time made, even though later revised. So the evidence of these wills can provide some indication of Venetian patricians' involvement with young girls' dowries.

There are in the wills many bequests to unmarried girls, and in view of the principle that a girl's dowry represented her share of the patrimony, most of them probably amounted to contributions to the legatees' dowries.[20] Nevertheless, to avoid ambiguity the analysis is limited to 125 bequests, in 79 wills, that the testators destined explicitly for the dowry purpose. Forty-two of the wills were drawn up by men, the remaining thirty-seven by women. Table 1 gives the distribution of the bequests among the various recipients.

Table 1 shows that though they were about equally generous to granddaughters and nieces, men outdid women in bequests to daughters by a ratio of 5:3. In fact, that ratio is only slightly larger than that of about 3:2 between the total number of children named in the forty-two men's wills and those in the thirty-seven women's wills.[21] Thus, part of the reason that men gave more in dowry bequests lies in the apparent fact that they had more children than women when they wrote their wills. How can this be explained? For one thing, women had a tendency, as we shall see below, to draw up wills during their first pregnancies, when, of course, their only

TABLE 1

Dowry Bequests

Beneficiaries	Male Testators	Female Testators	Totals
Daughters	50 (61.7%)	31 (38.3%)	81 (100%)
Granddaughters	7 (46.7%)	8 (53.3%)	15 (100%)
Nieces	11 (52.4%)	10 (47.6%)	21 (100%)
Sisters	4[a] (80%)	1 (20%)	5 (100%)
Cousins	—	3 (100%)	3 (100%)
	72	53	125 (100%)

[a] Includes one sister-in-law.

children were *in utero*. Men generally testated after their families were already born. However, we should not make too much of this difference; only four of the thirty-seven wills in the present sample were written by women apparently in their first pregnancies, and more generally women—like men—wrote wills at all points throughout their adult lives and at all points in their families' developmental cycles.[22]

A better explanation is that men on the whole named their children individually and made specific provision for their respective legacies. Women, by contrast, tended to make blanket bequests to their offspring, with equal shares to boys and girls alike. In this connection it is worth noting that young married women in their first pregnancies, like other female testators in later pregnancies, did make generalized bequests for their daughters' dowries. All four of the women in their first pregnancies mentioned above provided for the dowries of their unborn children should they be girls.[23] Thus, the appearance—to judge from dowry bequests—that men had more children may be illusory, a result of different habits of testation by men and by women.

In fact, the primacy of paternal involvement in dowry raising that the figures in Table 1 reveal—50 percent of the total—is even more clearly reflected in the amounts of dowry bequests.[24] Table 2 shows that throughout the period fathers continued to discharge their patrimonial responsibilities as leading contributors to their daughters' dowries, and that the size of the contributions rose with the inflationary trend in dowries. But the table also shows that though nonpaternal bequests did not increase in size to the same extent, they did increase in numbers—to the point that in the fifteenth century they outstripped bequests of fathers. The effect was to give nonpaternal bequests, small in average, considerable aggregate importance in the total amounts bequeathed for dowry purposes, as indicated in the bottom row of the table.

This substantial, and growing, involvement of kin other than fathers in the accumulation of dowries, coinciding as it did with an alarming rise in dowry levels, must have been welcome to hard-pressed fathers of daughters. But it raises an important question in the general context of family and kinship relations. The compensation that fathers and brothers traditionally had received for dowry expenditures was the acquisition of economic, social, and even political allies in the persons of their new sons- and brothers-in-law.[25] Did the growing involvement in dowry raising of kin from outside the patrimonial group—or, in its identity over time, the lineage—now attenuate the lineage's expectations from the marriage alliance? The answer to the question requires a closer look at the kinsmen who contributed to girls' dowries.

Since we want to discover whether the patrimonial group's concern in girls' marriages diminished as the pool of dowry contributors increased, it makes sense to divide contributors into those who belonged to the endowed girl's lineage, and those who did not. What this means in practice, since we are concerned with dowry bequests from kinsmen, is a division between the legatee's paternal and maternal kin. With that in mind, a nice parallel emerges with Table 1: Just as fathers dominated among contributors within the lineage, mothers were the foremost contributors from outside the lineage, accounting for nearly one quarter (24.8 percent) of all dowry bequests.

It is something of a moot point whether a married woman belonged to her husband's lineage.[26] For our purposes, however, differences on the one hand between statutory regulations governing succession to intestate fathers and those governing succession to intestate mothers, and on the other hand between men's and women's general bequest patterns, indicate that married women did not demonstrate the same patrimonial and patrilineal concern that characterized their menfolk.[27] So their participation in the dowry-raising process lay outside of the interests of the lineage. Why then did women contribute to their daughters' dowries? There was an obligation attached to dowries that required wives to benefit their children with them; some jurists even held that a woman enjoyed only the usufruct of her dowry, its real proprietors being her children. Venetian law seems to have stopped short of that view, but statutory provision for succession to the estates of intestate women was completely in favor of their children.[28] These maternal bequests are interesting less because they were made (there are, after all, cultural as well as legal reasons for that), than because of their size and importance, and the timing of their appearance as an important element in the assembling of dowries.

Women, in general, were at first slow in contributing to dowries, but in the course of our period they came gradually to represent an increasingly important source of dowry money. In part this can be attributed to a constant rise in the ratio of women's wills to men's (see Table 3). The

TABLE 2

Paternal and Non-Paternal Dowry Bequests

	to 1330	1331-1370	1371-1410	1411-1450
Largest bequest	p[a] -769[b] (I)[c]	p-1,000 (5)	p-2,300 (22)	p-4,500 (9)
	n[a]- 4[b] (I)	n- 769 (6)	n-2,000 (27)	n-2,000 (26)
Smallest bequest	p-269	p-382	p-1,000	p-1,000
	n- 4	n- 4	n- 1	n- 10
Median bequest	p-509	p-576	p-1,350	p-2,000
	n- 4	n-634.5	n- 200	n- 500
Average bequest	p-535	p-606.4	p-1,340.9	p-2,244.4
	n- 4	n-500	n- 589.6	n- 569.2
Total amounts	p-3,214 (99.9%)	p-3,032 (50.3%)	p-29,500 (65.7%)	p-20,200 (57.7%)
bequeathed	n- 4 (0.1%)	n-3,000 (49.7%)	n-15,379 (34.3%)	n-14,800 (42.3%)
	3,218 (100%)	6,032 (100%)	44,879 (100%)	35,000 (100%)

[a] p = paternal; n = non-paternal.
[b] All amounts are in ducats.
[c] The number of bequests in this category, during this period.

TABLE 3

Men's and Women's Wills

	to 1330			1331-1370			1371-1410			1411-1450		
	no.	%	ratio	no.	%	ratio	no.	%	ratio	no.	%	ratio
Men	8	57.1	1.3	22	44.0	1	40	33.1	1	34	28.3	1
Women	6	42.9	1	28	56.0	1.3	81	66.9	2	86	71.7	2.5
	14	100.0		50	100.0		121	100.0		120	100.0	

relative stabilization in the number of men's wills is curious. It could be simply an accident of documentary survival, although why should women's wills have survived more than men's? There is, however, another explanation. The most dramatic increase in the number of wills of both sexes occurred in the decades after the Black Death.[29] It is probable that the experience of the great mortality that accompanied the plague in 1348 induced survivors, and especially their descendants, to look to their own estates with greater attention. One result would be more will-making. Another would be more will-making by younger people, with the specific effects of: 1) more multiple wills (i.e., several wills written by the same individual over a number of years); and 2) more women's wills, as pregnant wives, concerned over intestacy, drew up their first wills during first pregnancies, modifying the intentions contained therein in later wills, also written during pregnancy.

The evidence of the 305 wills examined here documents both these effects. Eighty-seven, or 28.5 percent, were written by thirty-six individuals. Moreover, seventy-seven of these multiple wills were bunched between 1371 and 1450, constituting 32 percent of all wills written during those years. In fact, among the Morosini no series of wills by a single individual was begun before 1360—close enough to 1348 to suggest the influence of that year's events, and long enough after it for an institutionalized reaction to have taken hold.

Women dominated among the multiple testators. Twenty-eight of the thirty-six individuals who wrote more than one will were women. This fact adds credibility to the hypothesis about increased will-making following the Black Death. Women in Venice had a greater opportunity to write multiple wills than did men, by reason of their earlier entry into adulthood. In the fourteenth and fifteenth centuries the preferred nuptial age for patrician girls was thirteen to fifteen, and, as far as their elders were concerned, marriage meant that they became mistresses of their own affairs.[30] A young wife's first occasion to exercise this mastery would present itself during her first pregnancy; if she survived that and subsequent pregnancies she would have occasion to write a number of wills as her intentions regarding her bequests changed with changes in the life cycles of her kin.[31] As it happens, twenty-eight of the 202 women's wills in our group were written, by the testatresses' own explicit affirmation, during pregnancy; and another thirty-one were written by wives who may well have been pregnant but did not say so in their wills.[32]

This statistic is even more impressive in view of the fact that only 120 of the women's wills were written by wives; of the rest, 76 were by widows and 6 by single women or nuns. One of the pregnant testatresses was, in fact, a widow, but her example seems unique in our sample.[33] So the representation of pregnant women among married testatresses was at least 23.3 percent (28 out of 120) and, considering also those possibly pregnant, may have been as high as 49.2 percent. Moreover, this pronounced tendency to draw up wills during pregnancy was a development of the later fourteenth century; in the period 1331–70, pregnant women wrote one of twenty-eight women's wills (3.6 percent); in 1371–1410, thirteen of eighty-one (16.4 percent); and in 1411–50, fourteen of eighty-six (16.3 percent).[34] There are grounds, then, for arguing that the shock of the Black Death—and each successive visitation of the plague—induced Venetians to concern themselves more regularly than before with the disposition of their property by testation. And the fact that the increase in women's wills outstripped that of men's simply reflects women's more numerous encounters with the prospect of death because of pregnancy.[35]

But a more compelling acquaintance with mortality during the plague years only partially explains the increase in women's wills. Equally important is the consideration that in the second half of the fourteenth century, and especially during its last quarter, they had more property to dispose of. Here we are brought back to dowry inflation. Most simply, once women started bringing larger dowries to their marriages, by that fact they became more economically substantial persons, with a greater capacity to influence the economic fortunes of those around them. Once begun, dowry inflation was a self-accelerating process.[36] That is, when wives who had brought large dowries to their own marriages thought of disposing of their own estates (and, as we have noted, they started thinking of it sooner and more frequently in the later fourteenth century), they naturally thought of their own daughters. We shall see that they also thought of others, but their own knowledge of the importance of large dowries would incline them similarly to look after their daughters. And the existence of their dowry money, protected by law from husbandly rapacity and, often, enlarged through fruitful real estate and commercial investment, added a further impulse to well-considered testamentary disposition in favor of daughters.[37]

There was thus a self-reinforcing spur built into dowry inflation, derived from a woman's right to dispose of her own property, her concern for daughters, and the increased dowries that she was bringing to marriage. To illustrate the extent of this important dimension of dowry inflation—of which women were not only the objects but the effective agents as well—we can compare paternal and maternal dowry bequests in tabular form.

Table 4 reveals three things. First, mothers began bequeathing money toward their daughters' dowries only after the middle of the fourteenth century; but from then on, the frequency of their contributions grew rapidly, both in absolute terms and relative to father's dowry bequests. Second, the size of these maternal bequests was also on the rise, in keeping with the general trend in dowries. Finally, until the middle of the fourteenth century, mothers' dowry bequests had little impact on the total amounts bequeathed

TABLE 4

Paternal and Maternal Dowry Bequests

	to 1330	1331–1370	1371–1410	1411–1450
Largest Bequest	p[a]-769[b] (6)[c] m[a]- —	p-1,000 (5) m-200 (1)	p-2,300 (22) m-1,500 (8)	p-4,500 (9) m-2,000 (12)
Smallest Bequest	p-269 m- —	p-382 m-200	p-1,000 m-200	p-1,000 m-400
Median Bequest	p-509 m- —	p-576 m-200	p-1,350 m-891	p-2,000 m-900
Average Bequest	p-535 m- —	p-606.4 m-200	p-1,340.9 m-897.8	p-2,244.4 m-991.7
Total amounts bequeathed	p-3,214 (100%) m- — 3,214 (100%)	p-3,032 (93.8%) m-200 (6.2%) 3,232 (100%)	p-29,500 (84.1%) m-5,582 (15.9%) 35,082 (100%)	p-20,200 (62.9%) m-11,900 (37.1%) 32,100 (100%)

[a] p = paternal; m = maternal.
[b] All amounts are in ducats.
[c] The number of bequests in this category, during this period.

for dowries; but starting in the last third of that century, they accounted for an increasing share of parental contributions—more than one third in 1411–50. So from all three standpoints, frequency, size, and relative importance, mothers' dowry bequests were enabling their daughters to meet the challenge of dowry inflation—an inflation to which the mothers, as dowry recipients themselves, were indirectly contributing.

The importance of this maternal involvement in providing relief for Dante's frightened fathers is obvious. But it has considerable social significance as well. It means that an increasingly larger role in the critical (and to some, central) social fact—marriage—was being played by individuals whose commitment to the brides' paternal lineage was much less intense than that of the brides' fathers.

It is a question of lineage orientation. In the patrilineal order of Venice fathers never left their lineages, and they could attend materially to the interests of a wide range of kinsmen without this attention ever exceeding the realm of lineage interest.[38] Their bequests to members of their natal families and to those of their marital families alike remained within the lineage. As we have seen, men were tied to both by the *fraterna*, and the hereditary nature of patrician status in Venice only strengthened their commitment to the male line. In this context, a bequest to a daughter or sister was not essentially less beneficial to the interests of the lineage than one to a son or brother. In the latter case, the lineage benefited directly; in the former, it stood to benefit indirectly from the matrimonial alliance thus established.

With mothers the case was different. They were members of two conjugal families from two different lineages, and the result was a freer, less lineage-centered social orientation. The statutes, for example, did not exclude married daughters from succession to intestate women; women's property, lacking the patrimonial quality of men's could more readily be diffused into the families of sons-in-law.[39] And women's habits themselves attest to a more flexible social attitude. The general pattern of their bequests reveals a nearly equal regard for their natal kinsmen and thus for two distinct lineages.[40]

It would be valuable to know whether the increased maternal role in dowry accumulation equipped women with a greater voice in the choice of husbands for their daughters, as is the case, for example, in modern rural Greece.[41] Although there is some evidence of general motherly interest in whom their daughters married, the documentation does not reveal the extent to which mothers actually participated in matrimonial decisions. It seems reasonable to conjecture, however, that the concern that mothers demonstrated in the form of dowry bequests and the impact of their increasingly weighty contributions at a time of dowry-raising difficulty were negotiated into greater influence in the arrangements of their daughters' marriages.

More fundamentally, the contributions of mothers to their daughters' dowries may have helped to alter the social posture of the elementary conjugal family. In a widely held view, the Italian family during the twelfth and thirteenth centuries was subsumed under and, in important social matters, subordinate to the larger kinship group—clan, consortery, etc.[42] With mothers now counting for more in marriage—the most socially involving family enterprise of all—the importance of the larger kinship group, to which intermarrying women demonstrated a relatively weak allegiance, may have diminished. To see if this was the case, we can now turn to the dowry contributions of kinsmen other than parents.

Whatever long-range effects mothers' growing contributions to their daughters' dowries had in raising dowry standards, in the short run fathers must have welcomed them. But fathers had additional cause for happiness in the dowry contributions from a wide variety of other kinsmen as well. On the whole, women contributed to the dowries of girls other than their own daughters at a higher rate than did men: 41.5 percent of women's dowry bequests were external to the marital family, as against 30.6 percent of the men's. This is consistent with what we observed about wives' enduring attachment to their natal families. But, in fact, all Venetians, regardless of sex or marital status, were stimulated to help their nubile kin. Altogether 44 of the 125 dowry bequests, more than one third, were to girls other than the testators' daughters. And nowhere is the complexity of Venetian kinship patterns and of the bonds existing among kinsmen better illustrated than in the wide variety of relationships that existed between girls receiving dowry bequests and their benefactors and benefactresses.

One group of nonparental dowry bequests was consistent both with the spirit of Roman law and with general patrimonial principles: bequests from paternal grandfathers and uncles. Eighteen of the sample's twenty-two nonparental bequests from men were of this relationship. In the context of the undivided fraternal patrimony, such bequests made good sense. A father's contribution to the dowry of his son's unmarried daughter, a type of bequest encountered seven times in the sample, amounted to a farsighted arrangement for money that would have gone to the son anyway, and would ultimately have served him for his daughter's dowry. But the concern that grandfathers manifested in these bequests suggests that granddaughters' dowry prospects had a more than casual importance to them. For example, Alessandro di Michele Morosini, in his will of 1331, bequeathed his entire estate, less pious and charitable bequests, to his only child, Paolo. According to the instructions in the will, Paolo was not to come into his inheritance until age twenty, except for one eventuality: if he should marry and have a daughter before his twentieth birthday, he was to make a will and in it provide for the girl's dowry in the amount of 653 ducats together with a *corredum* "worthy of a noble woman"—all from Alessandro's estate. Seventy years later, Gasparino di Bellello Morosini added 800 ducats to the dowry left to his granddaughter, Franceschina, by her late father, and this at a time when Gasparino had three living sons of his own, at least one a minor.[43]

There is a clue to the reasons for such grandfatherly concern in Gasparino's will. He declared that he wanted Franceschina to marry a "Venetian gentleman worthy of her status and acceptable to my sons." Gasparino and, presumably, Alessandro and other grandfathers like them, were willing to cut into the property of the male line—the jealous preservation of which was a toughly held principle in many wills—and to alienate wealth by sending it into other men's families because such expenses were investments that promoted the interest of the lineage in two ways.[44] First, it ensured that the line would not lose status through unworthy marriages. Second, it provided the direct male heirs with affinal connections that, precisely because they were expensive to come by, promised social and economic benefits to the lineage.

This transgenerational solicitude for the well-being of the lineage, as expressed in dowry bequests to granddaughters, is even more striking in the case of men who had unmarried daughters of their own. An example of such a man is Andreasio di Michele Morosini, brother of the Alessandro whose will we have just considered. In his will of 1348, Andreasio left his own unmarried daughters dowries of 692 and 382 ducats, respectively, at the same time he willed a dowry of 616 ducats to any of his sons' daughters who should be her father's sole heir.[45] In such cases, the testators appear to slight their own daughters in the interest of their granddaughters. That they did so indicates that Venetian patricians had a sense of lineage as a sort of superpersonal abstraction that would live on after the testator but the well-being of which was nevertheless in his interest and deserving of his efforts on its behalf. It also indicates that they viewed its well-being not only in narrow terms of retaining wealth among males but also in a more sophisticated sense of social and economic alliances of the kind built up through marriage.[46]

The same sense is evident in the dowry bequests of uncles to nieces. There are eleven such legacies in our sample, and eight of them were given by the testators to their brothers' daughters.[47] Of these testators, five had children of their own to provide for, including, in three cases, unmarried daughters. Yet, the avuncular providence could be impressive: in 1413 Giovanni di Piero Morosini willed 1,200 ducats toward the dowry of his late brother's daughter while bequeathing his own daughter a dowry of 2,000 ducats.[48] The reasons for such generosity were twofold. The continued existence of the *fraterna* long after the father's death meant that the dowries of all daughters of a group of brothers came, to some extent at least, from the same common estate. But along with the common dowry burden went common advantages—the second reason for men's dowry bequests to their brothers' daughters. The economic and social benefits that a bride's father might harvest from a good marriage—at the price of a large dowry—were shared by his brothers. These were the considerations underlying Gasparino Morsini's instructions that any husband of his granddaughter Franceschina had to be approved by his surviving sons, the girl's uncles.[49]

The mutual involvement of brothers in the marital destinies of each other's daughters was complemented by their collective involvement in the marital destinies of their sisters. Indeed, it can be argued that the ones who bore the brunt of the entire dowry system, and especially of the inflationary trend, were the brothers of endowed girls. It was the inheritance theoretically devolving upon them, as continuers of the lineage and of the patrimony, that was diminished by each dowry that accompanied a sister to her marriage. It was probably recognition of this potential clash of interests that prompted the legislators to guarantee the inheritance rights of daughters *vis-à-vis* their brothers. On the other hand, Pertile observed that it was to protect brothers from the effects of dowry inflation that governments, such as that of Venice, attempted to put restraints on dowry amounts.[50] Yet despite the grounds for brother-sister rivalry, there are instances of brothers helping their sisters' marriage prospects from what seems to be a view of family advantage that extended beyond a narrow, and self-serving, emphasis on male inheritance. In the 1374 will in which he bequeathed 1,500 ducats to his newborn daughter, Gasparino Morosini gave 100 ducats to each of his nubile sisters.[51] In 1416 Nicolò di Giovanni Morosini, with no children of his own but with two living brothers and a sister, wrote in his will some instructions that testify to the broad view that Venetian men could hold of the interests of the lineage. After making some pious bequests, he willed the rest of his estate to his two living brothers, under two conditions. One was that from that inheritance the two brothers were to add enough to the 1,400 ducats which their father had left their sister to enable her to marry "in a way that befits the condition of my house and brings honor to it."[52] The other condition was that some of the money was to augment the dowries that their late brother had left to his daughters, who were Nicolò's and his brothers' nieces.

The case of solicitous brothers, like that of grandfathers and uncles, demonstrates a commitment to the continuing interests of the patrilineage. That much is consistent with the patrilineal traditions of medieval European society.[53] Even if Venetian patricians extended the range of lineage-promoting tactics to include investment in good marriages for social and economic reasons, the orientation was toward the lineage. If an occasional patrician bequeathed something toward the dowry of his wife's sister, as Fantin di Giovanni Morosini did in 1413, that was a remarkable exception.[54] The dominant impulse among males making dowry bequests, whether to daughters, granddaughters, nieces, or sisters, was to bring honor and profit to the male line to which they belonged and which they regarded as their duty to preserve. When hard-pressed fathers were helped in meeting the challenge of dowry inflation by their own fathers, brothers, or sons, this help had its roots in a long of male kinship solidarity.

But among women the pattern was different. And in the context of women's increasing prominence in dowry raising, the differences are important for an understanding not only of how this major aspect of the familial experience developed but of changes in the family's place in the larger kinship system and in society. In certain respects, of course, women did resemble men in their dowry bequests. We have already seen the priority that they gave to their daughters. But they also resembled men in some of their express motivations in making such bequests. Like men, they regarded social suitability, marrying according to one's station, as a major desideratum for their daughters. Lucia, wife of Roberto Contarini, made a forthright statement of this sentiment in her will of 1413. If at her death her daughters did not have dowries adequate to permit them "to marry well, according to their station," then they were to get more from her estate, "in order to marry better."[55] Superficially, women also resembled men in their dowry bequests to girls other than their own daughters. Against seven bequests to granddaughters by men, there were eight by women; against eleven bequests to nieces by men, there were ten by women.

It is among these nonfilial bequests, however, that some interesting differences occur. A closer look at the bequests to grandchildren reveals that both women and men divided their bequests evenly between sons' daughters and daughters' daughters. But the three men who made bequests to their daughters' daughters had no sons, whereas in three of the four cases of male bequests to sons' daughters, the testators also had daughters of their own (in two instances, married daughters) for whose living and prospective female offspring no dowry provision was made in the wills.[56] The eight women's bequests to granddaughters make an interesting contrast. In three cases, the testatress had only one child. But of the remaining five, only one made a bequest to the granddaughter by one child without also remembering the granddaughters by her other children of both sexes. To illustrate this difference more clearly we can glance at the wills of Giovanni, son of the Doge Michele Morosini, and of his widow, Novella, who wrote hers in 1420. Giovanni bequeathed 2,000 ducats to any of his sons' daughters who might be her father's only child. Novella also made a bequest to a son's daughters: she willed 500 ducats toward the dowries of her son Marino's daughters. But at the same time, and unlike her husband, she bequeathed the same amount to the daughter of her daughter.[57]

The indication is clear: in their nonfilial bequests men showed a prejudice in favor of the interests of lineage, which benefited from dowry assistance given to the daughters of its male members. Where male testators helped their daughters' daughters—and thus, indirectly, the lineages to which their sons-in-law belonged—they did so only when they had no sons to carry on their own lineages. Women, however, demonstrated no such prejudice. Their contributions to their granddaughters' dowries were not governed by consideration either of lineage or of the sex of the child whose daughter was benefiting.

But does that mean that married women substituted loyalty to their natal families' lineages for that of their husbands'? Certainly they maintained close ties to their natal families. The wills reveal that nearly half of the testamentary executors chosen by married women were primary natal kin (parent and siblings); and this was true both of women with living husbands and of widows.[58] But such continued rapport makes sense in the context which we are considering. A family investing a substantial dowry in a socially and economically desirable marital alliance could be expected to keep in touch with its son-and brother-in-law; *a fortiori*, contact would be maintained with his wife. Moreover, the wife herself, as a propertied person with the capacity to make testamentary disposition of and, provided her husband consented, to invest her property, could be expected to maintain economic ties to the family that had been the source of her property.[59]

However, women's social and economic contact with their natal families is not the same as identification with the continued interests of the natal family's lineage. In this connection, a comparison between men's dowry bequests to their nieces, already discussed, and those of women to their nieces discloses a significant difference. We noted that of eleven male bequests to nieces, eight specified the girls' precise relationship to their benefactors, and in each of these eight cases she was the daughter of the benefactor's brother. By contrast, only two of the ten women's dowry bequests to nieces went to daughters of brothers; three are unclear about the relationship, and five went to daughters of the testatresses' sisters. If we regard a bequest of this kind as helping a lineage, the lineage to benefit was neither that of the benefactress nor her husband, but that of her sister's husband. So although women were relatively more active than men in making dowry bequests to consanguines other than their own daughters, their motives were different from those of men. Although men emphasized their own lineages, women did not share this priority. For them, considerations of the lineage, whether natal or marital, seem to have been relatively unimportant. But family ties, whether male or female, natal or marital, represented an important imperative.

What conclusions can we draw from these differences between men's and women's dowry bequests? The most important is that a distinctive, feminine, social impulse was coming to have considerable influence in patrician social relations. The aspect of this feminine orientation that set it apart from that of men was a comparatively weaker sense of lineage. Women's relative lack of concern for the interests of the lineage did not mean indifference to kinsmen. It did mean, however, that the principle of selection governing their testamentary beneficence—in the context of our discussion, their dowry beneficence—was different from the commitment to kin-group interest that characterized men. It was the principles of "religion, morality, conscience and sentiment"—the sanctions that govern relations not of the kin group, but of the family.[60] And of these, in the case of Venetian patrician women, personal regard—affection—seems to have been critical.

It can be seen in a special bond that existed among women. This point must not be exaggerated, Women did demonstrate concern and responsibility for their male kin, sometimes even attaching greater importance to them than to the females.[61] But the attachment between women was both different from and, in important ways, stronger than the attachment between a woman and her male kin. We can see this by taking another look at the wills, this time focusing on bequests in general. A group of ninety-seven wills of wives and widows contains a total of 415 individual bequests to primary and secondary kin.[62] Of these, 218 or 52.5 percent, went to women and only slightly fewer, 197 (47.5 percent), to men. There does not seem to be a great difference. But if they are divided into bequests to primary and to secondary kin, the results indicate more clearly the special relationship among women. In the 302 bequests to primary kin (parents, siblings, husbands, and children), males and females benefited almost equally, receiving 154 and 148 bequests, respectively. But among the secondary-kin beneficiaries (aunts and uncles, nieces and nephews, cousins, grandparents, grandchildren, and first-degree affinal kin: children-, siblings-, and parents-in-law), females outnumbered males by a considerable margin, receiving seventy bequests compared with forty-three to males, or 61.9 percent to 38.1 percent.

The discrepancy between the sex ratio in women's primary-kin bequests and that in their secondary-kin bequests is revealing of the motives behind women's choices of beneficiaries. When they bestowed equal testamentary largesse on the men and women of their primary kin, they were acting under the natural impulses of loyalty and affection that domestic proximity stimulated. Young wives, married at age thirteen or fourteen, would naturally hold tightly to the reassuring ties to their parents and siblings regardless of sex.[63] Mothers would naturally feel affection for both sons and daughters. But though the preferences for females among more distant kin also reflects affection, it is of a more discriminating kind resulting from association by choice, not by biological chance. These preferences are in keeping with the indications of women's relative indifference to considerations of lineage. Women left property to their female relatives not to advance the interests of the lineage, but because they felt affection for these relatives. There may have been a sense of kinship responsibility at work, for example, toward aged grandmothers; and the apparent tendency of women to outlive their husbands may have provided testatresses with a number of elderly widowed kin toward whom they could discharge that responsibility. But such gestures are still not sufficient to account for the five-to-three ratio of females to males among women's secondary-kin beneficiaries. Moreover, even the type of motivation in bequests to aged female relatives is different from lineage allegiance, because it has a personal rather than institutional object.

In the context of the growing importance of women's property, organized in wills and particularly directed toward dowries, the impulse of personal affection that is apparent in the pattern of their bequests has a special significance. It means that a richer and more complex set of social forces was at work within the Venetian patriciate in the later fourteenth and especially the fifteenth century than had been the case earlier. The male commitment to the lineage still persisted, as indeed the endurance of the patrimonial system and the hereditary nature of Venice's ruling class dictated that it would. But alongside the lineage orientation of males, and complementary to it, there was appearing—in a position of considerable social influence—the more personal attitude of women. This may have bearing on the old but recently rekindled discussion of the emergence of a more intense family consciousness on the part of fifteenth-century Italians.[64] The heightened personal affection that, as some writers have argued, constituted the hallmark of the resurgent elementary family may have its origin in the enlarged role of women. Yet, in Venice at least, this greater influence commanded by women and by their distinctive social orientation did not replace attention to lineage; it simply blended with it another set of concerns.

In the light of these considerations, the dowry inflation that caused Venetian and other Italian fathers such anxiety can be seen leading to a number of developments that together contributed to a reordering and an enrichment of the social relationships within the Venetian patriciate.[65] It strengthened the traditional kinship bonds by inducing kinsmen to aid beleaguered fathers of marriageable daughters. It created stronger interlineage ties by increasing the expectations that families of effortfully endowed girls entertained vis-à-vis the girls' husbands. And by encouraging women themselves to take a substantial part in the accumulation of their daughters' and other kinswomen's dowries, it created a condition in which impulses of personal regard, both within and between families (and lineages), assumed a larger place among the principles governing patrician social relations.

NOTES

1. There is disagreement among historians of law about the degree to which Roman dowry practice, as opposed to Germanic institutions such as the Lombard *faderfio*, survived in the early Middle Ages. By the twelfth century, however, the Roman institution seems to have regained ground lost in earlier centuries: and the comeback involved more of a blending with Germanic law than a wholesale rejection of it. See Francesco Brandileone, "Studi preliminari sullo svolgimento dei rapporti patrimoniali fra coniugi in Italia," *Archivio giuridico* 67 (1901): 231ff; Francesco Ercole, "La dote romana negli statuti di Parma," *Archivio storico per le province parmense*, 8 n.s. (1908): 21-23. For the early Renaissance, see Lauro Martines, *The Social World of the Florentine Humanists, 1390-1460* (Princeton, 1963), pp. 19, 37-38; Frederic C. Lane, *Andrea Barbarigo, Merchant of Venice, 1418-1449* (Baltimore, 1944), p. 39.

2. The dowry figures are taken from Archivio di Stato, Venice (henceforth cited ASV), Notarile, Cancelleria inferiore (all henceforth abbreviated CI and followed by the bundle number and the notary's name) 114, Marino, S. Tomà, protocol (henceforth, prot.) 1366-91, *passim*. This source records the repayment of dowries to widows or their heirs upon the death of husband or wife. The entries usually mention the date on which the dowry had been paid to the husband, normally at or around the time of the wedding. The fifty cases studied represent marriages contracted between 1346 and 1366.

In this and in all other monetary references, the various Venetian moneys have been converted into ducats, for purposes of uniformity and comparison. For these conversions, see Nicolò Papadopoli-Aldobrandini, *Le monete di Venezia* (Venice, 1893-1907), pp. 383-85; Frederic C. Lane, *Venetian Ships and Shipbuilders of the Renaissance* (Baltimore, 1934), pp. 251-52. See also correspondences noted in the records of estates administered by the Procuratori di S. Marco. Thus, in 1347 the gold ducat was worth 2.63 lire *a grossi*, the Venetian money of account (ASV, Procuratori di S. Marco, Commissarie [hereafter abbreviated PSM], Miste, B. 70a, Nicolò Morosini, account book, fol. 2r).

3. We have been unable to find a fifteenth-century equivalent to the records in CI 114 cited above. However, already in the late fourteenth century the standard had risen. In twenty-five patrician marriages contracted between 1370 and 1386, the average dowry was 1,000 ducats (figures again taken from CI 114, Marino, prot. 1366-91). It is clear that by the fifteenth century 1,000 ducats was something of a minimum for respectable patrician dowries. Cf., in addition to examples cited below, Lane, *Andrea Barbarigo*, pp. 23-41, *passim;* Andrea da Mosto, "Il navigatore Alvise da Mosto e la sua famiglia," *Archivio veneto*, 5th ser., 2 (1927): 168-259, *passim*.

4. For the fifteenth-century law, see Marco Barbaro, "Libro di nozze patrizie," MS in Biblioteca Nazionale Marciana, Venice, MSS italiani, classe VII, 156 (8492), fol. a; the sixteenth-century law, dated 4 Nov. 1505, is in *ibid.*, fols. a-b.

5. Jacques Heers, *L'Occident aux XIVe et XVe siècles: Aspects économiques et sociaux* (Paris, 1966), pp. 294-99; Gim Luzzatto, "Il costo della vita a Venezia nel Trecento," in Luzzatto, *Studi di storia economica veneziana* (Padua, 1954), pp. 285-87. A graphic picture of the changing relations between gold and silver in Venetian moneys can be found in Carlo M. Cipolla, *Studi di storia della moneia*, vol. 1, *I movimenti dei cambi in Italia dal secolo XIII al XV* (Pavia, 1948), pp. 44-47.

6. The data are fragmentary, regionally selective, and sometimes contradictory. See Harry A. Miskimin, *The Economy of Early Renaissance Europe, 1300-1460* (Englewood Cliffs, N.J., 1969), pp. 89-92; Robert S. Lopez, in *The Cambridge*

Economic History of Europe (Cambridge, 1952), 2: 343-47; Gino Luzzatto, (trans. Philip J. Jones), *An Economic History of Italy* (New York, 1961), pp. 138-46.

7. See Léopold Genicot, in *The Cambridge Economic History of Europe*, 2nd ed. (Cambridge, 1966), 1: 688-94. On Venetian economic fortunes in the fifteenth century in general, see Luzzatto, *An Economic History*, pp. 150-55; in greater detail, Luzzatto, *Storia economica di Venezia dall' XI al XVI secolo* (Venice, 1961), pp. 146-79; Luzzatto, "Il costo della vita," p. 290. For the monetary conversion, see Papadopoli, *Le monete*, 1: 383-85. The equivalence of the *staio* is in Lane, *Venetian Ships*, p. 246. In 1390 the estate of Simone Morosini sold nine *staia* of wheat to the grain office for 1 lira, 10 soldi *di grossi* (one lira *di grossi* equalled 10 ducats) (PSM Miste, B. 128, Simone Morosini, Register, fol. 5r). The 1432 figure comes from Lane, *Andrea Barbarigo*, p. 67-68.

8. On wheat prices as general index, see Heers, *L'Occident*, p. 295; Luzzatto, "Il costo della vita," p. 286. See the regional variations in grain prices in Genicot, *Cambridge Economic History* (2d ed.), 1: 683. On dowries see Francesco Ercole, "L'istituto dotale nella pratica e nella legislazione statutaria dell'Italia superiore," *Revista italiana per le scienze giuridiche* 65 (1908): 191-302; 66 (1910): 167-257. These two parts shall be referred to as "Istituto dotale," I, and "Istituto dotale," II. The present reference is in "Istituto dotale," I: 280-84.

9. The main study of *prestiti* and their economic impact is Gino Luzzatto (ed.), *I prestiti della Repubblica di Venezia (sec. XIII-XV)* (Padua, 1929), esp. pp. clx-clxxv of Luzzatto's "Introduzione storica." See also Frederic C. Lane, "The Funded Debt of the Venetian Republic," in Luzzatto, *Venice and History* (Baltimore, 1966), pp. 87-98; Roberto Cessi, "La finanza veneziana al tempo della guerra di Chioggia," in Luzzatto, *Politica ed economia di Venezia nel Trecento. Saggi* (Rome, 1952), pp. 172-248. The fruits of Luzzatto's researches on this question are presented briefly in his *Storia economica di Venezia*, pp. 140-45.

10. A measure authorizing a revision of the fisc's estimate of private wealth, passed after the War of Chioggia, indicated that the total could be as much as 1.5 million lire less than the total of 6 million lire reached in the previous estimate of 1379, at the beginning of the war (*ibid.*, p. 145). But see the cautionary comments of Cessi, "La finanza veneziana," pp. 192-98.

11. Luzzatto, *Storia economica*, pp. 147-48; Lane, "Funded Debt," pp. 87-89.

12. ". . . propter importabilem sumptum dotium" (Barbaro, "Libro di nozze," fol. a). Especially noteworthy in this act are the suggestions that this practice is of relatively recent origin ("orta sit") and the clear indication that high dowries damaged a man's other heirs—presumably the male ones.

13. Ercole, "Istituto dotale," I, 197-98. See also Enrico Besta, *La famiglia nella storia del diritto italiano* (Milan, 1962), pp. 143-51.

14. Ercole, "Istituto dotale," I, 212-13, 218-32. The main study of the *fraterna* is Camillo Fumagalli, *Il diritto di fraterna nella giurisprudenza da Accursio alla codificazione* (Turin, 1912). Among more general literature, see Besta, *La famiglia*, pp. 207-9; Antonio Pertile, *Storia del diritto italiano* (Turin, 1894), 3: 282, 322. On the *fraterna* in Venetian practice, cf. Marco Ferro, *Dizionario del diritto comune e veneto* (Venice, 1779), 5: 276-78.

15. ". . . la dote è un diritto della figlia, cui il padre non può mai sottrarsi" (Ercole, "Istituto dotale," I, 334).

16. Felix Gilbert, "Venice in the Crisis of the League of Cambrai," in J. R. Hale (ed.), *Renaissance Venice* (London, 1973), p. 275; PSM Miste, B. 127, Leone Morosini, parchment no. 2.

17. *Volumen statutorum, legum ac iurium D. Venetorum* (Venice, 1564), Bk. II, ch. 8, p. 17v. See also Ercole, "Istituto dotale," I, 238-46; Ferro, *Dizionario*, 4: 385-86.

18. Pertile, *Storia del diritto italiano* (Turin, 1893), 4: 93–94; Ercole, "Istituto dotale," I, 237. "L'avo ed ascendenti materni sussidiariamente sono tenuti a costituire la dote alla nipote in mancanza degli ascendenti paterni, e della madre" (Ferro, *Dizionario*, 4: 386). It should be noted, however, that we have not seen this principle mentioned in any other source.

19. In a fiscal census (*estimo*) conducted in 1379, the Morosini estimates ranged from 500 to 38,000 lire *a grossi* (equal to 192–14,615 ducats). The basis of the estimate was real property. The Morosini in the *estimo* dwelt in twenty-four different parishes (*contrade*), in five of Venice's six *sestieri*, or administrative zones (Luzzatto, *I prestiti*, doc. 165, pp. 141–86, *passim*). For a full-length study of patrician kinship, based on the experience of the Morosini, we have isolated more than twenty different lineages within the clan. In our use of the terms "clan" and "lineage" we follow Robin Fox, *Kinship and Marriage* (Harmondsworth, 1967), pp. 49–50. For a fuller discussion, see Geroge Peter Murdock, *Social Structure* (New York, 1949), pp. 46–78. The 140 women's wills are, of course, distinct from 62 wills of Morosini daughters, twelve of whom married Morosini males.

20. See *Volumen statutorum*, Bk. IV, ch. 25–26, p. 73v. For the principle that dowries were women's only claim on their fathers' estates, see Nino Tamassia, *La famiglia italiana nei secoli decimoquinto e decimosesto* (Milan, 1910), pp. 292–95.

21. Thirty-six of the forty-two men mentioned children, totalling 129. Thirty-four of the thirty-seven women mentioned children, a total of ninety-one. Included in these figures are unborn children of pregnant wives—whether mentioned in the wives' or in the husbands' wills.

22. Thus, of the eighteen mothers whose husbands were still living when the women wrote their wills, four were pregnant with their first child, four mentioned one child, three mentioned two children, one mentioned four, one mentioned seven, and the remaining five made general reference to their children without specifying their names or numbers. Taking another perspective, five of the thirty-seven female testators mentioned grandchildren, against six of the forty-two men; and ten of the women mentioned living parents, against eight of the men.

23. The four are: Elena, wife of Andrea Morosini (ASV, Notarile, Testamenti [all henceforth abbreviated NT and followed by the bundle number and the notary's name] 466, Benedetto Gibellino, no. 5, 12 July 1417); Fresca, wife of Roberto Morosini (NT 1230. Federico Stefani, no. 207, 22 Dec. 1433); Franceschina, wife of Berto Morosini (NT 721, Andrea Marevidi, no. 145, 3 Dec. 1444); Maria, wife of Nicolò Morosini (NT 746, Marciliano de'Naresi, no. 83, 27 Nov. 1426).

24. Based on 102 bequests in specific amounts; the remaining 23 dowry bequests did not specify amounts.

25. For examples of economic and political returns on dowry investments, see, respectively, Lane, *Andrea Barbarigo*, pp. 28–29; Lane, "Family Partnerships and Joint Ventures in the Venetian Republic," in Lane, *Venice and History*, pp. 38–39.

26. In Roman law during the Republic, a wife might be absorbed into her husband's family or not; by the Empire, the tendency was for her not to be so—to remain, rather, either under her natal *paterfamilias* or, if none existed, to be *sui iuris*. In either of the latter two cases, she was not considered agnatically related to her husband's family. See J. A. Crook, *Law and Life of Rome* (London, 1967), pp. 103–4; Barry Nicholas, *An Introduction to Roman Law* (Oxford, 1962), pp. 80–83. In Lombard law, wives passed over to their husbands' families by reason of the husbands' purchase of the *mundium*—roughly, protective domination—from the wives' fathers; by the time of the restoration of Roman law, however, this practice no longer prevailed in the Veneto, if indeed it ever had. See Pertile, *Storia del diritto*, 3:

234-40. In practice, women retained ties both to their natal and to their marital families and lineages.

27. Succession to an intestate father excluded married daughters, whose share of the patrimony had already been advanced in the form of dowries. Married daughters were, however, admitted to equal shares in the succession to their intestate mothers' property since this property did not have the patrimonial character. See *Volumen statutorum*, Bk. IV, ch. 25, p. 73v; ch. 28, p. 74v. The same relationship holds true regarding emancipated and unemancipated sons (Roberto Cessi [ed.], *Gli statuti veneziani di Jacopo Tiepolo del 1242 e le loro glosse* [Venice, 1938], p. 207, gloss 173). On general bequest patterns, see below, n. 40.

28. Besta, *La famiglia*, pp. 149-50; Tamassia, *La famiglia italiana*, p. 289. Already in 1060, Venetian women were regarded as the proprietors of their dowries (Pier Silverio Leicht, "Documenti dotali dell' alto medioevo," in *Scritti vari di storia del diritto italiano* [Milan, 1943-48], 2: pt. 2, p. 294). The statute governing inheritance from intestate mothers is in *Volumen statutorum*, Bk. IV, ch. 28, p. 74v.

29. There was a momentary decline in the period 1351-70, from which twenty-two wills survive, as compared with twenty-eight for 1331-50, sixty-five for 1371-90, and fifty-six for 1391-1410. However, this relative decline can be attributed to the mortality itself; moreover, the great leap in the period 1371-90 strengthens the argument advanced below.

30. This is consistently apparent in the wills. For example, Marco di Gentile Morosini in 1359 instructed that his daughter Beriola come into her inheritance at age eleven (NT 1023, Ariano Passamonte, no. 23). Moisè di Piero Morosini specifically instructed that his daughters marry at age twelve (NT 572, Giorgio Gibellino, no. 23). One exception was Silvestro di Marco Morosini, who in 1432 instructed that his daughters were not to marry until age sixteen; he increased their dowry legacies by 250 ducats for every year that they waited after that. This may suggest a changing attitude in the fifteenth century. (NT 486, Francesco Gibellino, no. 45. See also Tamassia, *La famiglia italiana*, pp. 197-98.)

31. To cite just two examples: Beruzza, wife then widow of Marco Soranzo, who was unmarried in 1374, wrote wills in 1380, 1385, 1388, and 1401 (NT 108, Giovanni Boninsegna, no. 84; NT 921, Nicolò Saiabianca, no. 519; NT 108, Giovanni Boninsegna, no. 296; NT 575, Giorgio Gibellino, no. 704). Beruzza's nubility in 1374 is indicated in the will written that year by her brother, Gasparino di Bellello Morosini (NT 1062, Lorenzo della Torre, no. 300). Another example is Cristina, wife then widow of Vettor di Lodovico Morosini, who wrote wills in 1382, 1399, 1423, and 1432 (CI 36, Giovanni Campion, 3, I, no. 71; NT 571, Giorgio Gibellino, no. 118; NT 560, Francesco Gritti, no. 346; NT 215, Giovanni Campisano, no. 34).

32. That is, the thirty-one possibilities had no children or named their parents as executors—an indication of relative youth—or both.

33. This was Agnesina, widow of Marco di Gentile Morosini (CI 143, Stefano Pianigo, no. 41), whose will is dated 7 Jan. 1360 (1359 Venetian style). That of her husband (cited above, n. 30) is dated 21 Aug. 1359.

34. In the pre-1331 period there are six women's wills, including one written by a pregnant testatress.

35. In fact, wives generally seem to have outlived their husbands. In an as yet uncompleted analysis, we found that of 110 patrician marriages terminated by the death of one of the spouses between 1366 and 1380, 77 ended with the death of the husband and only 33 with the death of the wife (CI 114, Marino, S. Tomà, prot. 1366-91, *passim*). However, these data need to be examined carefully before the results are fully acceptable.

36. A consideration of some importance in this regard may be the effect of increased state-bond holdings (*prestiti*) on dowry amounts. From 1343 to 1381 the state's indebtedness, and thus the amount invested in it by citizens, jumped over 1100 percent; and although it oscillated thereafter, by 1438 it was nearly 16 times as much as in 1343 (F. C. Lane, "The Funded Debt," esp. p. 88). See above, 174–75.

37. To protect wives' dowries, the statutes required a deposit by the husband in the amount of his bride's dowry. They also assigned priority among all claims on a man's estate—including those of his children and his creditors—to dowry restitution, and made the husband's ascendants and descendants financially liable if the husband's estate was not sufficient to repay the entire dowry of his widow (*Volumen statutorum*, Bk. I, ch. 34, 56, 61, 62, pp. 17v, 26v–29v). An example of enforcement of the statutes is that of Marina, widow of Pangrazio di Benedetto da Molin. Although her late husband had been emancipated ("filius divisus") from his father, the latter was nevertheless forced to make up the difference when Pangrazio's own estate was inadequate to Marina's dowry claim (CI 114, Marino, S. Tomà, prot., 1366–91, n.p., 10 May 1368). A wife was unable to invest her dowry without her husband's consent; but in compensation, he was obliged to pay her interest when he invested it (*Volumen statutorum*, Bk. I, ch. 39, p. 19v, Bk. III, ch. 28, p. 48v; NT 579, Giovanni de Comasini, no. 95: will of Goffredo di Francesco Morosini, 21 Feb. 1349 [1348 Venetian style]).

38. In strict anthropological terms, of course, a husband was just as much a member of two conjugal families as his wife. Legally, however, a man could belong to a marital conjugal family and still be under his father's *patria potestas*, with all of its economic effects. In any case, descent in Venice was patrilineal; to the extent that Venetian husbands remained unemancipated from their fathers, as seems to have been the rule, it seems fair to speak of extended families in the male line, even when common residence did not prevail (see Murdock, *Social Structure*, pp. 2–10).

39. See above, n. 27.

40. This conclusion arises from an examination of the bequests in the first fifty (by alphabet) wills of married women in the sample. Of 215 total bequests to first- and second-degree relatives, 107 (49.7%) went to natal kin, 96 (44.7%) to marital kin, and 12 (5.6%) to affines. These bequests are analyzed more fully in Stanley Chojnacki, "Patrician Women in Early Renaissance Venice," *Studies in the Renaissance* 21 (1974): 176–203.

41. Ernestine Friedl, "The Position of Women: Appearance and Reality," *Anthropological Quarterly* 40 (1967): 108.

42. See Tamassia, *La famiglia italiana*, pp. 111–14. See also the valuable discussion of David Herlihy, "Family Solidarity in Medieval Italian History," in Herlihy, et al. (eds.), *Economy, Government and Society in Medieval Italy: Essays in Memory of Robert L. Reynolds* (Kent, Ohio, 1969), pp. 173–84.

43. NT 1189, Piero Cavazza, no. 83; NT 571, Giorgio Gibellino, "Carte Varie," dated 28 April 1401. Gasparino's bequest complemented some real estate that Franceschina had been left by her late father.

44. *Ibid.* In his will of 1348, Andreasio di Michele Morosini bequeathed all of his real estate to his four sons with the provision that if they all died without issue, the property was to be sold, at a discount of 25 percent off the assessed value, to "aliquibus vel alicui de propinquioribus, de stipite, prolis mee" (PSM Miste, B. 182a, Andreasio Morosini, account book, n.p.). For similar sentiments, see the wills of Nicolò Morosini dottor in 1379 and of Albertino di Marino Morosini in 1450 (CI 97, Francesco Gritti, no. 1; NT 986, Francesco Rogeri, no. 110).

45. PSM Miste, B. 182a, Andreasio Morosini, account book, n.p.

46. In this respect the Venetian lineage, and the clan to which it belonged,

contrasts with the consorteries of Lombardy and Tuscany. See Franco Niccolai, "I consorzi nobiliari ed il comune nell'alta e media Italia," *Revista di storia del diritto italiano* 13 (1940): 119–24, and *passim*. On the restrictions that corporate kin groups, such as the consortery, place on relations with affines, see Eric R. Wolf, "Kinship, Friendship, and Patron-Client Relations in Complex Societies," in Michael Banton, ed., *The Social Anthropology of Complex Societies* (New York, 1966), p. 5.

47. Of the other three, two are unclear about the testators' relationship to the legatee and one bequest went to the daughter of the testator's brother-in-law—it is not clear whether a sister's husband or a wife's brother is meant.

48. CI 168, Marco de Rafanelli, no. 93.

49. Legally, the *fraterna* lasted for two generations of the male line (Lane, "Family Partnerships," p. 37; Pertile, *Storia del diritto*, 3: 282). The principle of grandfatherly bequests was prescribed in the statutes. *Volumen statutorum* (Bk. IV, ch. 25, p. 72v), stated that the unmarried and orphaned granddaughters, through the male line, of intestate men possessed a right to shares of their grandfathers' estates for dowry purposes (in effect parts of the shares that their deceased fathers would have inherited had they been alive). The principle was important enough to have been included in the additions and amendments to the statutes carried out under the Doge Andrea Dandolo in 1343 (*ibid.*, Bk. VI, ch. 53, p. 110v).

50. The statute-makers devised a long and complex set of principles to guarantee that the son of an intestate father made a sufficient amount available to his unmarried sister for her dowry (*ibid.*, Bk. IV, ch. 25, p. 71v; Ercole, "Istituto dotale," I, 241–46). Pertile, *Storia del diritto*, 3: 322.

51. NT 1062, Lorenzo della Torre, no. 300.

52. ". . . cum honore et prout congruit conditionem domus mee honorificientius maritetur" (NT 1234, Francesco Sorio, no. 509).

53. On the patrilineal traditions, however, see the debate between Leyser and Bullough: K. Leyser, "The German Aristocracy from the Ninth to the Early Twelfth Century: A Historical and Cultural Sketch," *Past and Present* 41 (1968): 25–53; D. A. Bullough, "Early Medieval Social Groupings: The Terminology of Kinship," *ibid.* 45 (1969): 3–18; K. Leyser, "Debate. Maternal Kin in Early Medieval Germany. A Reply," *ibid.* 49 (1970): 126–34.

54. He bequeathed 100 ducats to his "madona" for her daughter's dowry (NT 1233, Francesco Sorio, no. 257). The source for the meaning of *madona* as mother-in-law is Giuseppe Boerio, *Dizionario del dialetto veneziano* (Venice, 1856), p. 381.

55. "E in caxo che si al maridar de mie fie le non avesse tanto che le podesse ben maridar segondo la so condition voio che lo i se possa azonzar la parte che i tocasse de questo mio residuo in la so impromesse per maridarle meio" (NT 1255, Pietro Zane, fol. 194r).

56. However, one of them, Giovanni di Marino Morosini, in 1397, was very generous to his brothers' sons (CI 242, Giacomo Ziera, 5. prot., c. iv).

57. Maria, widow of Matteo Morosini, in her will of 1431 bequeathed 500 ducats toward the dowry of her son's daughter without reference to either her own daughter or that daughter's children, although the daughter, who was married, was to act as executor. However, the daughter was living with her husband in Negroponte (Euboea), and distance may have weakened contacts; the daughter was to be an executor only if she returned to Venice (CI 24, Rolandino Bernardi, 16. c. 41, no. 99). Novella's will is in *ibid.*, 16. c. 67, no. 184. For Giovanni's, see PSM Miste, B. 2, Giovanni Morosini, account book.

58. Based on examination of primary-kin executors in ninety-seven wives' and widows' wills—those whose first names begin with the letters A–E. The results can be seen most clearly in tabular form:

| | | | All Women's |
Executor	67 Wives'	30 Widows'	Executors
Parents and siblings	91 (52.3%)	32 (42.7%)	123 (49.4%)
Husbands	53 (30.5%)	—	53 (21.3%)
Children	30 (17.2%)	43 (57.3%)	73 (29.3%)
	174 (100%)	75 (100%)	249 (100%)

It is noteworthy that one out of every five wives (14 of 67) failed to name her husband among her executors.

59. For example, Tomasina, widow of Albano Zane, made business loans to her father, Andrea di Dardi Morosini, at least twice in the 1380s (CI 20, Giovanni Bon, fasc. 4, n.p. 21 March 1380; fasc. 5, n.p., 27 April 1382).

60. Meyer Fortes, "The Structure of Unilineal Descent Groups," *American Anthropologist* 55 (1953): 34. He contrasts these principles governing the family, the nucleus of the "complementary line of filiation" which ties husband and wife together, with the principles that govern the descent group's interests—law and public institutions.

61. Making provision for her unborn child in her will of 1385, Cristina, wife of Antonio Querini, bequeathed it 300 ducats if a boy, but only 200 if a girl (CI 22, Miscellanea Testamenti, Notai Diversi, no. 747).

62. This is the same group as that used above, n. 58. Excluded from consideration are unborn children and generalized bequests to groups unspecified as to number, e.g., bequests "to all my children."

63. Evidence is the tendency in wives' choices of executors, indicated above, n. 58, and the patterns of their bequests, analyzed above, n. 40.

64. See Herlihy, "Family Solidarity," *passim;* Richard A. Goldthwaite, *Private Wealth in Renaissance Florence: A Study of Four Families* (Princeton, 1968), esp. pp. 255–58; Randolph Starn, "Francesco Guicciardini and His Brothers" in Anthony Molho and John A. Tedeschi, eds., *Renaissance: Studies in Honor of Hans Baron* (DeKalb, Ill., 1971), pp. 411–44.

65. For reasons of space, we have not discussed the growing practice, engaged in by both men and women, of allotting a certain amount of money to the dowries of poor girls, both patrician and plebeian. We have found thirty-four such generalized bequests in the Morosini wills, or almost one for every ten wills. The impulse behind these and the bequests to kinswomen that we have been considering were doubtless encouraged by the dowry inflation of the time. However, there is a difference between general charitable bequests, usually made in the category of bequests *ad pias causas,* and those to kinswomen made among the other specific bequests to family and friends. The former fall into the category of generalized charity that was growing in importance at this time. See Brian Pullan, *Rich and Poor in Renaissance Venice: The Social Institutions of a Catholic State, to 1620* (Cambridge, Mass., 1971), p. 183, and *passim.*

Susan Mosher Stuard

⚜ Women in Charter and Statute Law: Medieval Ragusa/Dubrovnik

Aristocratic women within the social context of medieval Ragusa (present day Dubrovnik) enjoyed the perquisites of upper-class life, citizenship, wealth, and family solidarity. They suffered under the burden of strict legal restriction, if Statute Law is to be believed. Social history, through interpreting the substantial chartulary resources of the Dubronvik State Archives, can help determine what balance was achieved in society between the advantages and the restrictions on their lives. Ragusa, small, aristocratic, and ambitious for a greater role in Mediterranean life, provides an excellent case study of the social position of the upper-class, urban woman.

Venice is frequently chosen as the model of a successful aristocratic city-state in the Middle Ages, but perhaps the very success of the Venetian Republic and its concomitant population growth should prompt us to look elsewhere in the Adriatic for a model of a town controlled by a mercantile elite. Ragusa comes closer to the medieval ideal of aristocratic government in that its patrician families formed a greater proportion of the town's population and through the centuries maintained dominance over the town's Councils, with no apparent need to legally close the ranks of the nobility. More significantly they monopolized long distance trade.

In the early fourteenth century, at the inauguration of Ragusa's great maritime expansion, the town incorporated, conservatively, about 3,000 inhabitants.[1] The aristocratic male population is estimated at 300 in 1310; figuring a woman and child for each adult male, the aristocratic class numbered about 900 or close to one-third of the town's overall population.[2] Within the next one hundred years, due to the Plague and its periodic reoccurrence, the aristocratic class shrank to 800 members (an estimate made in 1423). The fifteenth century witnessed recovery; Soloviev estimates the nobility at 1,100 members by 1442, an increment of 43.7 percent in nineteen years.[3] Even at the height of expansion in the sixteenth century, the population within the town's walls reached only about 6,000 inhabitants.[4]

To exercise political control, while maintaining the impetus for commercial expansion, taxed the capacities of this class in the years before 1442. With the exception of a few outstanding families of the *populi*, nonaristocratic persons were excluded from trade.[5] The merchants guarded the town's commercial leadership on the Dalmatian coast by also excluding most foreign competitors. If they did not turn to the lower classes within the town for personnel, who was available to promote expansion? The extant records of the chancellory, dating from the late thirteenth century, show that women of the aristocratic families were sometimes drafted to help in this capacity. This provides the historian with an opportunity to view the behavior of women within the medieval urban setting, a rare occurrence, since women do not frequently appear in public records. Despite the paucity of records for the late thirteenth and the fourteenth centuries, an attempt at reconstructing women's role can be made.

In suggesting that women of the aristocratic class in Ragusa did anything as practical as assist men in the mundane concerns of business life is to tamper with prevailing opinion concerning their role. Like their sisters in Venice, Ragusan women were generally regarded as mere ornaments to society, the expensive and exotic symbols of their father's or husband's mercantile success. Philip de Diversis, a fifteenth-century master of Latin who served Ragusa as school teacher, described the hauteur of Ragusan women.[6] According to his account, women who figured among the "supremi," that is, from branches of aristocratic families which had attained outstanding wealth by the fifteenth century, disdained to speak to others when they walked the streets of Ragusa. Their presence in public places was of utmost importance nonetheless, for on their persons they displayed the wealth of their husbands' mercantile empires. As a result of de Diversis' account, the prosperous goldsmith industry at Ragusa has been regarded largely as serving their needs. Cvito Fisković, in his study of the industry, compiled a list of over one hundred goldsmiths active in the town in the fourteenth century.[7] The noblewomen would be hard put to consume the industry's entire production of luxury goods. Highly specific restrictions had been set on dowries as early as 1235 and remained in effect through the era, regulating the jewelry and clothes a woman might own. This tended to limit women's ostentation, even though it is unlikely that the sumptuary law was obeyed to the letter.[8]

In reality gold and, more important, silver smithery was an export industry in the years following the adoption of the gold standard in the cities of northern Italy.[9] Silver, which had previously been sought for currency and represented a significant export from the Balkan interior, was fabricated into wares, particularly after 1310. If Ragusan women wore some of the locally fabricated wares, they served as excellent advertisement to foreign traders visiting the town. Sumptuary law at Ragusa applied only to dowries; husbands were free to give earrings, bracelets, *frontale*, crowns, and rings to their wives. This calculated display may help explain the growth of the myth concerning the elegance of Ragusan women's apparel.

This myth was not the only mask concealing the aristocratic woman's role in the practical concerns of the community. The law itself, codified in 1272, would indicate that women had no significant public, much less commercial, role to play in the town. A Ragusan woman was legally defined by the extensive and highly specific laws governing dowries.[10] While her rights to a dowry outweighed the rights of her brothers when she reached marriageable age, her dowry marked her final legal claim on her parents, as prescribed by Roman tradition.[11] At marriage she passed to the custody of her husband or the head of her husband's household, insuring that she be a private rather than a public person all her life. If her husband's debts came due in his absence she was not held responsible; rather, a term was set for her husband's return so he might answer the debt himself, and a relative might answer a debt for a woman as well.[12] In fact, following the principle established by the Roman jurist, Ulpian, in the third century, a woman was represented by a male advocate if it became necessary for her to appear in court.[13] Her own personal indebtedness could not amount to more than fifteen *hyperpera*, which would of course prohibit her from entering long-distance trade.[14] She did maintain authority over her minor children on the death of her husband, except in the significant question of the division of the children's patrimony.[15] Minors who were fatherless were appointed male tutors (by the town authorities) to oversee their estates.

Divorce was not practiced, but a woman expelled from her husband's home, who could not find a place to receive her, was entitled to have her husband assume responsibility for her expenses.[16] A woman might own her own clothes and jewels and a domestic slave brought with her as part of her dowry. If her dowry included land or movable goods she might continue to own and control them after marriage. Money brought as part of the dowry came under her husband's authority. He might invest it, or the courts might ask it as surety if he were brought before the law.[17] In this commercial town, where only limited land was available, noble dowries were much more likely to consist of money than land or movable goods, giving a significant advantage to the newly married man.

A dowry of a second wife might be entailed if a first wife's children had need of it, so, in a strict sense, the dowry was not the possession of a woman and her kin.[18] If she or her husband did not have heirs, a woman might dispose of her dowry as she pleased.[19] In men's wills, a deceased wife's dowry was treated separately, held apart from his other assets to serve the needs of the children.[20] Women frequently provided their daughters' dowries, thus allowing some Ragusan capital to follow a matrilineal pattern of descent.[21]

The sum of the laws regulating a woman's life would indicate that she could not participate in business life at all, but a different picture emerges from the chartularies. Women did participate to a limited extent in business, even if it conflicted with the tenor of the law. In order to give some coherence to the various examples within the extant chartularies, I have chosen one family, the de Mence, probably Ragusa's most numerous aristocratic family, as a point of concentration. They survived the years of the Plague due to their considerable number, and some branches were listed among the affluent "supremi" in the fifteenth century. They represented the "supremi" well since many of their members dealt in the luxury trade, particularly trade in precious metals from the Balkan interior. They are equally representative of the class as a whole since they intermarried extensively with other aristocratic families. Certain de Mence branches were not fortunately connected or accumulators of great wealth; some contented themselves with local trade in commodities as homely as fish.[22] All the men of the family conscientiously fulfilled their civic obligations, taking turn in office with the sons and fathers of other noble houses. As a family they were remarkable only in their fecundity.

A dowry received by Blasius de Mence in 1282, from a kinsman of his bride, reveals that infusions of capital through dowries were by no means inconsequential in the family's success. This particular contract includes the acknowledgment from Pasque Volcassio, the bride's kinsman, that the 600 *grossi* and 100 *exagia* of gold were over the limits set by law. The notary, Thomasini de Savere stated, "said kinsman confirmed this [standing] before the statute in which it is written that no one may give or receive over 40 *hyperpera* in a dowry."[23] The notary fulfilled the responsibility of his office, but the contractors showed little concern since there are no prosecutions for inflated dowries in the records of the chancellory, thus justifying the attitudes of Pasque Volcassio and the bridegroom, Blasius de Mence. Both contracting families traded in gold and silver; this dowry represented a pooling of capital between two affluent branches of two aristocratic families. Glaring inequalities in wealth did not exist in the noble class in the late thirteenth century, but it is readily evident that illegally high dowries could concentrate the wealth of the aristocracy in the hands of a relatively few persons within a century or so.[24]

An interesting case of a businesswoman exists in another early fourteenth-century branch of the de Mence family. Boni de Mence, wife of Nicola, who died in 1310, and mother of at least five children, outlived her husband by nearly twenty years. Her husband's estate was not divided upon his death but kept intact and invested by his two older sons, Marcus and

Domagna, who were later joined by a younger brother, Marinus, in the family business. They held the estate in a ocietas, closely resembling the *compagna fraterna* favored at Venice to maintain an undivided inheritance. Both older sons achieved success, traveling to the interior and doing business with the Serbian monarch in Domagna's case. Marcus traveled at least once to Venice. Possibly it was due to her sons' peripatetic habits that Boni entered their business domain.[25] In the 1320s she appeared in court and satisfied debts held by her husband's relatives with land settlements. One contract stated that she was absolving a debt held by her son, Marcus, with the permission of her second son, Domagna.[26] Given the joint nature of the family holdings, such an acknowledgment would be necessary to make her action binding. In 1329 she settled matters pertaining to her dowry and is heard from no more.[27]

Were her appearances before the court, without an advocate, illegal? During these years Domagna, her son, represented the wife of a business associate as advocate before the court, a far more mormal occurrence.[28] The records of Boni's transactions do not give the amount of indebtedness, but since they entailed land transfers there is a good possibility that they amounted to more than fifteen *hyperpera*, a woman's legal debt ceiling. Still, there is no clear-cut case of illegality—her actions violated the spirit more than the letter of the law and were never challenged. The record of her court appearances, and that of other women, indicate that the procedures prescribed by law to protect a woman from public responsibility could be ignored for a woman who was performing strategic services for a family enterprise. Her help was probably enlisted because of the strains of manning the family's far-flung commercial network.

In 1344 the wife of Lampre de Mence gave three pieces of silver, weighing twenty pounds and eleven ounces, to Dominicus (?) de Mence at her husband's request. While she is nameless in the contract, she was a participant in a major transaction, evidently trusted to assume a business responsibility.[29]

In 1351 a partition of estate was drawn up for the recently deceased Michael de Mence. His assets were considerable, a great house with offices on the *Platea* at Ragusa, a home in Venice, movable goods, and other assets. He had no sons, and a court case brought by his married daughters, Franussa and Dobre, ruled that his property be divided between his two sons-in-law (to the exclusion of his surviving de Mence cousins). There is no provision for daughters dividing a Ragusan estate and, to be completely accurate, the daughters did not do so in this instance—their husbands did. Michael de Mence's assets were extensive enough to be important to the overall economy of the town and it is therefore interesting that the judge's solution to the inheritance of his estate recognized the right to inherit through the female line, however indirectly.[30]

These four cases in the de Mence family raise a question: why not amend the law to conform more closely with the actual and accepted social patterns within the town, particularly in regard to the personal and public rights of women? The Eighth Book of Statute Law, which contains additions and revisions, and the *Libri Reformationes* indicate that the law was amended and updated in other instances. The failure to amend in the case of women may lie in the fact that only a few women behaved in a manner contrary to the spirit and provisions of the law, and then only in the interests of the family. Consequently it was in the interest of the mercantile class to make exception or ignore the law in certain specific cases rather than amend it. This is well illustrated by the case against Nicoleta de Mence, initiated by her husband, Jache de Sorgo, in 1390.[31] No information is provided in the *Libri Reformationes* concerning Nicoleta's reasons for removing herself and her goods from her husband's home, but her husband brought suit before the Small Council because of her behavior. The Council tried sending two representatives, one a relative, to reason with her. They next gave her fourteen hours to return to her husband's home. Then they resorted to sending her "old mother" to influence her. When that failed, in response to Jache de Sorgo's continued suit, she was held *inclusa*, (imprisoned) in the small palace, under guard. The Council referred to its own action rather dismally as the martyrization of Nicoleta de Mence, and she was later exiled, her goods confiscated. The *Libri Reformationes*, despite the cryptic nature of the account, reveal a concerted effort on the part of the Small Council to avert the severity of the law in Nicoleta's case. But her husband continued to bring suit, and he had the law on his side; Nicoleta had no right to deprive him of her dowry or her person, and there the case rested. The law might be stretched or ignored to further the interests of family business and the larger interests of the mercantile class; it could not accommodate to a woman's demands for her individual freedom.

Nicoleta is an exception, but one which serves to illustrate the degree beyond which the law could not be bent. Most women of the aristocratic class made no such demands upon the law and custom—in fact they appear to have assimilated the values of their class to a high degree. Even those who never participated actively in trade or public life made a significant contribution to the solidity and homogeneity of the merchant aristocracy.

Ragusa never experienced a "serrato" or closing of the ranks of the aristocracy in the constitutional sense as Venice did in 1297. To some limited extent the aristocracy closed its ranks in the 1330s by excluding nonaristocrats from the right to trade, but the social cohesion of the Ragusan aristocracy was sufficient to maintain the class's identity and authority without recourse to constitutional sanction.[32] Marriage within the class insured this continuation of class strength. Few exogamous marriages occur; if a Ragusan woman married outside her town, she did not marry outside her class.[33] These few exogamous marriages formed excellent ties with noble families from neighboring towns: for instance, Ragusan women married into the noble de Buchia and Thoma families from nearby Kotor. Both these neighboring aristocratic families were granted citizenship at Ragusa in the fourteenth century, the Thoma after considerable intermarriage with the Ragusans. In their case the grant of citizenship was merely recognition for an already existing acceptance into the social and economic life of the aristocracy, effected through marriage.[34] Other Ragusan daughters were married to noble Venetians, creating a bond of good will between business associates of the two Republics.[35]

Beyond this, Ragusan noblewomen helped maintain the widely touted homogeneity of the aristocratic class. They named their children with a startling admixture of Latin (or Italian) and Slavic names. A fifteenth-century list of noblewomen gives two forms for their names: Latin and Slavic.[36] Philologists are at a loss to decide the actual speech of the aristocratic class in the medieval period, but the merchant aristocracy attended school in Latin and knew enough Slavic to trade with ease in the Balkan interior.[37] Domestic servants and slaves from the interior insured verbal knowledge of the Slavic tongue in aristocratic households. The origins of the noble class itself, while obscure, point to a dual heritage, both Slavic and Italian. This diversity of origin failed to cause rents and divisions within the class because family origin was ignored in arranging marriages. The resultant cohesion of the noble families was so great that class identity is best understood as the cooperation of extended and interrelated families. Reinforced by a government policy of limiting population growth in the other classes in the town through control of immigration, the social cohesion of the aristocracy eliminated the need for strong constitutional sanctions for continued dominance.

Women also served to maintain the numbers of the aristocratic class. Prosperity, and an imported and subsidized grain supply, provided Ragusan homes with good nutrition. Domestic slaves and contract labor from the interior eased the burden of domestic labor for noblewomen, and the law made all but the exceptional woman a private domestic person.[38] Thus, noblewomen did what one would expect—they produced large families. Irmgard Manken's study of the patriciate comes complete with genealogies in which large family patterns tend to dominate in the late thirteenth and fourteenth centuries.[39] Since Ragusa underwent mercantile expansion during the era of the Plague, a high birth rate maintained the aristocracy's high proportion in the town's total population and produced the numbers necessary for overseas trade. The image of the elegant, jeweled woman sits uncomfortably on the reality of large families of surviving heirs. The statistical data is not sufficient to establish comparative mortality rates for men and women, but the pattern of serial marriages for men suggest significant instances of maternal death in childbirth. In the fourteenth century the overwhelming proportion of persons who survived childhood married; not until the mid-fifteenth century, with its sudden increment in the noble population, do families become smaller. Then significant numbers of sons and daughters begin to enter religious houses.

By this date the strains of expansion were largely over and the Plague no longer recurred every other decade. The noblewoman was free to retreat into private luxury and conduct her life according to an elegant and aristocratic pattern, cushioned from the reality of the commercial network which provided her privilege. This era conforms far more readily with the literary image of aristocratic society in the Adriatic or Illyrian cities, but it contrasts with the earlier centuries of Ragusan expansion. [40]

In the Ragusa/Dubrovnik archives, as in most urban archival collections, the record of women's history is scant. The essential question of whether women were largely passive or played a vigorous, even dominant, social role at odds with their legal rights can only be answered, quite tentatively, in favor of the latter. But a study of women does provide us with a new perspective from which to view medieval urban life. The extent to which social life in Ragusa did not conform to Statute Law becomes apparent in examining the case of women; it is much less apparent in regard to business life or other aspects of communal behavior. The cohesion of the aristocratic class in Ragusa takes on new meaning when we consider that the noble merchant would rather enlist the help of his women relatives than permit men from nonaristocratic or foreign families into partnership with him.

NOTES

1. S. Stuard, "A Communal Program of Medical Care: Medieval Ragusa/Dubrovnik," *Journal of the History of Medicine and Allied Sciences* 28 (1973): 138.

2. Irmgard Manken, *Dubrovački Patricijat u XIV Veku* (Belgrade, 1960), pp. 14–16.

3. Alexandre Soloviev, "Le Patriciat de Raguse au XVe siècle," in M. Vidoević and J. Tadić, eds., *Rešetarov Zbornik iz Dubrovačke Proslosti* (Dubrovnik, 1931), pp. 64–66.

4. J. Tadić, "Le Port de Raguse au Moyen Age," *Le Navire et l'Èconomie Maritime au moyen âge au XVIIIe siècle* (Paris, 1958), 18. 25,000 more are estimated to have lived in Astarea and on the nearby islands.

5. Desanka Kovačević, "Zore Bokšić: Dubrovacki Trgovoc i Protovestijar bosanskih Kraljevo," *Društvo Istoričara Bosne i Herzegovine Godišnjak* 13 (Sarajevo, 1962): 289–310, is an example of a successful, nonaristocratic Ragusan merchant.

6. Philippus de Diversis, *situs Aedificiorum, Politae et Laudabilium consuetudinum inclytae civitas Ragusii*, ed. V. Brunelli (Zara. 1880–82), c. XVI, pp. 124–25; c. XX, p. 130.

7. Cvito Fisković, "Dubrovački Zlatari, XIII-XVII Stoleca," *Starohrvatska Prosvjeta* 3 (1949): 143–249.

8. *Liber Statutorum civitatis Ragusii*, ed. V. Bogošić and C. Jireček, Monumenta Historico-juridica slavorum meridionalium, vol. 9 (Zagreb, 1904), p. lxiv; the law on dowries dates from 1235 and was added to the book of Statute Law when it was codified in 1272.

9. See forthcoming article, S. Stuard, "Ragusa and the Silver Trade, c. 1300," *Studi Veneziani* 17 (1975), pp. 1–40.

10. *Liber Statutorum*, p. lxiv.

11. *Liber Statutorum*, 4: cap. 13, p. 88.

12. *Liber Statutorum*, 3: cap. 7, p. 59–60; 8: cap. 7, p. 175; 8: cap. 9, p. 175.

13. *Liber Statutorum*, 3: cap. 9, p. 60.

14. *Liber Statutorum*, 8: cap. 7, p. 174; 8: cap. 32, p. 183.

15. *Liber Statutorum*, 4: cap. 20, p. 90.

16. *Liber Statutorum*, 4: cap. 10, p. 87.

17. *Liber Statutorum*, p. lxiv.

18. *Liber Statutorum*, 4: cap. 9.

19. *Liber Statutorum*, 8: cap. 95.

20. Gregor Čremošnik, *Spisi Dubrovačke Kancelarije, Thomasini de Savere, notarius*, (Zagreb 1951), doc. 1020, pp. 302–3; doc 1049, pp. 310–11. See also doc. 1117, pp. 333–34, for the investment of a woman's estate by the *thesaurarii de Santa Maria*.

21. *Spisi, Thomasini de Savere*, doc. 705, p. 220; doc. 743, pp. 234–35; doc. 866, p. 264; doc. 966, p. 290.

22. *Dubrovnik State Archives, Diversa Cancellariae*, 6: fol. 122; 8: fol. 82; 12: fol. 151b; (they dealt in oil and onions also).

23. *Spisi, Thomasini de Savere*, doc. 919, p. 278. See editor's notes at the bottom of the page. The sum of a legal dowry is clearly listed in the law as forty *hyperpera*, considerably more than the earlier dowry limit of the law of 1235, *Liber Statutorum*, p. lxiv. It is unlikely that the notary would make an error in this case, since he was standing in front of the statute in question. There is a strong possibility that the dowry law had been revised upwards, but the revision is not available.

24. This is by no means the largest dowry in the records of the late thirteenth century. The largest I can identify is listed in the will of Vitagna de Cerna: "In primis habui pro perchivio uxoris mee Marie de mobili et stabili ypp. tria milia, quod perchivium ante omnia set salvum." This may indicate the extent to which the dowry had grown over a life time, or the original sum; the latter is the more likely possibility. *Spisi, Thomasini de Savere*, doc. 1020, pp. 302–3. Note the sum was saved out before Vitagna de Cerna's debts were paid, to serve the purposes of the family (daughters' dowries, sons' inheritances.) See *Liber Statutorum*, 4: c. 57, part 4, p. 102. Again, there were exceptions to the rule. In 1341 gold from a wife's dowry was transferred to a husband, with the consent of the government. *Dubrovnik State Archives, Diversa Cancellariae*, 13: fol. 95b.

25. See the will of Domagna de Mence, T. Smičiklas, *Codex Diplomaticus Croatiae, Dalmatiae et Slavoniae*, vol. 2–15 (Zagreb, 1904–34), 12: doc. 496. See also *Dubrovnik State Archives, Diversa Cancellariae*, 12: fol. 201; 10: fol. 115b; 5: fol 32b; 4: fol. 40. See also V. V. Makušev, "Izprave za odnošaj Dubrovnika prema Veneciji," *Starine* 31 (Zagreb 1901), doc. 66.

26. *Dubrovnik State Archives, Diversa Cancellariae*, 8: fol. 27; 8: fol 25b.

27. *Dubrovnik State Archives, Diversa Cancellariae*, 9: fol. 21; 9: fol. 85.

28. *Dubrovnik State Archives, Diversa Cancellariae*, 8: fol. 4.

29. *Dubrovnik State Archives, Diversa Cancellariae*, 14: fol. 113b.

30. *Dubrovnik State Archives, Diversa Cancellariae*, 12: fol. 315.

31. *Dubrovnik State Archives, Libri Reformationes,* 28: fol. 47, 48b, 49, 50, (1390). This is the most extensively covered private issue in the *Libri Reformationes* for the fourteenth century. The issue would appear to be more appropriate for debate in the lesser court, yet it is heard before the Small Council sitting in public session.

32. For example, doctors who were salaried by the town were excluded from trade in this decade. See S. Stuard, "Communal Program," pp. 133–34.

33. A marriage contracted outside Ragusa was not subject to the law governing the size of dowries, *Liber Statutorum,* p. lxiv.

34. Irmgard Manken, *Dubrovačke Patrijicat u XIV veku* (Belgrade, 1961), part 2, genealogy no. 70 (Thoma); part 1, pp. 162–68 (Buchia).

35. For example, Margarita de Mence was married to Ludovicus Cornerii de Venezia in 1359. Irmgard Manken, *Dubrovačke Patrijicat u XIV veku,* part 2, geneology no. 42/1. An alliance with the Corner or Correr family of Venice would be a great advantage to the de Mence's trading interests.

36. P. Skop, "L'Importance de Dubrovnik dans l'Histoire des Slaves," *Le'Monde Slave* 8, no. 2 (Paris, 1931): 165–70.

37. Children of aristocratic families attended school in Ragusa, see Irmgard Manken, *Dubrovačke Patricijat u XIV veku,* p. 87. Did daughters attend as well as sons? There is no specific reference to daughters attending school in the fourteenth century, but no reason to believe they did not. In the fourteenth century, women won one positive right, the opportunity to be cared for by the communally salaried physicians, see S. Stuard, "Communal Program," p. 132.

38. Vuk Vinaver, "Trgovina bosanskim robljem tokom XIV veka d Dubrov-niku," Dubrovnik, *Anali* 2 (1953): 125–47.

39. Irmgard Manken, *Dubrovačke Patricijat u XIV Veku,* part 2, geneology no. 1. The heirs of Volca de Babalio, for example, numbered twenty in the fourth generation at the end of the fourteenth century; only one, Volca's son Domagna, is listed as a presbyter, and he had one daughter as an heir. The fourth generation, by contrast, saw four persons entering religious houses, and the tendency is even more pronounced in the fifth generation. Unfortunately Manken's genealogies are not complete or accurate enough to be the basis of statistical study of family patterns.

40. The artistic image also, see J. Tadić, *Grada i Slikarskij Skoli u Dubrovniku, XIII-XVI Veku* (Belgrade, 1952), 1: 3, 18, 19, 21, 51. Portraits of Ragusan women appear as early as 1296, but religious art tends to dominate in the fourteenth century.

Selected Bibliography

ABRAMS, A. "Women Traders in Medieval London." *Economic Journal* 26 (1916): 276-85.

ADAMS, HENRY. "The Primitive Rights of Women." In *Historical Essays*. New York, 1891.

AMUNDSEN, DARREL W. and DIERS, CAROL JEAN. "The Age of Menarche in Medieval Europe." *Human Biology* 45 (1973): 363-68.

BANDEL, BETTY. "The English Chroniclers' Attitude toward Women." *Journal of the History of Ideas* 16 (1955): 113-18.

BENNET, H. S. *The Pastons and their England*. Cambridge, 1951.

—— *Six Medieval Men and Women*. New York, 1972.

CHOJNACKI, STANLEY. "Patrician Women in Early Renaissance Venice." *Studies in the Renaissance* 21 (1974): 176-203.

COLEMAN, EMILY. "Medieval Marriage Characteristics." In *The Family in History*, edited by R. Rothberg and T. Robb. New York, 1971.

COLLIS, LOUISE. *Memoirs of a Medieval Woman, The Life and Times of Margery Kempe*. New York, 1964.

DREW, KATHERINE FISHER, ed. and trans. *The Lombard Laws*. Philadelphia, 1973.

DUCKETT, ELEANOR SHIPLEY. *Women and their Letters in the Early Middle Ages*. Northampton, 1964.

ECKENSTEIN, LINA. *Women under Monasticism*. Cambridge, 1896.

ENGELS, FREDERICK. *The Origin of the Family*. Translated by Ernest Untermann. New York, 1902.

FACINGER, MARION. "A Study of Medieval Queenship." In *Studies in Medieval and Renaissance History*, edited by William Bowsky. Lincoln, 1968.

FORBES, THOMAS. *The Midwife and the Witch*. New Haven, 1961.

GOLDTHWAITE, RICHARD. "The Florentine Palace as Domestic Architecture." *American Historical Review* 72 (1972): 977-1013.

GOODY, J. *The Developmental Cycle in Domestic Groups*. Cambridge, 1958.

Green, Mary. *Lives of the Princesses of England.* 6 vols. London, 1849-55.

Hanawalt, B. A. "The Peasant Family and Crime in Fourteenth Century England." *Journal of British Studies* 13 (1974): 1-18.

Hays, H. R. *The Dangerous Sex: the Myth of Feminine Evil.* New York, 1964.

Helmholz, R. H. "Infanticide in the Province of Canterbury during the Fifteenth Century." *History of Childhood Quarterly* 2 (1975): 379-90.

Herlihy, David. "Women in Medieval Society." Pamphlet: The Smith History Lecture, University of St. Thomas. Houston, 1971.

Himes, N. E. *A Medical History of Contraception.* New York, 1963.

Homans, G. C. *English Villagers in the Thirteenth Century.* New York, 1970.

Hughes, Diane Owen. "Urban Growth and Family Structure in Medieval Genoa." *Past and Present* 66 (1975): 3-28.

Hughes, Muriel Joy. *Women Healers in Medieval Life and Literature.* New York, 1943.

Kramer, H., and Sprenger, J. *Malleus Maleficarum.* Translated by Montague Summers. London, 1928.

Laeuchli, Samuel. *Power and Sexuality.* Philadelphia, 1972.

Lancaster, Lorraine. "Kinship in Anglo-Saxon Society." In *Early Medieval Society*, edited by S. Thrupp. New York, 1967.

Laslett, P., and Wall, R. *Household and Family in Past Time.* Cambridge, 1972.

Lewis, Archibald. *The Development of Southern French and Catalan Society.* Austin, 1965.

McDonnell, Ernest. *The Beguines and Beghards in Medieval Culture.* New Brunswick, 1954.

McNamara, Jo-Ann, and Wemple, Suzanne. "The Power of Women through the Family in Medieval Europe." In *Clio's Consciousness Raised*, edited by Mary Hartman and Louise Banner. New York, 1974.

McNeill, J. T., and Gamer, H. M. eds. and trans. *Medieval Handbooks of Penance.* New York, 1965.

Miller, B. D. H. "She who hath Drunk any Potion." *Medium Aevum* 31 (1962): 188-93.

Moller, Herbert. "The Social Causation of the Courtly Love Complex." *Comparative Studies in Society and History* 1 (1958): 147-63.

Morewedge, Rosemarie Thee, ed. *The Role of Woman in the Middle Ages.* Binghampton, 1975.

Noonan, John. *Contraception.* Cambridge, 1965.

Phillips, Dayton. *Beguines in Medieval Strasburg.* San Francisco, 1941.

Phillpotts, Bertha. *Kindred and Clan in the Middle Ages and After.* Cambridge, 1913.

Pollak, O. *The Criminality of Women.* Philadelphia, 1950.

Power, Eileen. "The Position of Women in the Middle Ages." In *Legacy of the Middle Ages*, edited by C. Crump and E. Jacob. Oxford, 1926.

PUTNAM, EMILY. *The Lady.* 2nd ed. Chicago, 1971.

RUSSELL, JOSIAH COX. *Late Ancient and Medieval Population.* Philadelphia, 1958.

STENTON, DORIS. *The English Woman in History.* London, 1957.

TOBIN, ROSEMARY BARTON. "Vincent of Beauvais on the Education of Women." *Journal of the History of Ideas* 35 (1974): 485–89.

THRUPP, SYLVIA. *The Merchant Class of Medieval London.* Ann Arbor, 1948.

IMPORTANT WORKS IN FOREIGN LANGUAGES

BESTA, E. *La famiglia nella storia del diritto italiano.* Milan, 1962.

CECCHETTI, B. "La Donna nel medioevo a Venezia." *Archivio veneto* 31 (1886): 33–69.

CORNUEY, LOUIS-MAURICE-ANDRÉ. "Le régime de la 'dos' aux époques mérovingienne et carolingienne." Thesis, Univ. d'Alger, 1929.

DAUDET, P. *Études sur l'histoire de la jurisdiction matrimoniale.* Vol. 1, *Les origines carolingiennes et la compétence exclusive de l'église.* Paris, 1933. Vol. 2, *L'établissement de la compétence de l'église en matière de divorce et de consanguinité.* Paris, 1941.

ERCOLE, F. "L'istituto doctale nella pratica e nella legislazione satutaria dell 'Italia superiore." *Revista italiana per le scienze giuridiche* 45 (1908): 191–392; 46 (1910): 167–257.

ERMOLAEF, AIMEE *Die Sonderstellung der Frau im französischen Lehnrecht.* Dissertation, Univ. of Bern, 1930.

ESMEIN, A. *Le mariage en droit canonique.* 2 vols. Reprinted. New York, 1968.

GANSHOF, FRANÇOIS. "Le statut de la femme dans la monarchie franque." *Société Jean Bodin, Recueils* 12 (1962): 5–58.

LEHMANN, A. *Le rôle de la femme dans l'histoire de France au moyen âge.* Paris, 1952.

MARONGIU, A. *La famiglia nell'Italia Medionale.* Milan, 1944.

METZ, RENÉ. "Le statut de la femme en droit canonique médiéval." *Société Jean Bodin, Recueils* 12 (1962): 59–113.

PORTMANN, MARIE-LOUISE. *Die Darstellung der Frau in der Geschichtsschreibung des früheren Mittelalters.* Basler Beiträge zur Geschichtswissenschaft. Vol. 69. Basel, 1958.

RITZER, KORBINIAN. *Forman, Riten und religiöses Brauchtum der Eheschliessung in den christlichen Kirchen des ersten Jahrtausends.* Münster, 1962.

SANCHEZ-ALBORNOZ, CLAUDIO. "La mujer en España hace mil años" In *España y el Islam.* Buenos Aires, 1943. Reprinted in *Del ayer de España.* Madrid, 1973.

SENN, NOEL. *Le contrat de vente de la femme en droit matriominal germanique.* Portentruy, 1946.

VOGELSANG, THILO. *Die Frau als Herrscherin im hohen Mittelalter: Studien zur "in consors regni" Formel.* Göttingen, 1954.

Contributors

BRENDA M. BOLTON is currently lecturer in medieval history at Westfield College, University of London. Her research interests lie in an examination of some of the popular religious and heretical movements throughout Europe in the late twelfth and early thirteenth centuries. Publications include a number of articles for *Studies in Church History*, a series produced by the Ecclesiastical History Society and providing a forum for the work of younger historians.

STANLEY CHOJNACKI is Associate Professor of History at Michigan State University. He is interested in the sociological aspects of medieval history and is completing a study of the Venetian patriciate in the Middle Ages.

EMILY COLEMAN is an Assistant Professor of History at University of Pittsburgh, and has published articles on medieval peasant demography and "Medieval Marriage Characteristics: A Neglected Factor in the History of Medieval Serfdom" (*Journal of Interdisciplinary History*). She has recently completed a manuscript on "A Peasant Society and Social Change: The Serfs of Saint Germain-Des-Prés," and is currently working on a study of death and suicide in the early middle ages.

HEATH DILLARD has studied with James B. Ross (Vassar), Sylvia L. Thrupp (U. Mich.), and Charles J. Bishko (U. Va.), and is currently completing a dissertation on "The Status of Women in Medieval Spain" at the University of Virginia.

BARBARA A. HANAWALT is an Assistant Professor in the history department at Indiana University and is now writing a book on fourteenth-century English

213

crime. "The Peasant Family and Crime in Fourteenth-Century England" (*The Journal of British Studies*), "Economic Influences on the Pattern of Crime in England, 1300–1348" (*The American Journal of Legal History*), and the present chapter represent various aspects of this study.

DAVID HERLIHY, Professor of History at Harvard University, is distinguished for his numerous articles and books on the economic and social history of medieval Italy. His more recent work on demographic history employs extensive quantitative analysis and has added further dimensions to our knowledge of the history of women.

JO-ANN MCNAMARA is Associate Professor of History at Hunter College. After the publication of *Gilles Aycelin: Servant of Two Masters* (Syracuse University Press, 1973), she turned to the study of medieval women. With Suzanne Wemple, she has published several studies on early medieval women prior to the present chapter.

SUSAN MOSHER STUARD is an Assistant Professor of History at SUNY, Brockport, N. Y. Her research work involves the archival collections in the Adriatic seaports, and she has published studies on economic and social history and the history of medicine.

SUE SHERIDAN WALKER, currently Associate Professor of History at Northeastern Illinois University in Chicago, has published articles on various aspects of feudal wardship in *Medieval Studies* and the *American Journal of Legal History* and has given a paper on "The Action of Waste in the Early Common Law" at the English Legal History Conference, Cambridge University, in July 1975. She is a Director of the American Society for Legal History, preparing a second edition of the *Checklist of Research in British Legal Manuscripts*, and editor and translator of the Court Rolls of the Manor of Wakefield 1333–34 to be published by the Yorkshire Archeological Society.

SUZANNE F. WEMPLE is Associate Professor of History at Barnard College. Her *Atto of Vercelli: Church, State and Christian Society in Tenth Century Italy* (Edizioni di Storia e Letteratura, Temi e Testi 20, Rome) is currently in press. She has published studies with Jo-Ann McNamara on the subject of early medieval women and is writing at present a book on women in Frankish society.

Index